Think
like a
Shrink
and keep
yourself
SANE

JOE DUNN

Newleaf

Newleaf
an imprint of
Gill & Macmillan Ltd
Goldenbridge
Dublin 8
with associated companies throughout the world
www.gillmacmillan.ie

A catalogue record is available for this book from the
British Library.

9 8 7 6 5 4 3

To Susan
and our children
Joni, Tom,
Liam, Harry
and Gabrielle

Contents

Introduction

So, why is this book different from any other self-help book? Make yourself comfortable. This is a long story, but I'll try to keep it short and sweet. Essentially this is a book written by a psychiatrist (that's me) about what psychiatrists do. Not the technical stuff about nerve cells, brain chemistry and medication, but the really interesting stuff about people, emotions, relationships and the 'Meaning of Life'.

I have written it because I'm fed up to the back teeth with the sort of preconceptions people have about my profession. I've also tried to give a broad overview of how we shrinks think.

And one more thing. Have you noticed how the writers of self-help books take themselves so seriously? Starchy lot. I have tried to write this book so that you can read it while standing half-asleep on a crowded bus. Not solemn or sober. If you can get a chuckle out of it, then that's a bonus.

About the case histories in this book: as you plough through the pages you will find that I've described a number of my patients to illustrate some point that I've been trying to make. Please take note that even though all of the information in the case histories is real and credible, none of the case histories describes any person who is real. Not only have I changed their names but I have had a good old tamper with the details of the case as well, so that the gist of the information is true but the person described is a figment of my fertile imagination. Sometimes they are a hybrid of two or three patients with a similar problem. Sometimes they are my garbage man or my brother-in-law's mate. Sometimes they are someone I met at a party who found out that I was a psychiatrist and spilled their guts all over me. Sometimes they even have a dollop of me in them . . . Whatever, get the clear message that I haven't described real patients here. If I had then I'd have a lot of fast talking to do to my patients. And their lawyers.

I ain't that stupid.

CHAPTER one

The subconscious mind

Myths, minds and mad psychiatrists

Everyone knows that only mad people go to see a psychiatrist.
Everyone also knows that most psychiatrists are a bit mad
themselves. They are peculiar people with goatee beards or
twin-sets and pearls. They walk with hunched shoulders. They take
themselves very seriously. When you go to visit them you are expected
to lie on a big leather couch and then you are asked why you hate your
mother. You deny you do. By the end of the session the only person you
hate more in the world than your mother is the psychiatrist.

Psychiatrists are also those people who give you drugs that make you feel and act like a zombie. And if that is not enough to reduce you to a state of benign, mindless compliance then a few thousand volts across your temples will do the trick.

I used to believe all these things about psychiatrists. Until I became one. I was fascinated by the character of Hannibal Lecter in the movie *The Silence of the Lambs*. He epitomised the image of the mad and bad psychiatrist. He was superhuman as an escapologist, totally capable of controlling the minds of all those around him and utterly insane in his cannibalism. I have worked in psychiatry for a few years now and I cannot for the life of me remember the last time that I came across a real-life colleague who ate his patients. In fact I have found my fellow psychiatrists to be a rather ordinary bunch. When you cut them, they bleed. They have mortgages and halitosis. They have holes in their socks and ladders in their tights. Their teenage children give them hell (as do all teenage children their parents). And they are not half as crazy as most surgeons.

Like all doctors, psychiatrists study hard to get their medical degrees, work long hours as interns and then embark on five or six or more years of study to become psychiatrists. They are a devoted lot with a sense of duty towards their patients. And in an inherently ambiguous world they also try very hard to be scientific — just as scientific, in fact, as any paediatrician or dermatologist.

So where did all this mythology come from? Why is it that society has built up all this nonsense around my profession so that patients enter my consulting room in such a state of apprehension? Why do they look around for the leather couch and breathe a sigh of relief when I ask them to sit down in a comfy armchair? Why do all the most needy patients invariably begin with the words, 'I really don't know whether I need to be here but . . . '?

The answer is that psychiatrists deal with your mind. More specifically, they often deal with that part of your mind that is chaotic, childlike, emotional and irrational, that is called your *subconscious*. Entrusting your mind to the scrutiny of someone else is an experience that makes you feel pretty vulnerable. It requires far more trust than letting them see into any orifice. This is because the fear of losing control of your mind or your emotions and the fear of becoming insane are not far removed in intensity from the fear of death itself. So that psychiatrists, like morticians, become the object of a morbid curiosity and a catalogue of mythology to match.

Imagine my frustration. I am at a cocktail party. Someone asks me what I do. I reply that I am a psychiatrist. Suddenly one half of the room has moved away and the other half has drawn closer. I would imagine that it would be the same if I were, say, a bishop or an undertaker. Sometimes it is better to go incognito. Be warned that if you are ever at a cocktail party and someone tells you that he or she is a 'health worker', you are probably talking to a psychiatrist.

You will have gathered by now that this book is primarily about your mind. I will start here and then move on to some insights about personal development, emotions, relationships, health, etc. But to begin with, let me dissect a mind.

In the simplest possible way, the mind is divided into two parts: the conscious and the subconscious (see diagram). The conscious mind is adult, rational and thinking. The subconscious, as I have indicated, is childlike, irrational and essentially emotional. When you do arithmetic you use your conscious mind. When you get annoyed at that person who looks over your shoulder (because they remind you of that dreadful teacher you had in sixth class) you use your subconscious mind. When you marvel at the engineering of a Mercedes-Benz engine you use your conscious mind. When you fantasise about

Your conscious mind is mostly:	Your subconscious mind is mostly:
adult	childlike
thinking	emotional
rational	irrational
aware	concealed
awake	dreaming/fantasising
transient	permanent

pulling up in your driveway in your new Merc so that all the neighbours can see, that's your subconscious kicking in.

As a generalisation the subconscious mind is a primitive, chaotic, disinhibited, illogical piece of kit. Like the proverbial elephant, it never forgets. Given half a chance it will throw up at you every memory of suffering that has ever gone into it. It can take over any bodily function and take it away from conscious control. It can cause you to have the most marvellous dreams and the most hideous nightmares.

You are unaware of your subconscious mind most of the time. It is not completely inaccessible since you can purposely draw some memories from your subconscious into your mind with conscious effort. For this reason Freud (or 'Saint Sigmund of Vienna' as he is affectionately known in psychoanalytical circles) divided the subconscious into the *preconscious* (from which memories could be drawn) and the *unconscious* (which could only be accessed in a regressed state in intense psychoanalysis).

To illustrate the power of the subconscious I will describe a number of patients who became all too painfully aware of this hidden side of themselves.

CASE HISTORY **Jenny the survivor**

Jenny was a very likeable woman, about forty-five years old. She lived in a de facto relationship with her supportive husband and worked as a computer programmer.

She came to see me ostensibly because she had experienced anxiety when her son had developed diabetes at the age of nineteen. When I investigated the history, however, it seemed that the young man had taken this health problem in his stride and adjusted very easily to his insulin injections with a minimum of fuss. The control of his diabetes was more than adequate and Jenny's anxiety did not seem too severe. She seemed to derive some comfort from having someone to talk to and returned to see me for five or six sessions at weekly intervals.

I found myself wondering why she kept coming back. An even more curious impression was that Jenny did not quite know either. I felt a little impatient and decided to suggest that we might continue our sessions at less frequent intervals or perhaps even terminate them altogether. But before I could raise this idea she was hit with a memory from her childhood. I use the word 'hit' because she felt bowled over by the significance of it. She had been sexually abused by her father, sadistically, horribly, consistently, over many years. Only after she had been seeing me for several months did she allow herself to remember other information from her past which led to an even more miserable realisation: her mother had known about it and had done nothing to protect her.

All of this horror had been held like a time-bomb in her subconscious mind, just waiting to go off. It had been these memories, not her worries about her son, that had brought her, quite unawares, to see me. Only after her subconscious felt comfortable with me did it allow the memories to explode. They had been quietly eating away at her for decades. They had to be released and dealt with.

I have found that this ability of the mind to 'forget' childhood sexual abuse is the rule rather than the exception.

CASE HISTORY   Cathy the shoplifter

Cathy was the archetypal businesswoman. She was driven by blind ambition and had done very well for herself. She had worked her way up from secretary to office manager, to staff trainer, and then formed her own business training bank staff in the mysterious ways of the international money market. And she made an absolute killing doing it.

At just the right age a handsome, intelligent and equally ambitious stockbroker had walked into her life. They made a striking couple and maintained the image and the trappings of status and self-esteem, including the big house with the obligatory tennis court and the prestige cars with the obligatory carphones. At a respectable interval after their marriage she gave birth to first a son and then, three years later, a daughter.

They had everything going for them and were the envy of all their friends. Then one day, as Cathy was leaving a department store, two burly store detectives walked up to her and arrested her for shoplifting. She had no idea what they were talking about until they reached into her baby's pram and pulled out four pairs of stockings. This was not a 'set-up' by the detectives because she had remembered looking at the stockings in the shop and thinking in passing how garish they looked. Her purse was stuffed with money. She had stolen the stockings and hidden them in the pram but had absolutely no recollection of doing so.

She did not need the stockings. She needed to be caught. She needed to be humiliated and punished. She did not know all this until her subconscious mind had made her steal some pretty ghastly hosiery under the very noses of the store detectives.

Why did she need to do this? Because she had grown up as the 'perfect child': intelligent, hardworking and obedient. All she really wanted was a bit of love and attention but, as we shall later see, many parents feel that they need to give less attention to children who are doing well and more to children who are in distress. Perfect children learn how to hide their distress but it tends to come out, eventually. In Cathy's subconscious mind was an immense amount of anger at her parents but an equal amount of guilt for feeling so enraged. She had to find a punishment to suit the guilt. Shoplifting, her subconscious mind thought. Now there's a good lark . . .

CASE HISTORY **Moyra who was mute**

Any of you who have ever been admitted to a large general hospital will know the indignity of being a guinea pig for junior doctors. Your case history and your carbuncle are described in detail to a group of intense young interns in white coats and every one of them is allowed to poke at it, especially at the painful parts.

We have a similar teaching process in psychiatry but we are a bit more dignified about it since we bring the patient in after we have discussed his or. her history so that the whole thing does not look so much like the Spanish Inquisition with stethoscopes.

I vividly remember a case presented at a hospital where I trained in psychiatry. The patient's name was Moyra. She was about 55, a machinist by trade, admitted because she had been unable to speak for the past two months. She had undergone every test known to medical science at the hands of the neurologists and the ear, nose and throat surgeons. They had found nothing physically wrong. They had made a diagnosis of 'hysterical mutism' and referred her to the psychiatrists, which is what happens to most patients who defy diagnosis by other specialists. There is usually some expectation that we humble psychiatrists with our holey socks and laddered tights will be able to work miracles.

This particular day a sort of miracle did happen. The patient was brought into the Grand Round, as it was rather pompously called, and the senior psychiatrist interviewed her. He was a particularly popular and sensible chap with a kindly manner and a respect around the hospital that put him somewhere just above the Pope and below Saint Peter. She indicated that she would like to be able to answer his questions but was simply unable to speak. He then encouraged her to try to grunt from deep inside her chest, which she managed to do. He then spurred her on to grunt even louder and louder and to try to form the grunt into a word. After a few minutes of grunting and hissing she managed to form a word that seemed to have been stuck in her throat. It emerged as a hoarse whisper at first but then became normal speech. The word was 'Help!' She was 'cured' in one fell swoop and the senior psychiatrist retained his godlike status.

It transpired that she had a 30-year-old daughter who had finally accepted a proposal of marriage. Her daughter's fiance was aged about forty and was a rather dashing character with a handlebar moustache and a soft charm with women. The patient had, quite simply, fallen in love with her own daughter's fiance and was completely incapable of handling the thrill of these feelings as well as the intense guilt that they engendered. Her subconscious mind had decided that she must say nothing about her love and had slapped a 'hysterical' ban on her vocal cords. No matter how hard she had *consciously* tried to speak, no words emerged.

You could deduce from these three cases that only women have a subconscious mind. Right? Wrong. Read on.

CASE HISTORY **Andrew the security guard**

Andrew was a security guard, not terribly bright, but an affable character. He looked very competent and paramilitary in his uniform, with peaked cap and 'nightstick' (euphemism for 'club'). He also wore a pistol on his hip and he harboured fantasies of catching intruders in the middle of the night, arresting a whole gang of them single-handedly the way they do in the movies, and then having his picture in the newspaper receiving a bravery award from the Governor-General. Some men are so predictable. Give them a uniform and a gun and they think they're Clint Eastwood.

Andrew worked in a large financial institution that prepared pay rolls for a number of smaller firms and distributed them in an armoured truck. The ritual was the same every week: the pay packets were made up on Wednesdays and kept overnight in a guarded office before being driven all over the city the following day. Andrew and his fellow guards would ride 'shotgun' . . .

On this particular Wednesday night Andrew was rostered on to the night shift and had to sit up all night 'baby-sitting' all these crisp banknotes in their yellow envelopes. One and a half million dollars. He sat inside an office with frosted glass and watched the late, late shows on a portable television. Now you would expect him to be disciplined and self-controlled because he looked as if he had just come out of the SAS. But Andrew coped with the boredom that pervades his industry by smoking large quantities of marijuana. So when the robbers struck that night Andrew was stoned.

Andrew noticed something move behind the frosted glass. The office door swung open and he found himself looking down the barrel of a shotgun. Twelve gauge and terrifying. On the other end was a man wearing a balaclava that revealed only a pair of angry eyes. The intruder's voice was croaky and deep: 'Onto the floor arsehole. Touch your gun and you're dead meat.' Our hero was rooted to the spot with fear. His breath stopped. His skin was suddenly wet with perspiration and his bowels turned to water. Then the end of the barrel was shoved into his face, cutting his cheek. He got down on to the floor about as fast as a man can and he conscientiously did not move his hand anywhere near his handgun. He had one burning ambition: to see Thursday morning. The next ten minutes were a blur. More men in balaclavas, pistol stolen, being tied up, telephone smashed, crowbars breaking locks, hundreds of yellow envelopes into a bag and off. But not before another hiss from the man with the angry eyes. 'I'll be back in a few minutes arsehole. If you've moved I'll shoot you into a hundred pieces. Got it?' Our hero nodded hurriedly. Then the eyes were gone. Silence. A minute seemed like an hour. Waiting for that barrel and those eyes again.

After what seemed like a long, long time, he got up. He was aware enough to wish that he had never smoked that joint. He felt numbed, shocked, out of control. Eventually he raised the alarm. He tried to look a little more composed when the police arrived and he blurted out what had happened.

Of course the crooks were never found. A car seen speeding away from the scene of the crime had been stolen from a nearby suburb a few hours before. Standard robbery stuff. Andrew regained his sanity and dignity over a few days. He managed to embellish the tale by claiming to have wrestled with old Angry Eyes before being pistol-whipped by his accomplice. It was all lies but it made Andrew feel less like a wimp and it sounded good down at the pub. He never did meet the Governor-General, but a couple of the women at the pub seemed more interested in him. It's an ill wind, he thought.

This would have been all very well, but stuck in Andrew's subconscious mind were a few memories that were not going to go away. His subconscious did not belch them out again for several months; but when the images came back they came with a vengeance. Nightmares, flashbacks, intrusive memories. Quite suddenly, after a period of coping just fine with work he found that he could not face it. He began to call in sick, but learned that you could not do that five days a week. Eventually he had to resign. He became moody and depressed. He could not get it out of his head: eyes, balaclavas, a croaky voice, a movement on the other side of frosted glass. Anything that reminded him of *that night* got him going: tremor, sweats, a feeling of sheer terror. No peace of mind, no tranquil sleep, a yearning to once again be able to relax. One evening he watched a TV movie about a bank robbery and found himself cowering under the dining-table.

His benign and blustery Aunt Ruth bullied him into seeing me. He did not take much bullying. By the time he got to my office he was well and truly depressed.

The diagnosis: post-traumatic stress disorder. Vietnam veterans' stuff. The treatment: re-visit the fear in his imagination. Describe it, feel it, talk about it. Again and again. Like letting pus out of an abscess. Except that the yukky stuff was in his mind and not his skin. And he learned the hard way that men have a subconscious mind too.

Each of these four cases illustrates the extraordinary power of the subconscious. They are used as rather dramatic examples to make a point but, in everyday life, your subconscious mind works in ways that are a lot more subtle. When we imagine the future, when we listen to our hearts more than our heads, when we go on 'gut feelings', then we are allowing our subconscious minds to guide us rather than the cold logic of our conscious minds. Car and real-estate salesmen know this all too well. We buy the two major investments of our lives on a mostly intuitive level because the choice 'feels good' rather than because it makes financial sense.

Clever salesmen do not point out the logic of a purchase in any sort of mathematical way; instead, they appeal to our emotions and fantasies. They invade our personal space and call us by our first names. They make us imagine sitting in this car or by this swimming pool and encourage us to feel how good it is. They make us believe that they are benevolent friends whom we have known for years so that we feel honoured by their help and advice. And then they make us sign our lives away. Nothing conscious or logical about that.

All human beings have a need to indulge in some venting of the subconscious from time to time. Mr Spock from *Star Trek* is a shining example of a being who does not have this need: soulless and logical. One of the most benign ways that we vent our subconscious is through imaginative escapism. By this I refer to all the forms of art, literature and entertainment that indulge in stimulating our feelings. Every time we collapse in front of the television and are mesmerised by its eerie glow we are giving our subconscious minds a well-deserved back-rub.

Dreams

It is worthwhile pausing here for a comment about dreams. Freud called these 'the royal road to the unconscious'. He spent many hours trying to analyse both his own dreams and those of his patients. He came to the conclusion that they were a chaotic tangle of events from the day, from your distant memory, symbolism and fantasy, and all compressed into a few seconds. Sometimes the hidden 'meaning' of the dreams was discernible, but, like your Christmas tree lights in early December, only when they could be untangled. Sometimes meaning remained a mystery. Either way there was a fair amount of subjectivity in dream analysis.

There are plenty of books around now that provide a blanket interpretation of the symbolism of just about any object or event that happens in a dream. Such generalised interpretations are pretty meaningless, rather like horoscopes. I really cannot believe that, say, every Virgo in the world is going to have a good day on Tuesday. Surely some of them must go bankrupt or be diagnosed with a terminal illness on that day. Similarly, the understanding of the contents of your dream world is entirely individual according to your personality and life experience. The appearance of a cat in your dream might mean something sleek, warm and homely. In my dream it just means hay fever.

Your dreams and nightmares give a window of understanding to your own subconscious world but they must be interpreted with the help of a trained professional. As they say on TV, don't try to do this at home by yourself, kids.

Quick-fix and Ripe Plums

We live in a hi-tech, whizz-bang scientific world. We like to believe that we are in control of ourselves and our lives. Given that the subconscious mind is so private and so unpredictable, and seems to be just a hair's-breadth from madness, it is little wonder that my specialty must be so mythologised. Unfortunately there has also been a trend towards an even more insidious belief system in recent years: people have tried to deny that we have a subconscious mind or to ignore its existence. They have attracted a large following, including some of my own colleagues who say that there is no point in dipping into the world of the subconscious since most human misery can be dealt with by using the conscious mind alone.

The technical term for such an approach is that it is 'cognitive/behavioural'. The 'cognitive' part refers to *thinking* and the 'behavioural' part refers to *doing*. The rationale behind the cognitive/behavioural stance is that feelings, personalities, life experience, habitual ways of relating to others and a search for meaning in your life are irrelevant. All that matters is what you think and what you do. Thus, if you think and behave in a sad manner but you want to be happy, you must *think* positively and *act* happy and if you do this conscientiously enough and for long enough then you will *feel* happy. If you feel defeated and wretched then all you need to do is to think and do things that are confident and motivated, and organised into appropriately graded goals, and you will eventually know unlimited success and wealth. Most of all you must *visualise* yourself driving that Jaguar, sewing up that deal and being promoted before the green eyes of your contemporaries.

The cognitive/behavioural approach therefore has immense appeal. It is quick and clean. It is superficial and not too personally challenging. It is quite effective in managing a specific problem for a specified period of time. But whether it leads to any true change of the patient's internal emotional world over a sustained period remains doubtful.

The excesses of the cognitive/behavioural approach are best seen in the business world. Companies have 'Personnel' departments while corporations have 'Human Resources' departments. In 'Personnel' departments a grouchy old clerk who smokes too much can painstakingly work out how much annual leave you've accrued. In 'Human Resources' departments brisk young executives talk about recruitment, motivation courses and time management. In this latter arena the merchants of cognitive/behavioural treatments have done a roaring trade. This is because people in business do not want to own up to the idea that they might have feelings and families and inner vulnerabilities. But they are also well aware that as they stare at themselves in the mirror in the morning and repeat their affirmations to themselves it all sounds a little corny. When they say 'I will love and accept myself in every way today' they hear a little voice within their subconscious minds pipe up and say 'No you won't!'

Pardon me if my scepticism is showing. I am sure that many cognitive/behavioural therapists will find my comments slanderous. I do not mean to offend and, in fact, I have a confession to make: I use the cognitive/behavioural techniques from time to time, but only on obsessional cripples and Ripe Plums (see page 10).

Obsessional cripples are people who are impeccably groomed, structured, organised, punctual, impossibly tidy and thoroughly, pedantically boring. Freud believed that they were stuck on the so-called *anal* phase of development because they were, quite literally, emotionally constipated. For a long time I thought that this simply reflected Freud's own bottom fixation, that is until I encountered a few obsessional cripples. Now I realise that obsessional cripples gather in groups at the proctology departments of hospitals. To the uninitiated, a proctologist is a doctor who specialises in treating diseases of the anus. No, I can't imagine spending a lifetime dedicated to the study of bums either.

Obsessional types form one end of a spectrum of emotionality that has histrionics at the other end. Histrionic types gush emotions, enter the room with a flourish, make sure that they are noticed by everyone in attendance and call everyone 'daaarling'. Obsessional people live in a structured world of thought and histrionics in a chaotic world of emotion. Obsessional cripples spend a great deal of mental energy trying to avoid feeling feelings. That is why the cognitive/behavioural therapies are so appropriate for obsessional people. Getting them to talk about their feelings becomes an intensely frustrating exercise for both patient and therapist.

Ripe Plums, on the other hand, are people who have often undergone a great deal of personal introspection before they even walk into my office. They've got most of the answers already but they seek the opportunity to bounce a few ideas off me in order to get to those last few perspectives or realisations. At some point during the consultation they get a particular look upon their faces. It's the same look that, I imagine, adorned Einstein's face when he realised what 'E' equalled. The Plum, like the penny, has dropped. And often the realisation can be summed up in a simple 'affirmation' such as:

- I don't have to stay in this job/marriage if I am unhappy.
- I don't have to be perfect for everyone all the time.
- The reason that my boss/wife/husband is such a bastard/bitch to me is that I don't stand up against him/her enough.

If, then, the cognitive/behavioural techniques are generally impersonal, superficial and transient, what is a person to do with their sadness, their anger, their insecurity, their bitterness, their frustration?

Misery is like fat. It builds up slowly and it must be discarded slowly. Crash diets work for a short time, but then you pretty quickly return to being just as rotund as when you started. Psychological quick-fixes are the same. Unless you are a Ripe Plum you have to be prepared to work at deeply felt emotions and deeply held misconceptions over a period of time to really erase them. There will be plenty of people who promise you a quick-fix for your personal or emotional problems. There are also plenty of crash diets. Get real.

Psychodynamic defences

It took me fifteen years of tertiary study to become a psychiatrist. I am now going to treat you to something that will save apprentices a couple of years of slog. I am going to tell you about psychodynamic defences. These are the rather dinky ways that your mind works to prevent all that subconscious anguish from bursting forth into your conscious mind. Society expects us to be fairly inhibited and genteel in company. We are not allowed to pinch people's bottoms or nick the silverware at dinner parties. It is frowned upon to punch the host. All of these spontaneous acts of unbridled lust or greed or rage will guarantee that we will never be invited back to dinner and we might end up in jail.

The subconscious mind, with all its distress and demands, must be tamed. That is what defences do. They create a protective wall between the two parts of the psyche. There is a variety of defences, some sophisticated and some primitive. I will describe the sophisticated ones first. They include:

Intellectualisation Anguish can be labelled, philosophised about and discussed over a civilised cup of tea.

Creativity The artist on the point of madness can splatter a lot of paint on to a canvas and as a means of self-expression and can earn a fortune in the process.

Humour Making human suffering look absurd is an effective way of taking the sting out of it. Groucho Marx's famous line 'I don't want to belong to any club that will accept me as a member' attracts laughter but, in the cold light of day, it is actually a statement of rock-bottom self-esteem.

This is all pretty humdrum stuff compared with the more primitive defences. There are three of these:

Denial This is the most primitive defence of all. We all use it when it comes to death. We do not wake up and wonder whether we are going to die today. That is why we react with such horror when we witness a fatal car accident. It stuns us. Our most reliable defence, denial, has been overwhelmed with cruel reality. It is also used by alcoholics who, in the face of their divorce, drink-driving charge and cirrhosis of the liver, will blithely claim that 'I know I'm a heavy drinker but I'm *certainly* not an alcoholic.' Look for it in your life tomorrow and you will find it everywhere: denial that your cheque account will be overdrawn; denial that you will get a parking ticket; denial that it will rain in the face of the darkening sky. Denial is our subconscious mind's oldest friend.

Splitting This is the tendency to see people as either all good or all bad. It is quite permissible when you are a child. You can play 'goodies and baddies'. Only the nerds get to be baddies. When Hollywood makes a movie with a 'hero' in it, then it is quite acceptable for him or her to blow away the bad guy with a jumbo-sized handgun in the final scene. The fact that the baddie's mother loved him dearly or that she was kind to animals becomes irrelevant. The baddie is 'split' into being all bad. But when we are adults we must handle the ambivalence of our relationships in a mature way. No one is either all good or all bad. In our heart of hearts we know that but sometimes we slip back into the old ways. There is only one time in our adult lives when we are encouraged and expected to view another person as being 'split' in this way and that is when we fall in love. In the initial, zany, besotted phases of a love affair we are allowed to fantasise that our lover is 100 per cent good. The hard work starts when we find out about their foibles and warts.

Projection This is the ability to disown an element of our badness and to dump it on to someone else. Many people cannot own their own anger but see it in all around them. They cannot own up to the fact that they have annoyed everyone else and it is their own anger that they are perceiving, mirrored back to them. If projection reaches monstrous proportions then it can become delusional. In this case it is called by another name: 'paranoia'.

So these are the most primitive and most sophisticated defence mechanisms. In between these extremes is a variety of defences. I will mention a few of them here simply because they are so damned interesting. By now you will be cottoning on to the idea that your mind is not just a rational, thinking, adult apparatus. Underneath that cerebral cortex is a swamp of wallowing emotional distress. You do a very good job just coping from day to day. Don't be alarmed or ashamed if you can't.

Repetition compulsion This phenomenon is epitomised by the adage that 'the person who does not understand history is condemned to repeat it'. The daughter of an alcoholic marries an alcoholic. And when that doesn't turn out she leaves him and marries another one. And another one. She can break out of this repetition compulsion only if she begins to understand that she is trying to 'undo' all that damage that her father inflicted upon her with his alcoholism but is marrying men who simply continue to hurt her. She needs to put her past to rest before she can get on with her future.

Reaction formation This is the process by which people act in a way that is completely opposite to the way they really want to behave. They have huge unresolved emotional issues in their subconscious minds. Like Ian and Adam.

CASE HISTORY **Ian**

Ian was a supple, aesthetic-looking young man. Ian was gay but he simply could not admit this to himself. When other men were attracted to him he became bewildered by his feelings. One half of him felt the pleasure and flattery of men finding him attractive while the other half was disgusted by these feelings. Ian's father, an inadequate, emotionally distanced, macho bloke, had passed on to Ian his own homophobia. Ian had ended up afraid of his own homosexuality.

Ian was in a bar one day with a few 'mates'. He chose his friends so that he could hide amongst them: they were all beer-swilling louts and if Ian left his beard to grow more than a five o'clock shadow and drank as much beer as they did (while stifling the bloated nausea) then he could feel like a real, sweaty, heterosexual man. He could talk about 'the talent' as if he was interested and he could howl with derisive laughter at all the 'poofter' jokes.

But one night in his favourite drinking hole with all his loutish friends, Ian noticed an Adonis of a young man at the bar and promptly fell in love. Just like *Death in Venice*. All that bewilderment about his sexuality came to a head. His subconscious mind was giving him hell. So what did he fall back on? Reaction formation.

He started to make crude remarks about the Adonis. He stirred his mates up by making the usual inferences: rear-gunner, pillow-biter, clay tracker, etc. The denouement was inevitable. They followed the Adonis out to the pub carpark and did him over in a 'poofter bashing'. Ian threw the first punch. A few minutes later the Adonis was unconscious and in a pool of blood. The blokes dined out on this for weeks — the night they taught that homo freak a lesson.

You guessed it. Ian became very depressed. He came to see me extremely reluctantly. That was the first step. It was an easy one, compared with what was to follow. Owning up to loving men more than loving women was the hard bit. Then there was the task of trying to forgive himself for what he had done to the Adonis. It was not this man he wanted to strike, but himself. He had so much pent-up anger. And his subconscious mind had found his own impulses so strong and so distasteful that he had to punch, rather than kiss, another man.

CASE HISTORY **Adam**

Adam was paraplegic. More specifically, Adam had been crippled by his own mother. Accidentally of course. You hear about this sort of accident as you drive along daydreaming and listening to your car radio. A parent backs the car out of the garage over the four-year-old playing in the driveway. As you hear it you wince, because you know that such accidents happen and that they devastate the family and that it could have been you.

Adam had no memory of his mother's car tyre crushing his spine as it came to a halt, just as she heard his scream. His subconscious mind had suppressed that memory. It was there somewhere but nothing, come hell or high water or in-depth psychotherapy, was going to get that one to budge. There are some things that are left well enough alone.

What Adam had to contend with was the rest of his life in a wheelchair. He missed out on most of the sport at school. He missed out on dating. He tried to get used to the way people always stare at someone who is even vaguely different from everyone else. And a young man in a wheelchair with two living but absolutely useless legs is more than vaguely different.

Adam loved his mother. He told me that he had forgiven her. But how do you *really* forgive someone whose mistake robbed you of the ability to walk and run and skip and look 'normal'. Human beings are simply incapable of unconditional love, unconditional trust and unconditional forgiveness. Call that cynical if you must, but it is true. Adam coped with his hurt and resentment by excelling. In fact he over-excelled. That's what turned his coping mechanisms into something more insidious: he used reaction formation.

Adam decided that there would be nothing that he would not or could not do. Rather than rolling over and giving up, or simply accepting his limitations, he displayed a dogged determination to act as if he had no handicap at all. He bungee-jumped. He went white-water rafting. He rode a specially modified Harley-Davidson motorcycle. He did a degree in accountancy and then threw it all in because he did not like the image of being boring, conservative and desk-bound. Then he seized upon the most outlandish plan of all: he hitch-hiked around the world.

His friends, and he had plenty, held him in awe. So what was so bad about what he was doing? He was *over*-compensating, that's what. He showed by his need to completely negate the importance of his handicap that he had not come to terms with it. He relied upon reaction formation: his subconscious mind wanted him to roll around in sadness and hurt. But he hid this, from himself more than anyone else, by being brave, smiling, over-ambitious and 'normal'. Don't get me wrong. I think handicapped people should take on as much as they are able to. But not over-compensate. And not over-compensate in an effort to hide the pain within.

The 'manic defence' This is the defence that people use when they laugh at a time when they should cry. The subconscious mind releases pain but somewhere between the murky interior of your feelings and the outward expression of them they mutate from being tears of pain to tears of laughter. We all do this at times. But some people do it because they are emotionally out of control.

CASE HISTORY **Sally and Sandra**

These two young women were best friends. They got together one evening to drink too much red wine and smoke too many cigarettes. They were both at a stage of complete turmoil. Sally had been having an affair with a married man. The affair was over, torpedoed out of the water by his wife, who had found out about it. Sandra, who was married, had been having an extra-marital affair and had now come to the conclusion that she must leave her husband to be with her lover. She had to tell him and she had to tell him soon. Judgment Day was upon them. They were both hurting like hell.

They looked each other in the eye. Then, in the same instant, they burst out laughing. They laughed so much that they nearly wet themselves. The manic defence.

CASE HISTORY **Norma**

Norma giggled uncontrollably all through her father's funeral. The minister's pompous expression, her mother's running mascara, the obligatory arum lilies in vases through the church; it all seemed so absurd. She imagined what her father looked like inside his coffin, all battered and bruised but ashen and white. He had committed suicide by leaping from a cliff. His body had landed on the rocks so far below and had to be extricated by police helicopter. Norma had to go the morgue to identify her father. They showed her only one side of his head, the other being draped in white linen. She knew why they had to do that and was quietly thankful for their discretion. She only had to see half of his face to identify the body. She knew it was him because he looked cold and cruel even when he was dead.

Norma had never been close to her father. She had not been flagrantly sexually abused by him, but his behaviour was intrusive and inappropriate enough so that she felt violated in his presence. He had had a nifty way of walking into her bedroom just as she was getting dressed. When she was fourteen he explained to her in graphic detail what boys would want to do to her when she went out on dates. She knew that he was getting off on it. After a shower he liked to parade around the house naked, ostensibly 'getting something from the living room', but his nudity was much more exhibitionist than natural and open. Norma came to despise him.

At his funeral, her subconscious mind was in a state of complete confusion. Here she was, in public, wanting to act like the dutiful daughter. Somewhere way back there, in the crevices of her emotions, she felt some sort of pity for him and she even remembered the few soft moments, when he had bounced her on his knee or called her 'poppet'. But for most of the time she hated him. She had often imagined him burning in hell and here she was, waiting for the crematorium curtains to slide back. In her mind's eye she could see his coffin disappearing into the flames.

Guilt, rage and sadness, all at once, smothered in giggles. The manic defence.

CASE HISTORY **Erma**

Erma had manic-depression. Diagnosed, signed and sealed. By me. I had seen her depressed and I had seen her in the manic phase of her illness too: overactive; not sleeping; talking incessantly; racing, irrational thoughts; laughing a lot; making grandiose plans and schemes; coming up with marvellous new ideas and inventions that would never materialise; spending too much; partying night and day and demanding sex from her ever-suffering fiance.

But Erma's manias were unlike those of the vast majority of people with manic-depression: they were predictable, down to the last hour. They occurred only once a year, on the anniversary of her first husband's death. Then she would slump into a depression that reflected her unresolved grief about losing him. The manic defence again.

Erma never did go through a satisfactory bereavement for that loss. Eventually she married her fiance and her anniversary reactions simply dwindled away over the years. She did not manage to sort out her feelings about husband number one, but compensated for this bewilderment by making sure that husband number two was a warm and loving man. Fair enough too.

These, then, are the commonly used defence mechanisms that we use every day to push our subconscious minds out of consciousness. Now . . .

A final word before we move on to the next chapter, which is all about the influence of your past upon your present and your future.

I have spoken here about the subconscious mind. I have railed against the simplistic idea that the problems of the mind can be addressed through the conscious mind alone. There is something that is much more subtle and yet much more powerful in your psyche than just thought and logic. In this respect I am simply letting you into a perspective that is much more prevalent in the USA than it is elsewhere. Americans are much more psychologically minded than the rest of us. They have that characteristic candour that many of us find peculiar, even abrasive. But they are far more willing than we are to be openly and honestly introspective about emotions and relationships. President Clinton has spoken publicly of the benefits of his own psychotherapy. Oprah Winfrey and Donahue always have a guest shrink.

America sets the trend for many ideologies in the Western world.

CHAPTER **two** Personality
development

Here-and-now and there-and-then

Everyone knows that psychiatrists love to live in the past. You bring us your here-and-now problems and somehow we end up talking about the there-and-then. I see it on the faces of my patients when I try to find out about their backgrounds. They are talking about how they are feeling this very minute when I begin to ask them questions about their childhood. There is a bemused look that they have. It says:

'Here we go. Blame it all on my poor old grey-haired mother. Tell me I hate her. Tell me she didn't potty-train me enough or that she was anally fixated on the damned potty. Tell me that I feel empty because I wasn't breast-fed. Tell me I want to castrate my benign bald-headed old dad because I envied the size of his penis. Then show me some ink-blots and nod seriously as I tell you all I can see is smudged ink. And if you think for one minute that I'm going to tell you about my long, red, hot sports-car . . .'

I frequently hear the suggestion that we should 'put the past behind us', forgive and forget, live for the present, etc. etc. So why bother raking over the coals? And over and over and over ... The answer is that *what happened in your past determines to a large extent what happens in your present and your future.* If we all carry our own invisible suitcase full of emotional baggage then that suitcase was filled when we cried ourselves to sleep at age four or sat outside our parents' bedroom door listening to them argue at age six. And the day that that old man next door touched you in a scary way was the day that your suitcase became much, much heavier.

Your past life experience shapes your personality, your habitual ways of thinking, feeling and relating and your sense of your own identity. No one, but no one, has a perfect childhood or perfect parents. We all have skeletons closeted away in the darkest recesses of our minds. For the most part we can live with them. But sometimes, in order to feel that life is worthwhile and satisfying, we must expunge these ghosts from the past. And it is usually a rather protracted and distressing exorcism.

In this chapter I want to explore the way personality develops, what kids need so they can grow up with confidence and a sense of self-worth, and how it all goes wrong. But before I launch into that, let me consider where all this navel-gazing came from.

Freud, Darwin and other hairy men

L et us presume for a moment that the Book of Genesis was written on a rainy Sunday afternoon by an unknown Hebrew with a vivid imagination and time to spare. Let us presume that God did *not* create man from a pile of dust on what was the equivalent of a Celestial Saturday but that humans evolved over about 200 billion

Saturdays. We began, so we are told, as a group of ambitious molecules hit by lightning while floating in some primordial puddle. We eventually dragged ourselves out of the sea (but physiologically maintain its salinity as a souvenir) and passed through a stage of looking like a bunch of squirrels before assuming an ape-like appearance and learning how to use large sticks to bash other apes. From here it was a short hop to becoming humans and replacing the sticks with nuclear arsenals. But not so long ago we were apes.

So what has all this got to do with psychoanalysis? When Charles Darwin proposed evolution he shook the scientific world. We take it for granted now; after all, who really believes that their ultimate ancestors were a couple of naive naked kids who shared an apple? But Darwin started to make a lot of sense of some puzzles that had been around for yonks. Why, for example, did humans possess an appendix and a pair of tonsils when their only purpose seemed to be to become infected and keep a whole heap of surgeons employed removing them? We came to see that they were evolutionary remnants of things that had been important to our hairy forbears.

Freud was heavily influenced by the work of Darwin. He came to see that a lot of emotional problems that he called 'psychoneurotic' were rather like an inflamed appendix: dangerous, potentially self-destructive and caused by some unwanted residue from our own personal pasts. He likened his early work to the process of lancing an abscess (stored up emotional distress) and letting the pus (tears) out in order facilitate healing.

And that, Virginia, is how psychiatrists came to be preoccupied by the past histories of their patients.

YURU: Why you are you

Motivation. That is what seems to have been the focus of attention of a lot of writers over the years. What motivates you to be, do, think, say, feel, etc. The operative word here is not what, when, how or where, but *why*.

Let me kick off with a very important point; it is a point that I will keep coming back to in this book so take it on board now and save flicking through pages later on. The point is that, in the final analysis, all

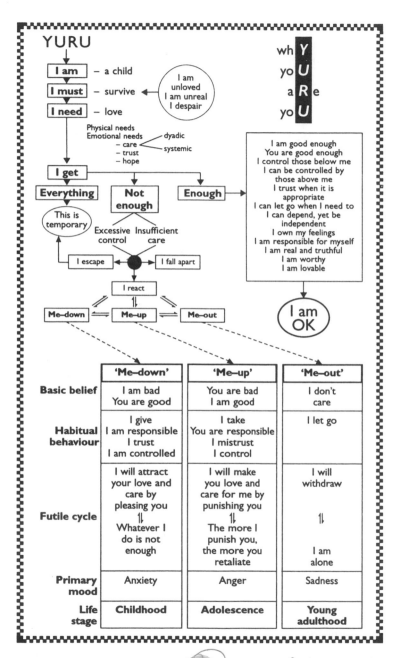

YURU

I am — a child
I must — survive
I need — love

I am unloved
I am unreal
I despair

wh **Y** — **why**
yo **U** — **you**
a **R** e — **are**
yo **U** — **you**

Physical needs
Emotional needs — dyadic
– care — systemic
– trust
– hope

I get

Everything   Not enough   Enough

This is temporary

Excessive control   Insufficient care

I escape   I fall apart

I react

Me–down ⇌ Me–up ⇌ Me–out

I am good enough
You are good enough
I control those below me
I can be controlled by those above me
I trust when it is appropriate
I can let go when I need to
I can depend, yet be independent
I own my feelings
I am responsible for myself
I am real and truthful
I am worthy
I am lovable

I am OK

	'Me–down'	'Me–up'	'Me–out'
Basic belief	I am bad You are good	You are bad I am good	I don't care
Habitual behaviour	I give I am responsible I trust I am controlled	I take You are responsible I mistrust I control	I let go
Futile cycle	I will attract your love and care by pleasing you ⇅ Whatever I do is not enough	I will make you love and care for me by punishing you ⇅ The more I punish you, the more you retaliate	I will withdraw ⇅ I am alone
Primary mood	Anxiety	Anger	Sadness
Life stage	**Childhood**	**Adolescence**	**Young adulthood**

23

Copy

human behaviour, action, endeavour is motivated by only two factors:
- the need to stay alive; and
- the need to keep others alive.

There. It's so fiendishly simple. The first is about survival of the self and the second is about survival of the species. In my everyday work I rename these two basic motivations. The first is called the need to control and the second is called the need to care. By the time you finish this book you'll be heartily sick of my harping on about this basic dichotomy: care and control.

So what do I need so that I can develop a personality and sense of my own identity, that's going to see me through my life and let me die with the belief that I've had a good innings? What factors need to be implanted in my psyche for me to feel that life is satisfying and worthwhile? Once again, the answer has a diabolical simplicity: I need to be loved.

Trouble is, 'love' is such a big word. It tends to be so abused in the English language. Greasy-haired rock singers use it and then smash their guitars on stage. Pimply youths use it in the hope of a grope. It appears in a syrupy greeting card given to some old aunt whom you don't particularly like. It is uttered from the lips of battered wives who keep going back for more: 'Because I *love* him.'

There are so many feelings that are love. There is erotic love, sibling love and love of God. There is intense love with racing heart and solid love with quiet sureness. There is gooey-eyed love with sweet nothings and weak-at-the-knees love when we see our baby's first smile. But in English we are stuck with this one four-lettered item that seems to have a thousand different meanings. Perhaps if there is a unitary concept of its meaning it may be that it is involved with a sense of pleasurable but selfless giving.

Now let me try to further analyse the components of love that I need to develop as a fairly contented sort of bloke. Essentially my carers (usually my parents) must satisfy certain physical and emotional needs and do this in a loving way. I shall dispense with the physical needs first because they are easy.

My physical needs are that I need a roof over my head and three square meals a day, preferably not all of which are fried chips with lots of salt. Or Brussels sprouts. I need clothes to keep me warm, liquids to prevent dehydration, fresh air, a bit of exercise from time to time as well as a warm dry place to sleep. This all sounds rather veterinary, and it is.

In our affluent Western civilisation people don't come to me because they have missed out on all these basic physical needs; they go to the State welfare agencies. Priority number one for them isn't to be introspective; it is just to survive.

What I do see, from time to time, are parents who have the mistaken belief that these physical aspects of care are all that are needed.

CASE HISTORY   Edith

Edith was a rather severe woman who looked a bit like a lower middle-class Margaret Thatcher. She had a tendency to dress in twin-set and pearls but the pearls were plastic and the handbag was vinyl. Somewhere beneath her cryogenic exterior was some sort of distant warmth but it showed itself only in momentary lapses when her harsh look would soften and there was a hint of a tear in her eye.

She came to see me because her two grown-up daughters had declared to her that they hated her and that they did not want anything further to do with her. That explained the tear. But why were the younger women so hurtful and angry?

As Edith spoke more she began to reveal the insidious belief that her girls did not need affection. 'I show them I love them by doing things for them. I have worked hard to give them a good home and education in the best private schools. I have never been one to hug or kiss. That doesn't come easily to me. Never has. But these girls should know that I love them. Why else would I have done so much for them?'

Wrong, Edith. Very, very wrong. The first tragedy was that she was inherently a well-intentioned woman who had never been hugged or cuddled by her own austere parents. The second tragedy was that she had reached the age of fifty-six and found herself all alone. Her daughters had grown up just as she had, carrying a quiet internal sense of being unloved and now they were showing their hurt in this angry rejection. How could Edith come to believe that she had to soften up and become more human towards them? She could not change what had happened in the past and the threat of admitting that she had made a series of sad mistakes was overwhelmingly threatening for her.

It took time but Edith worked away at it — what option did she have? And in the process she learned a lot about herself and her own feelings of neglect.

Are you leaving your run too late, as Edith did?

Enough with the physical needs, let us move on to an analysis of a child's emotional needs. As they say in investment jargon, this is where the money is.

I want to try to break down some of the basic concepts into smaller components so that I can form something of a 'checklist'. There are three types of emotional need that parents must address in their own children. They are *care*, *trust* and *hope*. You may have a sense of deja vu in seeing these three words together. They were written, in a different form, two thousand years ago:

> **'And now abideth faith, hope and charity, these three; but the greatest of these is charity.'**
>
> *I Corinthians 13:13*

Luba
Vera
Nada
(Generous giving)

For 'faith' read 'trust'. For 'charity' read 'care'. Bob's your uncle.

Care

Now feast your eyes on the diagram on page 23. Care can be further analysed into dyadic care (i.e. between two people) and systemic care (i.e. care that exists in a human group), and each of these can be further split up into a number of different factors.

I have to confess that I am borrowing heavily here from the work of an American psychiatrist called Heinz Kohut. Yes, his name sounds like a can of soup and when I call myself a 'Kohutian' that doesn't necessarily mean that I come from the planet Kohut. But this character has become very influential in the world of psychotherapy. In fact I think that in the next generation he will be recognised as the new

Freud, a household name in fact. Keep his name recorded in your memory banks for future reference.

Kohut distilled our need for care into three main categories:

- the need to have our valid good deeds and talents recognised;
- the need to have a strong person in our lives who makes us feel secure and protected;
- the need to be accepted by other human beings. *Respect*

It seems all quite straightforward, doesn't it? Now let me come along and offer my own variation on these themes.

Dyadic care comprises affection, positive regard, someone to look up to, and empathy.

Affection

This refers to common or garden hugs. Physical affection begins with the infant's feeling of being held closely. It feels just like that other great holding that we all received when we were foetuses. It must never end even when we learn how to walk and leave our mothers to explore the room, the house, the neighbourhood, then the world. Affection gives the message that you are *safe*.

This is what Edith's daughters missed out on. It seems so obvious, yet I find that in a surprising number of families it is simply missed out or, at best, saved for times when even Attila the Hun would get sentimental. Physical affection in all its forms does not come easily to some people; this is usually because they are damaged themselves.

Positive regard

Most of the patients who come to see me have problems with their self-esteem. They are trying to obtain in adult life what they should have been given in childhood.

Question: How do you get self-esteem? Answer: Self-esteem is rather like a statue. Your parents are the sculptors and with their praise and positivity they can shape the way that your self-esteem develops. But the stone that these sculptors use is the foundation of the statue. The 'stone' of your self-esteem is the feeling of being loved. If you feel loved then you feel lovable. If you feel lovable then that's a damned good start to developing a sense of self-worth.

The development of self-esteem starts even before you can talk. It is in your parents' tone of voice or the way they look at you with approving eyes. It is in the round of applause and appearance of the video camera that occurs when you take your first steps. It is in the smile in your parents' eyes when you show them your best drawing. To them it is the most insightful and creative scribble they have ever seen. It continues when you are driven to weekend sports and know that someone who cares about you is standing in the rain on the sideline (when they would much prefer to be sitting by the fire at home with a good book) just waiting for you to feature somehow so that they can cheer over all the other parents' voices, or simply because they care. It is in the knowledge that they are sitting there in the seventy-fourth row at your graduation with numbed palms because they have politely applauded several hundred strangers before you make it to the stage; and then the seventy-fourth row erupts in clapping. It is in praise where praise is due.

A hero

Every child needs someone to look up to. They need to be able to say 'I want to be just like you'. If you're the world's best bank robber and your kid asks to see your dynamite, you feel pretty chuffed. It's not only important for you to have flattery but it's essential for your kid to feel that there is someone who is competent and strong to look up to. So make sure the kid's not around when you get arrested . . .

If you don't provide a role model, society has provided a rather peculiar way of transmitting some alternatives to your children. It is called television and it allows kids to aspire to being as muscle-bound as Arnold Schwarzenegger, as thin as Elle MacPherson and as bright as Albert Einstein. Unfortunately the models that they provide might not be the best. They might set the standard as being too muscle-bound, too thin or too bright. They might also encourage your kids to be a Freddy Krueger or a Sid Vicious. Role models are best if they are home-made . . .

Empathy

In this analysis of dyadic care, I have saved the best until last. Empathy. It is a word that has been bandied around psychiatrists' conferences for the past decade. We take it very seriously. Esoteric papers with many multi-syllabled words have been written about it. We have only recently begun to appreciate the importance of empathy. It is crucial to the development of a self-respecting, whole personality. So what is it?

Empathy is the process by which one individual understands what it is like to experience life through the eyes of another. It is all about being on someone else's wave-length. It is not sympathy. It is not an intellectual understanding of what I would feel like if I were them. Empathy is *my attempt at feeling what it must be like to be you*. And you had better hope like hell that your parents had heaps of it when they were bringing you up.

As an example of how it goes right and goes wrong, I tend to take a lot of notice of how my adult patients' parents react to being informed that their son or daughter is seeing a psychiatrist. The empathic parent is alarmed and concerned. They recognise that their child, this living being whom they have brought into the world and cherished, is hurt. They tune in to their child's hurt. They want to know what they can do to help. They offer to become involved. They encourage communication.

The *unempathic* parent might react in one of the following ways:

- 'Don't be stupid, you don't need a bloody shrink!' The parent's message is that their child's suffering is trivial or unimportant. I have seen parents do this after their children have had a pretty good go at killing themselves . . .

- 'You think you've got problems! The person in this family who needs to see a psychiatrist is me!' The parent's message is that no one could ever suffer more than they have or need care and attention as much as they do. These are parents who have always given the message that no one, be they Kurd, Somalian, Serb, rape victim or HIV carrier, could ever have suffered as much as they have. Their kids suffer, but learn not to compete.

- 'I don't think that you should talk to anyone about this, dear.' The message is that of shame and embarrassment. Secrecy must be kept not for the patient's sake, but for family pride. The individual's well-being is unimportant.

- 'I suppose that all you do is sit there and bitch about me!' The parent is more concerned about their 'good name' than the sadness of their child. I have had parents phone me and ask to come to see me without their child (who is my patient) being informed. They want to tell me their 'side of the story'. Needless to say I always refuse. The irony is that they tend to be so controlling and preoccupied with their own self-esteem that their children always *do* sit there and bitch about them . . .

CASE HISTORY **Anna**

Anna wanted to try to bridge the gap between herself and her mother. She organised to visit her parents, who lived in a distant city, and found her opportunity when her father went out for his regular-as-proverbial-clockwork Rotary meeting. She was nervous and had a few glasses of wine before she broached anything painful with her mother. She told her how she had been feeling depressed and alone and that she had always wanted to be closer. Her mother cut her off in the middle of the second sentence: 'Don't be stupid, Anna, that's just the drink talking … '

CASE HISTORY **Frances**

Frances went to an exclusive girls' school and did her best to be 'good'. One Saturday when she was sixteen, she was allowed one of her few unchaperoned evenings out to go to a party. She celebrated this taste of freedom by drinking alcohol. It was her way of letting her hair down and rebelling. She awoke a few hours later in a confused state to find that a young man whom she hardly knew was having sex with her. She had been a virgin. The following Monday morning the senior common room noticeboard at the local exclusive boys' school was adorned with a notice announcing that 'Frank f***** Frances'. Frances had to keep this all to herself.

Later that week her mother, as intrusive mothers do, was 'tidying' Frances's bedroom and 'happened' to read her diary. She found out about what Frank had done and released a tirade of moralistic abuse at her daughter. Frances had been violated, degraded and technically raped. All her mother could think about was what her snobby friends would think. Frances had been violated twice in one week. She was referred to me by the hospital that treated her after the overdose. She had turned her rage on herself.

CASE HISTORY **Laura**

Laura was infertile. Her casenotes resembled a gynaecological textbook. When it came to her plumbing, Murphy's Law prevailed.

Laura had learned how to be a recluse. She had come to believe that what she called the 'three-pronged fork of tactlessness' was inescapable. She found that in most conversations with people whom she had just met she would eventually be asked how many children she had. That was prong number one. She would reply that she had none. Eventually she would be bled of the information that she had a problem with infertility. That was prong number two. They were the easy hurts compared to what would come next. People would always make some comment that showed a complete insensitivity to her suffering. The gist of this last sting would be that children were such a burden, so expensive, so naughty, etc. etc., that Laura was actually *lucky* to be infertile.

Laura was a successful businesswoman who had amassed a large personal fortune. She would gladly have given it away if she could have just one baby. She responded to the 'three-pronged fork' by avoiding people. She was afraid that if just one more person came out with anything intrusive, personal or unempathic she would have a homicide charge on her hands.

People in general have an amazing ability to be utterly insensitive if they are in a situation in which they are nervous and feel powerless. Just listen to the 'comforting' words that grieving relatives utter to the widow at a burial. Do not be surprised if she does not take long to join him.

CASE HISTORY Rachel

Rachel's parents had been about as emotionally alive as a couple of garden slugs. They were never cruel to her; they just hardly seemed to notice that she was there. In her teenage years she took to befriending and bringing home the most gruesome-looking guys that she could find in the hope that her parents would blanch and express some concerns about her safety and choice of boyfriends. But they never did. Deep inside she felt unloved and unnoticed and she compensated for this by leaving home, joining the workforce and becoming as promiscuous as possible. Her many lovers demonstrated their interest and attraction but, as might have been predicted, none of them actually made her feel loved.

Later she met Alan, who had just completed a doctoral thesis in some obscure topic in computer science. They got married. Early in the marriage things began to fall apart. Rachel was desperate for some emotional understanding. Alan was good at systems analysis. Rachel wanted to be held and listened to. Alan was good at problem-solving. Rachel yearned to have her childhood needs answered. Alan could not understand that his 'answers' did not seem to help. She did not need a 'bottom line'. She needed to be understood. She needed empathy.

Enough of dyadic care; now let us move on to the care that is elicited by being in a group. Systemic care consists of the provision of a sense of belonging, as well as protection.

Belonging

Belonging in this sense refers to the comfort that one derives from being in a group. Belonging implies acceptance, being given an identity and feeling that there is a sense of teamwork and co-operation. It is relevant to families in a number of ways. Family members might fight like cat and dog but they will never tolerate anyone outside the family criticising another family member. For the most part they all share a name which identifies them as being linked. When there is adoption, divorce, remarriage or the blending of children and step-children all of the usual rules become bent in some way (more about this in Chapter 7).

Protection

So far I have concentrated on *care* and used the notion of *control* as if it were a dirty word. We all know, however, that families that live in turmoil are not necessarily what we would choose to grow up in. Families that have a comfortable feel about them usually have some element within their functioning that is organised and, dare I say, controlled. A special type of control is needed within a family. Its ingredients are equal parts of care and control. The mixture results in the following formula:

Care + Control = Protection

Protection is controlling care, or perhaps caring control.

Does all this talk about care mean to imply that all parents must give unconditional, unadulterated, unwavering, unstoppable care? Like hell it does. No human being could provide such care. Unconditional love, like unconditional trust and unconditional forgiveness, is a goal that we all strive for but never attain. Nor should we attain them. Total, continuous care becomes smothering.

> **CASE HISTORY** **Luigi**
>
> Luigi was a middle-aged Italian man. He worked as an architectural draughtsman. He did not speak much so no one at work got to know him that well. He did not have many friends because he was a pretty shy bloke.
>
> Luigi lived with his widowed mother. When Luigi came home in the evening, Momma was there for him. She took off his shoes and fetched him his slippers. She puffed the cushions on his favourite easy chair and gave him home-cooked Italian food to eat in front of the TV. She combed his hair. She washed, she ironed, she bowed, she scraped. From the point of view of living in comfort, Luigi seemed to have it all.
>
> But really he had nothing. No friends, no family, no confidence, no dignity. From the outside it seemed that Momma was loving in an unlimited way and

that Luigi had hardly had to move from the all-giving breast. But Luigi stayed at home to keep his mother happy, not himself. When he wanted to go out to socialise she made him feel so guilty that he had to stay at home. This was love that had a lot of strings attached. It was love that was selfish. It was controlling rather than caring. In jargon terms, it was 'smother mothering'.

The moral of the story? The moral is that damned-near perfect love is like a sale-priced bargain: it is only on for a limited time. Furthermore, *parents must fail in their ability to provide perfect love for their children.* If nothing else, it forces the child to grow up, to individuate and to stand on his or her own two feet.

Trust

After care, the next factor that I need in order to feel loved is a sense of trust. For 'trust', read also *honesty* and *realness*. Care becomes destructive if it is perceived as being false or dishonest. The child feels betrayed.

The most catastrophic betrayal is one that I have already described in case histories: it is sexual abuse of a child by an adult. Children have their finger on the pulse. They may seem unsophisticated but they have a very strong instinct about what is honest and what is not. No matter how much an abusing adult tells a child that this sexual act is normal, every child knows that this touching does not feel good. No kid is bluffed and every kid ends up feeling betrayed.

There are many other, less dramatic, ways in which parental care can be perceived as false.

CASE HISTORY **Warren**

Warren's parents had read Doctor Spock. They knew that they should be very wary of allowing sibling rivalry to develop. So they treated Warren and his only brother Bruce with Solomonic justice. If one received something good then both had to receive it. To be fair.

The problem was that Warren was not as good as Bruce at most things. He was not much of a runner and he did not come top of the class as Bruce did. But the boys' parents were determined to avoid sibling rivalry. When Warren came sixth in his running race on school sports day, his parents bestowed no end of praise upon him. When Bruce received a prize at the school prize-giving both the boys were bought a special treat, so that Warren did not feel 'left out'.

This was obviously very caring on the part of Warren's parents. What a pity it backfired in their faces. Warren derived no pleasure from their praise or gifts. In his heart he knew that he had not earned them. Bruce became quietly resentful that he was not given special treatment when he had done especially well. He decided that he must double and treble his efforts to do better so that he would be noticed for having more talent than Warren. But their parents did not get the message that by being dishonest in their avoidance of sibling rivalry they had actually increased it.

What should they have done? They should have rewarded Bruce for winning his running races and for coming top of the class. They should also have noticed that Warren had talents too. He was a very handsome child with a placid disposition. He was very popular with his classmates at school. He was talented at artwork. He needed recognition for the elements of his personality and identity that were special. He knew that coming sixth in his running race was not good, so his parents' applause sounded hollow, even deceitful. In a paradoxical way it made him feel even more of a failure.

The road to hell is paved with good intentions.

All families have secrets and all families have a set of beliefs that might be called the '*family mythology*'.

Family *secrets* might be that:

≡ Mum and Dad had to get married because Mum was pregnant with Abigail.

≡ Freddy is really adopted.

≡ My older sister is seventeen years older than me because she is not really my sister but my mother.

You will see that many family secrets are associated with some old-fashioned idea of what is 'shameful'. Some family secrets are quite appropriate. It may not be in the best interests of the children to know that Mum and Dad are having trouble paying the mortgage this month. This will all pan out in the end and the kids do not need to be confronted with insecurity like this if it is temporary. But most family secrets are destructive, such as the darkest of secrets that is called 'incest'. Secrets are like time-bombs: they do their most damage when they reveal themselves.

Family *myths* might be that they were all descended from, say, the Kings of Ireland. The most insidious family myths are:

≡ 'We are all one big happy family.'

- 'You can come and talk to me about anything, anytime.'
- 'We are right (in religion or politics) while the rest of the world is wrong.'

Myths might be fervently believed by some members of the family, but usually because they have some problem that *requires* them to hold these beliefs to be true. Children know from an early age and with considerable conviction what is true and what is false. Family mythology exists to bolster the fragile egos of parents, not children. Children who are overly controlled might buy into these myths to please their parents. If they are not allowed to rebel and look for their own beliefs in adolescence then they will, reluctantly, mouth the myths even if they do not believe them in their hearts. When they eventually allow themselves to speak the truth ('our family has huge problems ... I cannot talk to either of my parents because they are more interested in themselves than in me ... I cannot identify with my parents' religious or political beliefs ... ') then they are often left with an insidious sense of betrayal. And it becomes very hard to trust anyone ever again.

Now having said all this about the need for truth, let me confuse you with another paradox. You will remember that I extolled the virtues of care but explained that *perfect* care from a parent to a child was unattainable. The reality is that children need to realise that their parents will never be able to love them in an unconditional and everlasting way. Parental care comes with strings attached, and so it should. This helps the child to grow up beneath the umbrella of care but also to individuate and, in time, to become independent of his or her parents' care.

The same applies to truth. A child can never grow up in a family that is 100 per cent honest all the time. The 'truth paradox' is that a child must learn to mistrust and to lie. Not a lot, just when it is necessary to save the backside and, on the balance of probabilities, it can be got away with. This usually attracts the label of telling 'white lies'; these are untruths that we can feel a bit uncomfortable about but not worry that for saying them we will burn in hell forever. They are adaptive talents if they are not taken to extremes. Kids who lie frequently, because they are skiting or because they have no conscience or because they want to be just like Dad (who is in jail), tend to end up in strife in later life. In a similar vein, kids who do not mistrust tend to become abused. Or they grow up into the victims of con-men. As Barnum, the circus proprietor

of Barnum and Bailey fame, said, 'There's one born every minute ... '
He was talking about suckers. They are the people who do not mistrust
enough.

My kids are taught in school about 'stranger danger'. Good show.

Hope

Hope is the fuel that keeps us going. The poet Alexander Pope
claimed that it 'springs eternal' but by the time most of my
patients get to see me their needle is on 'E'.

Hope is all about projecting the present and the past into the future
and estimating what life will be like on the basis of what it is and
has been like. There is a natural human tendency, the 'human
spirit' perhaps, to be hopeful. People have an extraordinary ability
to forget pain and suffering. Most people spend the decade between
fifteen and twenty-five years of age entering and exiting intimate
relationships before they finally decide to commit themselves to
another person indefinitely. Exiting each preceding relationship is
associated with pain and despair, but it does not stop them from
launching headlong, filled with besotted hope, into the next one. Along
the way a few people drop out. They are the most hurt of all. They are
called 'cynics'.

CASE HISTORY **Drew**

Drew was a compulsive gambler. Poker machines beckoned him. The betting
shop would lovingly breathe his name as he tried to walk by. Down at the
racetrack he felt alive.

Drew was trapped into frantic cycles of hope and despair. When he put
money on a horse, life seemed worthwhile. Like all compulsive gamblers he
always had to bet so much money that winning would be spectacular and
losing it would hurt. He hung around the one dollar pokies and looked
sanctimoniously at those who bet in ten cent lots. Like all gamblers he spoke
proudly of the $1000 he had won last Saturday, but never of the $5000 he
had lost the week before.

Why did he do this? Because inside he felt unimportant, unlovable and
worthless. Most of all there did not seem to be any point to his life. He was
alone and unhappy. He could not see that this situation would ever change.
He had no hope. And gambling was his *escape*.

> Compulsive gamblers never take it up as a lifelong profession. The ones who claim to are lying to you. Eventually they all lose it all. Gambling is a very poisonous drug. It is the mistress who will always betray you.

So what has all this got to do with childhood? The answer is that life is full of disappointments. Buddha said that 'life is suffering'. I think that he might have overstated the case a bit, but he was on the right track. No one, not even that spoilt brat who lives on the corner and seems to have all the toys that were ever invented, can escape some sort of hurt or misery in life.

Over the centuries humans have tried in a hundred different ways to predict the future. No one ever has. Astrologists speak in such vague terms that you could identify with their predictions for me and vice versa. The writings of Nostradamus are held up as evidence of his being a prophet; but closer examination shows them to be a lot of nebulous waffle.

If you were offered a crystal ball and could see your own future would you accept the offer? I doubt it. I do not want to see what illnesses I will suffer. I would prefer not to know if one of my children is destined to die in an accident in ten years' time. Most of all I do not want to know how long I will live or how I will die. I know that I must die eventually, but I would prefer to leave the details to God, whatever he/she/it may be. Fixing a date and time of death is the cruellest element of capital punishment; more callous, I suspect, than the execution itself.

What we do know is that life is not a rose garden. Or if it is the thorns must dig into our fingers from time to time. And when it comes to families, no one has the perfect family, no one has the perfect parents and no one can be the perfect parent. We all strive to have a good-enough life with good-enough parents in a good-enough family. Given that start, we can handle a few disappointments yet still hang on to that hope that is the 'human spirit'. If we have too many disappointments then there is a chance that we will find ourselves

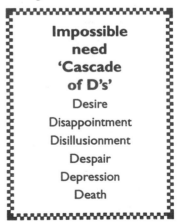

Impossible need 'Cascade of D's'

Desire

Disappointment

Disillusionment

Despair

Depression

Death

tumbling down what I call the 'cascade of D's' (see diagram on page 37). Sometimes the disappointments are a continual assault on us such as the everyday pattern of being ignored that existed for Rachel, who could not even get her parents' attention with Hell's Angels. Sometimes the disappointment comes as a handful of catastrophic 'thuds' in our lives, such as the death of a parent, developing a serious illness or being put into a class with a particularly sadistic teacher who picks on you. Either way, it is difficult to hang on to hope when the people who are responsible for our upbringing are, quite simply, not good enough.

How it all goes right — or wrong

So far in this chapter I have mused about what children *need* so that they feel loved. Kids who feel loved tend to be kids who feel lovable and able to love. Now I want to move on to what kids *get*. If all children got what they needed then psychiatrists would never have been invented. The people whom I see are grown up kids who didn't *get* what they *needed*.

You will see from the diagram on page 23 that when it comes to love, children fall into three groups:
≡ those who get everything;
≡ those who do not get enough;
≡ those who get enough.

Let me dispense with the first category. Getting unlimited, unconditional, unfailing love is something reserved for babies. Sad but true, it does not last.

Cast your minds back. Your arrival was celebrated with flowers and cigars. Wherever you went, people crowded around and went 'Ooh!, Aah!' They spoke to you in funny squeaky voices and proclaimed how cute you were. And what a nice name you had. They passed you around so that everyone could 'have a hold'. All you had to do was squawk to obtain food and comfort. You didn't even have to get up to go to the bathroom.

But perhaps the most luxurious sensation of all was being held at your mother's breast. What a *cornucopia*. So soft and warm and yielding. So safe. So pleasurable. Remember? No, neither do I. Rather a pity, don't you think? Because this was our finest hour. This was the time when we were special with a capital 'S'. This was when we were loved with a capital 'L'. No responsibility, no worries, no pain. Why, oh why, did we ever have to grow up?

Who knows, but grow up we did. And many of us have spent much time and energy trying to return to this state. It is called 'escapism'. More of this below.

The children who did not get enough love

I know these children well. I spend hours every day sitting in my comfortable leather chair listening to them speak. It takes time, but eventually I hear how they did not get enough love. There are only two ways. You will recall that I mentioned earlier that, in the final analysis, human beings relate to each other in only one of two very instinctive ways. They either care for each other or control each other. Control is about making sure that I survive. Care is about survival of the species.

Children who do not get enough love tend to get either *an excessive amount of control* or *an insufficient amount of care*. The former group are criticised, judged, attacked and abused. The latter group are neglected and ignored. That all sounds rather dramatic but it can actually be very subtle and very long-standing.

When this happens children invariably know somewhere in their hearts that 'this is not the way it is supposed to be'. Young children usually speak the truth but try to keep their parents happy by spouting all their parents' rationalisations to convince others, and themselves, too, that 'this is the way it is supposed to be'. At the same time they may become uncomfortably confused when they begin their early attempts at individualising. This might involve playing with the kids up the street or going to kindergarten. As these children get older it dawns on them that not everyone's dad gets drunk and not everyone's mum yells at their kids all day. They may see that they have all the toys but none of the hugs and bedtime stories.

> **CASE HISTORY** **Catherine**
>
> Catherine came to see me but brought her five-year-old daughter Sasha with her. Catherine was anxious and depressed. Sasha stood silently by her mother's chair as Catherine spoke to me. The two seemed bonded in some unhealthy way. I interrupted Catherine and began to involve Sasha. Did she go to school or kindergarten? 'No', replied Sasha. 'I have to stay at home to look after my mother. She gets too scared when I go away.'

From the mouths of babes. Here was the sad truth. It was a reflection of Catherine's own misery that she had given birth to a child with the intention, consciously or subconsciously, that this daughter would look after her rather than the other way around.

If I had encountered Sasha two or three years later, when she had joined that unhappy group who are called 'school refusers', then I would have found a whole different story. The truth would have remained the same, but both Sasha and Catherine would have a variety of rationalisations as to why Sasha did not go to school. 'Sasha is sick a lot.' 'Sasha is too bright to go to a school that does not treat her as special.' 'The kids at that school are too rough.' 'My mother does not like my teacher.' And so on.

Sometimes the distress gets covered by these rationalisations. Sometimes it is simply too awful to bear so it is stuffed deep into the subconscious mind and 'forgotten'. It might be forgotten for decades, but not forever.

CASE HISTORY **Jeanette**

Jeanette attended her school's twenty-fifth jubilee celebrations. There she bumped into James who had been her sweetheart when they were both thirteen years old. There was still a lot of warmth between them. They split off from the main group to sit down and catch up with all the news of the past two decades and to have a heart-to-heart.

James told her that he had hoped that she would be at the reunion because there was something that he had remembered from all those years ago that had been troubling him. He wanted to clear it up with her.

He said: 'Do you remember when we decided in the playground that we would be boyfriend and girlfriend? You said to me: "If I'm your girlfriend does that mean that we have to have sex? I don't know whether I want to do that because it hurts too much." What did you mean by that?'

Jeanette was riveted to the spot, speechless. All of a sudden he had opened a door into her subconscious mind and excruciating memories began to flood back. You can guess what they were about. Jeanette had not had such a nice childhood as she had preferred to remember. Incest again. All those years she had been sad. All those male friends whom she had not allowed to touch her. The horrible gut-wrenching numbing feeling she felt after going to bed with the handsome chap she met in the bar. It all made sense. But what a ghastly sense.

So if I, as a child, receive excessive control or insufficient care, what happens next? I have only three options:

40

- I must either escape from the scene; or
- I must fall apart in a decompensation; or
- I must react to the situation.

I escape In the first chapter I mentioned the phenomenon of escapism. It takes many forms but all have the following elements in common:

- Escapism takes us from a world of pain into a world of pleasure. The pain is often simply boredom or monotony. The pleasure is associated with some form of relief, hope or fantasies of love.
- Escapism often develops into a compulsion; one is compelled to pursue this exit from pain. In its worst form it is called 'addiction'.
- Escapism may be harmless or harmful. Harmless efforts at escapism might be fantasising about seducing or being seduced by that delectable person you saw on the bus, or switching on your favourite comedy program on television so that you do not notice how lonely you are. Harmful escapism comes under a variety of names including 'philandering', 'alcoholism' and 'a heroin habit'.
- Escapism is, at some level in your subconscious mind, a trip to that utopian world of infancy in which you were loved and pleased in an almost unlimited way.

Escapism has one over-riding drawback: the pleasure never lasts. If it did, we would all be escaping all the time. Such a situation was depicted in Aldous Huxley's book *Brave New World* in which a drug called *soma* was put into the world's water supplies. *Soma* made everyone feel relaxed and happy and loving. If anyone out there finds the recipe, please let me know ASAP. The nearest that we have got to *soma* is probably cocaine, which would be a marvellous substitute if it did not wear off rapidly and leave people depressed and irritable and, in some cases, addicted. These days there is no such thing as a free lunch or a trouble-free psycho-stimulant. As they say in the gangster movies, them's the breaks.

I fall apart You will recall that in the last chapter I described the subconscious mind and how we all have a repertoire of coping strategies called 'defences' to protect ourselves from having to deal with the harsh emotional realities of life. Sometimes, if we are exposed to enough stress, our coping strategies are overwhelmed. Our subconscious mind, that vulnerable, childlike part of us, is exposed. Emotionally, if not physically, we feel as if we are falling apart.

How much stress is enough to knock down all our defences? This depends very much upon the stability of the individual. We all know people who seem to be unflappable. They make good surgeons and airline pilots. We also all know people who make a life crisis out of finding that their cheque account is overdrawn. They make good actors. Between these two extremes are you and me. We are threatened by the sudden death of a loved one, by witnessing a serious car accident, by learning of the infidelity of our spouse or by finding ourselves lost in the outback. Come to think of it, even surgeons and airline pilots get rattled by these stresses.

As a child we might be overwhelmingly threatened by the death of a parent, by serious physical or sexual abuse or by finding ourselves lost in a crowd. We might *seem* to cope well at the time but, as I have described above, all of these traumas are recorded in that unfailing hard disc that is called the subconscious mind. Later when we are threatened with similar traumas in later life there is a tendency to react to them by readily *decompensating*. In this reaction to crisis all sorts of thoughts and behaviour are revealed. We may decide that we are worthless, unloved and unlovable. In a particularly severe decompensation we may come to believe that either we are unreal or the world is unreal; when taken to an extreme this is called a 'reactive psychosis'. Stress can be so great that it sends us mad.

CASE HISTORY **Gillian**

Gillian came to see me because she could not stop crying. She was an insurance broker and found that tears and business were an unholy mix. Her sadness had come to the point where she could no longer work. Gillian was a stoic and highly suspicious of psychiatrists, so it had taken her some time, with coercion on the part of her GP, to even set foot inside my office. This began a long and arduous association between us.

Gillian's father had been an alcoholic who had died, predictably, of cirrhosis of the liver not long after Gillian was born. Her mother, as is the trend with the wives of alcoholics, suffered from an almost unremitting depression. Quite apart from this she was an extraordinarily harsh woman who spent most of her time either punishing or ignoring Gillian. Gillian lost that wonderful naive innocence of childhood. Her home became a prison. Her mother, who was a suspicious recluse, became her only cell-mate.

Gillian was an unwanted child and her mother reminded her of this daily.

Many, many sessions into her psychotherapy, Gillian described through almost uncontrollable tears that she had passed through a phase of her childhood, at age eight or nine, of becoming convinced that she was invisible. This was the only way that she, in her childlike way, could rationalise why her mother neglected her as she did. Gillian's emotional neglect was of such severity that she lived most of her childhood years in a state of near decompensation into an unreal world.

Psychiatrists must keep a certain personal and emotional distance from their patients in order to maintain objectivity. That way we can provide a safe, containing environment for both ourselves and our patients. With Gillian it was a struggle to hide the horror and the pathos that I felt in hearing her story. Once again the words crossed my mind. Familiar words. They said:

'How could anyone do that to a child? ... '

I react   Falling apart, decompensating, is what happens when we are overwhelmed. For the most part, though, people develop a habitual way of reacting to the hurts of attack and abandonment. These habitual reactions over many years become personality styles. Emotionally healthy people have a bit of each of these personality styles at various times, but they do not become trapped in any particular one. Problems arise when people cannot move out of one specific way of thinking and relating. In the simplest of simplifications there are only three. Let me describe them.

The 'Me-down' personality   These people make a habit of giving, loving, caring, rescuing and supporting. Their greatest pleasure is in pleasing others. Unfortunately they take all of these honourable behaviours to an extreme and they cannot be downright self-centred when they need to be. They believe that they are responsible to everyone in their lives. They are trusting, loyal and dutiful. They are also invariably downtrodden. Their most commonly felt emotional distress is anxiety.

The 'Me-up' personality   These people are takers. They are conscience-free takers too. They bring people into their lives who are 'Me-down' personalities and make them responsible for their well-being. They are controlling and mistrusting. They are often ambitious and narcissistic. Their most commonly felt emotional distress is anger.

The 'Me-out' personality   These people do not play 'Up' and 'Down' games. They pick up their bat and ball and go home. Sometimes it is appropriate for all of us to withdraw from an intolerable situation ('I quit') or a bad relationship ('I'm off'), but 'Me-out' people are always alone. In their worst extreme they become hermits. Sometimes they are the peculiar pensioner whom the neighbours hardly ever see. In less extreme forms they simply avoid any great emotional contact with anyone. In a quiet way their most commonly felt emotional distress is sadness.

When you delve into the subconscious minds of people with these personality styles it is often possible to discern a rather peculiar basic belief. For 'Me-down' people the basic belief is 'I am bad and you are good'. They are stuck in childhood. 'Me-up' people harbour the belief that 'I am good and you are bad'. They are stuck in adolescence. 'Me-out' people often do not seem to have a basic belief possibly because they do not come near enough to someone like me in order to reveal it. If it *is* there then perhaps it can be stated quite simply as 'I don't care'. Maybe these people are stuck in early adulthood, which is when most of us withdraw from our families in the process of individuation. The problem is that 'Me-out' people usually individuated in childhood.

All of these personality styles become involved in what I call a 'vicious cycle'.

- 'Me-down' personalities decide that they will attract love and care by pleasing everyone around them. Unfortunately they learn that, when they are around a 'Me-up' personality, no matter how much they try to care and please, it is never enough.
- 'Me-up' personalities become angry and decide that they will punish the people who are supposed to love and care for them; that way these stupid carers will get the message and front the goods. Unfortunately the carers usually get angry as all hell and retaliate, so 'Me-up' people have to punish them even more.
- 'Me-out' personalities withdraw. And then they get lonely.

As you can see, becoming 'stuck' in any one of these personality styles does not lend itself to a happy life. Just in case this all sounds dreary and theoretical, I shall put flesh on to these people and give them names.

CASE HISTORY **Rita**

Rita was a mousy woman. So mousy was she, in fact, that as she spoke to me, I sometimes found myself drifting off into a daydream in which she had long whiskers. Even her voice was squeaky. She spent a lot of time apologising to me but most of the time I had no idea what she had done wrong. Her demeanour screamed of submission. Rita was well and truly 'Me-down' . . .

She came to see me with, you guessed, depression. A few weeks before her first appointment she had been beaten up by her son, who was a heroin addict. He had then emptied her purse of money and disappeared. She had not seen or heard from him since. Despite all this she felt that she had lost her 'only friend'.

Rita lived with her husband Tom. In fact Tom was her ex-husband since they were divorced but in truly masochistic style she had gone back to live with him. Do you think that he treated her well? Like hell he did. He was an alcoholic. He criticised her. He ignored her. He sometimes punished her by the 'silent treatment'. He could be unbelievably cruel while saying nothing. For days and days on end.

Rita seemed to have a neon sign on her forehead that said 'Kick me'. And everyone that she encountered seemed to oblige. The most extraordinary thing was that Rita seemed to think that this was all that she deserved. Rita did not realise that *people respect people who have self-respect*. Rita had no self-respect and people could pick this up a mile off. When she was around other 'Me-down' people they would try to rescue her. But for the most part she was treated with contempt.

Trying to win people's love and respect by being so submissive is a futile exercise. Rita's task was to delve into her anxiety and then into the anger that lurked underneath. The rage was there but it was too threatening to Rita to even begin to touch.

Rita illustrates an important feature of her personality style: within every 'Me-down' person there is a 'Me-up' person trying to get out . . .

CASE HISTORY **Adolf**

Adolf was never my patient. He was, in fact, the leader of a rather large military organisation called the Third Reich. Adolf had major personality problems. He had a grandiose image of his own self-importance. He harboured fantasies of gaining limitless power and prestige. His ability to empathise with the suffering of anyone else rated a 'zero'. He reacted catastrophically if anyone criticised him. He required continual praise and admiration to feel real and alive.

Adolf was the world's most famous 'Me-up' personality. He was also the world's worst. But when you look at *all* cult leaders and most of the world's leaders they certainly have a 'Me-up' flavour about them. And notice how many of them are men.

CASE HISTORY **Christopher**

Christopher was a bit of a suburban Adolf but with some redeeming features. 'Me-up' personalities can often be thoroughly charming. They tend to use that to manipulate people by gentle seduction. Chris presented himself immaculately. Not one of his dyed hairs was out of place. He shook my hand warmly and immediately called me by my first name. That always gets my alarm bells ringing.

Chris was a salesman. Funny lot, salesmen. They know how to get under your skin. But you always feel that beneath *their* skin is very little. Their charm is superficial, as they are.

He informed me that he had come to see me to 'prepare' me for seeing his girlfriend Anna, who had an appointment to see me next week. Bollocks he had. Chris's real agenda was to take control of Anna's treatment. He was not concerned about Anna, but about how Anna would describe him to me. He oozed charm from every pore. He wanted me to see him as the 'good guy' that he wasn't. He asked me to keep it a secret from Anna that he had come to see me. My alarm bells were going crazy. I declined. Chris's reaction was predictable. He was quietly incensed, flushed red, and ended the consultation shortly after that. I never saw him again. I also never saw Anna. I can only suppose that he 'forbade' her to see me, telling her what an absolutely hopeless psychiatrist I was. And all because I prevented him from being in control of my dealings with her.

Chris was a 'Me-up' person. I will bet ten-to-one that Anna was 'Me-down'. Any takers?

Chris illustrated two important features of 'Me-up' people. Firstly, they rarely come to see me of their own accord unless they are in absolute crisis. They make life comfortable for themselves by always having a 'Me-down' person around to look after them. The crisis happens when the 'Me-down' person gets fed up with of all this and moves out. Then the 'Me-ups' form a queue at my door. Secondly, 'Me-up' people must *always* be in control of a relationship.

If you are reading this, Anna, get out now while the going is good.

CASE HISTORY **Louise**

Now for an example of a 'Me-out' personality. Louise looked like everyone's maiden aunt. She looked this way because she had been caught in a time warp and still wore her hair in a bun. She had not gone to any lengths to make herself attractive for many years. Her clothes were simple and dowdy. She had stacked on a bit of weight.

Louise was professional and composed at the start of her first session with me. She worked as a publisher's secretary. She had worked for the same boss at the same desk in the same building for fifteen years. Security was a big deal to Louise.

Fifteen minutes into this session she began to cry. A couple of dozen tissues later it was time to go. She had blurted out a wretched story. In her teens she had fallen in love with a man who rejected and hurt her. The pain was so intense that she had quietly vowed to herself that she would never again let another man get close to her. At the time of consultation she was fifty-four years old and still living with her aging mother. Over the past year she had developed a friendship with Frank, a middle-aged divorcee whom she had met at her bridge club. Bridge was her one and only social outing. He had been a newcomer to the club and they immediately found that they had many things in common. He impressed her as being soft and sensitive. Slowly she came to trust him. They would go out for dinner and to movies. The relationship grew more intimate. She was doing things that adolescents usually do, but that she had busily avoided for the past thirty years.

Eventually she gave him her most prized possession: her virginity. Two weeks later he told her that he was going back to his wife. Her hurt was immeasurable and unceasing. She never spoke to him again. She never went back to the bridge club. Her world had been turned upside down. She spent all day, every day, by herself and in tears.

The tragedy was that she was a hell of a nice woman, with homely warmth and humour. She had spent her life as a 'Me-out' personality and taken one brief and disastrous excursion back to the real world. She retreated to the 'Me-out' stance and is almost certainly still there.

Most 'Me-out' people were sent there because they were hurt by letting people get too close. There is a natural human tendency to seek emotional intimacy but it is inherently a vulnerable and risky business. Just ask Louise.

I cannot move on until I mention two unusual 'Me-out' personalities. They illustrate how subconsciously crafty 'Me-out' personalities can be.

CASE HISTORY   Sister Mary

Sister Mary was a middle-aged nun. When she was a novice (which is the convent jargon for a 'rookie nun') she fell in love with a handsome young priest. She used to flirt with him, in the most benign nunly way, after mass on Sundays. She then took to visiting him and slowly a real bond of affection grew between the two of them. Eventually in a moment of great distress she told him she loved him. To her delighted surprise, he returned the sentiment. Talk about star-crossed lovers. This was real Mills and Boon stuff with a religious twist.

They both agreed that they must pursue their respective vocations. There was never any contact between them that was intimate enough to be risky. They have loved each other from afar for nearly thirty years.

Now read on.

CASE HISTORY **Belinda**

Belinda was a very beautiful woman who was a nurse. Nurses do not scrub floors or empty bedpans any more. They are specialists in their own right and Belinda's specialty was intensive care nursing.

All women want to be attractive but only really beautiful women know what a millstone this can be. They become the object of men's desire. After a few years of this the novelty wears off and they yearn to be wanted for their minds and personalities rather than just their faces and curves. Belinda had been hurt by so many men who simply wanted to possess her that she had 'given up' on men.

One day a young man was admitted to the intensive care ward of her hospital under armed guard. He was from the local prison. He was a convicted murderer who had tried to hang himself in his prison cell. A chance inspection by a warder had saved him just in time.

The patient remained unconscious for an hour or two more before waking to look into the beautiful face of Belinda. He was happy. He had succeeded in killing himself, had gone to heaven and he was looking at an angel. He had escaped the next fifteen years of misery in jail. Then he realised that he had an intravenous line in his arm and an oxygen mask on his face. Damn!

You know the rest of this case history. The two fell in love. Mills and Boon again but without the suggestive words like 'throbbing urgency' and 'heaving breast'. No sex or physical contact because there was always a guard with them. When he recovered, Belinda visited him twice a week in prison. Only another fifteen years before they could be together . . .

The cases of Sister Mary and the beautiful Belinda indicate how people with a great fear of the vulnerability of intimacy can skilfully avoid it. They fall in love with people whom they simply can never have. The subconscious avoidance in all of this is something that they would never admit to. But the distancing effect of a nun's habit or prison bars saves them from having to confront the reality of a mature relationship.

The most damaged personalities: borderlines and psychopaths

Now go back to the diagram on page 23. If children do not get enough love they have only three choices. They must either escape or decompensate ('fall apart') or react. I have described the three 'Me' personalities, 'Down', 'Up' and 'Out', which is how people try to cope with their deep feelings of being unloved. Now let me describe the most damaged personalities of all.

They become stuck in life at the level of the black circle in the middle of the diagram. They spend their lives behaving as if they are running frantically all over the diagram. At times they will isolate themselves, then go on a drug-binge of escapism, then become attracted to someone and assume a victim-like 'Me-down' position or a brutal, controlling 'Me-up' position, but never something decent and mutually respecting in the middle. Then they fall apart by becoming hysterical or destructive or enraged. In women this personality disorder tends to become what is called 'the borderline personality'. If men suffer this way they tend to be labelled 'psychopaths'. Some men are borderlines and some women are psychopaths. And sometimes the personality styles almost merge.

Borderlines come to see psychiatrists. Psychopaths go to prison. Borderlines enrage psychiatrists and their own families. Psychopaths enrage society.

CASE HISTORY **Penny**

My first impressions of Penny were of how warm and charming she was. She had a way of making me feel like the most competent and good-looking psychiatrist in the world. Silly, silly me. It did not take long before Penny and I were doing battle head-on. That is the way with these people's relationships. They are chaotic. They are filled with charm and seduction but this alternates with rage and manipulation. If borderlines stick with any particular personality style they will tend to be 'Me-up' personalities. Their internal psychic world is in such a state of wretched turmoil that they must always be in control. In my practice they always end up wanting to set the appointment times and durations, the fees, when they will pay me, how I will treat them, who they will bring along with them, etc. etc.

Borderlines drive me crazy. Some psychiatrists specialise in the psychotherapy of borderline personalities. They must be crazy too. How many thorns can their sides take?

Borderlines tend to waltz around personality styles depending upon what stage of the relationship they have reached with you. They start off as seductive 'Me-down' types. When they are disappointed in a relationship they tend to fall apart pretty decisively and then they become 'Me-up' people: critical, controlling, even degrading. They have a way of knowing how to flatter you and how to demolish you. They know your Achilles heel and when you disappoint them they will remind you that they know. They know how to mock and humiliate. How do they know this? I wish I knew. They seem to have some sort of perverse instinct.

At the end of Chapter 1, I described some psychodynamic defences. Borderlines rely heavily on the defence that is called 'splitting', i.e. the need to see everything and everyone as good/bad, right/wrong, black/white. There is no ambivalence and no shades of grey. When they meet and like you they see you as all good. When you disappoint them (which any human being must invariably do) they see you as all bad. Then they punish you. And then they discard you and go off to find someone else. 'Me-down' becomes 'Me-up', then 'Me-out'. *All of their intimate relationships become intense and transient.*

So why did I persevere with Penny? Because Penny, like all borderlines, lives in a state of chronic depression. Borderlines attract that name because they are always on the borderline of madness. Penny would occasionally fall apart so much that she would become transiently psychotic.

Even though borderlines wreak havoc upon their families and get right up my professional nose, there is a certain sense of pathos about them. They are the world's greatest deceivers. They often seem externally integrated and highly functioning. Inside they feel hollow, empty and bored. Penny, like many borderlines, developed the bizarre habit of mutilating herself. She would go into intense decompensations in which the world became strange and unfamiliar. She found out by trial and error that the only thing that she could do to stop this state of anguished suffering was to cut herself. She did not feel any pain when she did this, just an immense relief. But the crucial element in this ceremony was that she had to see her own blood. It made her feel real.

Penny was not really mad. Just very, very damaged. How many Pennys are there in the world? Plenty. But they are good at disguising themselves. Penny is an extreme case but if the essential features of this personality style are their chronic emptiness and boredom and the instability of their relationships, they probably make up five per cent of the population. Scary thought, that.

CASE HISTORY **Geoff**

Geoff was bad. But he also had had a bad start to life. I saw him in prison at the request of his solicitor. In psychiatric terminology I labelled him as having an antisocial personality disorder. In other words he was a psychopath.

He was the third child of a prostitute. Neither he nor his mother ever had any idea who his real father was. Geoff showed the world from an early age that he was not going to be a professor or a saint. He had huge problems with reading. He became impossible to teach because of his disruptive behaviour. Eventually he simply did not go to school and, while the headmaster made the usual noises about how bad this was, his teacher was quietly relieved. Geoff had started a fire in the school toilets and by the age of eight had twice been caught in the playground with a knife in his possession. The local police knew him well. He was aggressive and a loner. He was 'farmed out' by government welfare agencies to well-meaning and stable foster-parents but none of them could put up with him for long. His most disturbing behaviour was his cruelty to animals. Most of the cats in the neighbourhood were canny enough to avoid him and the ones that did not had had their ears cut off . . .

Geoff's life was characterised by fairly frequent jail sentences, impulsive violence, alcohol binges, dabbling with drugs and a series of de facto relationships with girlfriends whom he would frequently beat up. He was an artful liar and had a profound disregard for the feelings or welfare of anyone else, including his own children. Perhaps most disturbing of all was the impression that he could do horrible things and *never feel guilty*.

Geoff was emotionally unreachable. The only glimpse of the embittered child within him was a tattoo on his cheek. The tattoo was of a single teardrop.

Yes, Virginia, there are psychopaths. But if you stay away from prisons and back alleys in seedy inner-city suburbs you might not have to meet them. Rather paradoxically, however, some psychopaths wear suits and ties and earn huge amounts of money. They habitually lie, but never with little fibs; they work on the principle that people will only believe them if they tell real whoppers. They are called 'creative psychopaths'. They reveal themselves by their extraordinary lack of guilt or empathy. They make the newspapers because they have just skipped the country with a squillion dollars of stolen money in a suitcase. Sometimes they make the newspapers because they have just been elected to government . . .

Kids who get enough love

Borderlines and psychopaths are *the* most damaged personalities. Most people who consult me professionally are slightly more sophisticated. Lots of them have become stuck in the 'Me-down' position. They try to attract love and attention by being good, loving, giving, caring and rescuing. In the process they become quietly resentful and depressed. Usually they have never been allowed to go through a healthy adolescent rebellion. *They have been under-loved and over-controlled.*

So what about the majority of the population who never get to my office? I can only presume that most of them get enough love. Their parents have respected them enough to allow them to individuate and be independent. They have an inherent and unshakable appreciation of their own worth, entitlement, goodness and integrity. Their relationships are relatively equitable and stable. They know about truth and trust. They are in touch with their feelings and can communicate them, even the bad ones. They cope. Deep inside they hold the conviction that they are *loved, lovable and able to love.* They turn out OK.

My patients often ask me how many people out there in society are really 'normal'. How should I know? Obstetricians see pregnant women and can formulate the belief that all the world is pregnant. Paediatricians begin to believe that the world is a metre tall and dermatologists believe that the whole world has dermatitis. Psychiatrists believe that the world is sad, mad or bad. This is only because we spend our lives becoming involved in the lives of people who are one or more of these. But I am not that pessimistic because there is something that is inherently hopeful and spirited in most of the people I see. They consult me because they want their lives to improve.

That is why I hold a very deep belief in the basic benevolence of humankind. Among all the woes of the world, hang on to this idea. *Most* people are *mostly* good *most* of the time.

CHAPTER three

Emotions

The red, blue and yellow of emotions

Everyone knows that emotions are like bowel gas: they are better out than in, but releasing them can be a fairly alarming process.

In the preceding chapters I have looked at the structure of the mind (conscious and subconscious) and also the effect of your personal past on the development of your personality. Now it is time to look at emotions. They are my bread and butter. People bring me their emotional distress. They use a variety of words to express it. Cast your eyes over the selection here and choose a few to bamboozle your psychiatrist.

I am a rather simple-minded chap. I become overwhelmed with all these words. Not only is the patient confused, but so am I. And a patient who feels that his or her psychiatrist is confused tends to quickly find another psychiatrist.

I have found that I can take all these words and reduce them to three. I believe that there are only three primary types of emotional distress, rather like there being only three primary colours, from which all shades and hues are developed. The red, blue and yellow of emotional pain are *anger*, *anxiety* and *sadness*.

> ### Doctor, I feel a great sense of . . .
>
> . . . restlessness, doubt, animosity, apprehension, grief, hostility, dismay, melancholy, burnout, indignation, fear, sorrow, resentment, trouble, frustration, suffering, bitterness, stress, concern, wrath, strain, torment, rage, tension, guilt, bother, distress, worry, confusion, annoyance, outrage, concern, disquiet, bewilderment, reservation, pointlessness, emptiness, irritation, aggression, insecurity, depression . . .

≡ For 'anger' read annoyance, irritation, frustration, aggression and rage.

≡ For 'anxiety' read fear, stress, worry, insecurity, restlessness and concern.

≡ For 'sadness' read depression, burnout, grief, dismay and sorrow.

During this chapter I intend to explore each of these three emotions, to give them each a flavour and a meaning and to let you know how they present to me clinically.

First of all, let me suggest that these three inter-relate in

> ### Three types of emotional distress
>
> Anger   Anxiety
>
> Sadness

a predictable way. Anger and anxiety are about excitation and overactivity; sadness is about depletion and underactivity and the three can be conceptualised as forming the corners of an upturned triangle (see diagram). Anger and anxiety run on adrenalin. This induces our most primitive animalistic response to any sort of threat: fight (anger) or flight (anxiety). We see these feelings in animals every time we encounter a dogfight or watch a cat pounce on a mouse. Do animals suffer sadness? They seem to have a bewildered feel about them when they encounter the death of one of their kind. But from a bodily, physiological point of view the nearest thing to depression that animal behaviour displays is actually *hibernation*.

About anger

In the business world I am frequently bemused by the emphasis that psychologists and counsellors put upon 'stress management'. Squillions of company dollars are spent every year encouraging executives to think positively, manage their time and do relaxation exercises. But they still look pretty burnt-out to me.

More recently there has come a trend (all these things are so faddish) to seminars about 'conflict resolution'. In this, warring factions within a corporation are encouraged to communicate their disagreements and to seek mediation so that a compromise can be reached and everyone can leave the room in a 'win–win' frame of mind.

All this is just so much bunkum. The human subconscious can be a highly illogical and rather vicious piece of kit. Businessmen may leave the mediation with a 'win–win' frame of mind but the petty resentments and underlying state of anger within a company may seethe on quietly only to erupt at a later stage. Most fights in the business world have little to do with the matter at hand but more to do with rivalry between two forceful personalities, or a deficiency in the dynamics of the organisation: a 'power vacuum' develops in the managerial hierarchy that has to be filled.

In the old days it was so simple. Two managers would take off their Zegna suit jackets, meet in the carpark after work for a punch-up and then go off for a beer. This technique had a certain pristine simplicity about it but was not good for the company image, even if it did get the decisions made.

So how should we handle our anger? Let me introduce you to the three steps:

- own it;
- understand it; and
- deal with it.

Own your own anger

I never fail to be staggered by the number of my patients who blithely announce to me that they do not possess any anger. Invariably, as the layers of their defences peel back, what is revealed, deep within their subconscious minds, is unadulterated rage, suppressed and repressed for years. Own up. Within *any* relationship or *any* human group there is always some sort of power struggle. Human beings at an instinctive level organise themselves subconsciously into some sort of pecking order. It can be so subtle or covert that it needs to be uncovered by a conflict of interests, *but it is there*. Like death and taxes, anger is a sure thing….

You must understand that anger, like ice-cream, comes in forty-one different flavours. The most superficial varieties are called irritation, annoyance, being narky, being scratchy or grumpy. The deepest layer is rage. Between the top and the bottom come nuances of resentment, bitterness and aggression. But they are all anger.

Also be aware that anger can be expressed either actively or passively. The latter variety is usually called 'passive aggression' and it can be so subtle at times that it is hardly noticeable.

In the vernacular this phenomenon has another name. It is called 'sabotage'. We all do it when we procrastinate, show up late or promise people that 'the cheque is in the mail' when

Levels of anger

Level I
Annoyance, irritation, resentment

Level 2
Anger, aggression, bitterness

Level 3
Rage

No ONE admits ... one ... only

we are skint. Workers do it when they go on strike. Children do it when they sit down in a crowded supermarket and refuse to budge, knowing full well that they cannot be disciplined in front of all these bemused shoppers. Mahatma Ghandi used it to get the British out of India, but he called it 'civil disobedience'. There was no point in throwing rocks at the British Army trucks when you and a half dozen of your mates could immobilise it by simply sitting down on the road in front of it. Passive aggression is a very powerful tool since you need express no anger yet utterly infuriate your target.

Some people, however, adopt passive aggression as a personality style. It is not 100 per cent efficient since it hurts both you and your target. Workers who go on strike do not get paid. People who are on a continual 'go-slow' or who habitually 'forget' their obligations do not progress in life. Most of the time these people are completely unaware of their own *modus operandi* but their hallmark is that wherever they go and whatever they do, *they are both frustrated and frustrating.*

CASE HISTORY   Mark the saboteur

Mark was a young man who came to see me on the recommendation of his careers counsellor. He was handsome and affable and he clearly had the intelligence and talent to do well. He also seemed to be highly motivated. His presenting problem was that he kept failing at university, but not enough so that he would be refused a re-enrolment. He failed just enough so that he had spent a lot of time at university and effectively got nowhere fast. He had the uncanny ability to snatch defeat from the jaws of victory. He had come within one examination of completing a degree before failing the exam and then, for a number of spurious reasons, promptly switched to another degree. Perhaps there was an element of avoidance in this young man, but what came over more and more was his own sense of helplessness at his own ability to sabotage his life.

Eventually what became obvious was that he was a very angry young man. His anger was contagious. Despite his smiling face I became aware of my growing desire to slowly throttle him. Within his therapy I had become ensnarled in the web of a passive aggressive personality. But who was he really angry at? It was his father, who had always given him the message that he had never been good enough and had shown him no genuine warmth or interest. Then, as Mark was about to become an angry adolescent and dump a few buckets full of anger on his father, the old man up and died. No way to get rid of all this anger but upon himself. And me.

For the Marks of this world, their anger is buried so deep in their subconscious minds that they are often not even aware of it themselves. If you find that people are angry with you wherever you go it is probably high time that you owned up to your own anger.

Understand your anger

What causes anger? A conflict of needs. Next question. What needs? Care, trust and hope. Those needs. If you feel that you are not being cared for in the way that you deserve, if you are being deceived or lied to, if you are being disappointed, you will feel angry, no matter how good you are at denying or suppressing it.

All anger is generated by finding out that someone else is putting their needs before yours. Nothing too esoteric about that.

Deal with your anger

Now for the hard part. What, I hear you ask, do I do with all this anger now that I have owned up to it and understood it? Stay with me.

There are four levels to the expression of anger. They are:

≡ suppression
≡ assertiveness
≡ aggression
≡ violence.

There is a time to suppress your anger. There is a time to be assertive and even aggressive. Apart from the time when you find that you are down a dark alley and half a dozen large men who cut the ears off cats are bearing down upon you, there is never a time to be violent. Yes, I take back what I said about the benefits of the punch-up in the carpark . . .

Sometimes it is necessary to suppress your anger. Only children and adults with out-of-order frontal lobes find this impossible to do. When a pushy driver pulls his car out

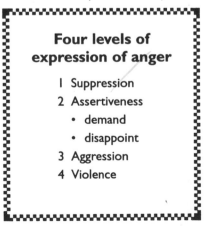

Four levels of expression of anger

1 Suppression
2 Assertiveness
  • demand
  • disappoint
3 Aggression
4 Violence

in front of you on the freeway you are sometimes left with the only option of tooting your horn at him when you would really like to let fly with a bazooka. When the nasty old man next door complains about the leaves from your mulberry tree dropping on his lawn you might have to smile in a neighbourly way but you are really fantasising about detonating a nuclear device beneath his house.

There is a time to suppress your anger, but most people are just too damned good at it. They suppress so well and for so long that their anger corrodes away inside them. It is a fast track to depression.

Most people also move rapidly from suppression to aggression. There is a middle step that is called assertiveness. How we all envy assertive people. They are the people who firmly tell the queue-jumper to go to the back of the queue. They politely (but with steely eye-to-eye gaze) remind that woman with the cigarette that smoking is not permitted in this submarine. They seem to have a quiet internal confidence that does not allow them to get rattled. Their anger is so socialised yet quietly ruthless. Ah, to be assertive.

Good news. There are courses springing up everywhere that teach some basic principles about assertiveness. As might be expected, they tend to be over-subscribed.

I cannot claim to save you the bother of going to an assertiveness-training course but I will sum up the quintessence of assertiveness in two words. I call them 'the two D's'. They are *demand* and *disappoint*. Let these words settle in your mind for a minute. In twenty years' time if you find this book shoved into a dusty bookshelf somewhere let its cover remind you of these two words. If you can feel comfortable in demanding and disappointing then you have this assertiveness thing licked. And you will probably have fairly hassle-free interactions with your boss, your staff and the tax department.

Demand is all about letting people know that you have needs and that you expect them to help you to meet these needs.

Disappoint is all about letting people know that you cannot answer all their needs. It is limiting *their* demands.

Remember the two D's. Practise them. See how easy it becomes?

Now to aggression. This is just as important as assertiveness and comes into play when the queue-jumper turns nasty and the woman with the cigarette stubs it out on the palm of your hand. One of the problems with this constrained world is that we have forgotten how to have a bloody good barney. Or at least we think it is uncouth. This also tends to be part of the Anglo-Saxon-Celtic tradition since most cultures of the world allow for the short, sharp expression of verbal aggression without too much of a fuss. They also tend to be cultures in which the aggression rapidly dissipates and everyone gets on with life as if nothing had happened. We more inhibited folk tend to be a bit bewildered by aggression and let it play on our minds long after the adrenalin has settled.

Unfortunately the teachers at the assertiveness-training course will try to convince you that any bone of contention can be dealt with by assertiveness. They are wrong. Well intentioned, but wrong nevertheless. There is still a time in this world to have a fight, particularly within marriage, and the art of letting off steam must not be neglected. When I describe the art of fighting below I shall relate this to marital conflict. That is simply for convenience' sake. Also because that is how I encounter it most in my practice. But the ideas below can just as readily be applied to conflict between parents and children, workmates, you and your boss, etc. etc.

'Catharsis' is a word that Freud (that grand-daddy of all psychiatrists) used to describe a sudden release of pent-up emotions. Having a weep is a type of catharsis. So, I suppose, is having a sneeze or an orgasm. I have long held the belief that people, especially couples, relate to each other in a *passionate* way with only two behaviours. I call them 'the two F's'. They are *fighting* and *making love* ... think about it. They both follow the same rules and the same time course.

The 'rules' for fighting and making love are:

≡ They are both to be carried out between consenting adults behind closed doors. While it is quite healthy for parents to show physical affection for each other in front of the children they certainly do not make love that way. Similarly, it is quite healthy for parents to disagree or bark at each other in front of their children. This shows the children in an honest way that anger, like sex, is an integral and natural part of any adult relationship. If a couple is going to have a ding-dong row, however, then this must be done behind closed doors. And that means out of earshot too. Kids have ears and, contrary to first impressions, they are not stupid.

≡ Each participant must try not to hurt the other, no matter how excited or how furious they might be. Sex can result in some fairly catastrophic pains when, say, someone falls from a chandelier or there is, for want of a better expression, a sudden disengagement. But it is not, unless you are slightly bendier than kinky, the prime motivation in the exercise. Couples must also retain *some* restraint when fighting. Physical violence is a definite no-no. So is sarcasm. So is dredging up every hurt or fight from the past. Fighters, like lovers, must live for the moment.

Now come out of your corners and start ... whatever. The diagram, 'The art of fighting', shows that fighting and making love follow a similar time course. There is an excitation phase, a plateau phase, a catharsis and then a resolution phase. In making love the excitation phase involves twinkles in eyes, sweet nothings, disrobing, etc. The plateau phase is foreplay, the catharsis is orgasm and the resolution phase is that state of totally relaxed intimacy that occurs when a couple lie together after making love.

In fighting the excitation phase occurs when someone puts their needs before the other's. This gives verbal and non-verbal clues between the couple that they had better get their adrenalin pumping because a bunfight is on the way. The plateau phase involves attack and counter-attack. At this time the couple are preferably standing a reasonably safe distance apart and the weapon that they are using

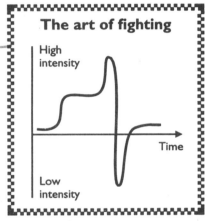

against each other is the raised voice. The human larynx is designed to create sounds that can be heard across a parade ground by a reasonably deaf soldier. God intended it to be used this way in the act of fighting, too, but humans confounded all this by inventing high-density housing. In this respect our country cousins, who have only the cows to scare, have it all over us.

The catharsis phase of the fight is the most important. Here a human invention becomes crucial. It is called a door and it is made for slamming. The catharsis of an argument must happen when the tension between the two becomes unbearable and it must occur before either becomes so upset or feels so vulnerable that they are tempted to hurt the other either verbally or physically. The time has come for one or other to exit the scene. If this involves wheelspinning the family car out of the driveway to go for a long drive by yourself, then so be it.

What follows is a resolution phase in which the adrenalin, like the dust, must settle. A respectable amount of time must pass, which must be minutes or hours but not days. The couple must then come together and work together *to end the argument.* One or other must begin the process by re-establishing communication. There must be some degree of apology which is followed by a counter-apology. In the excitation phase the fight is escalated by attack and counter-attack. Now it is resolved by apology and counter-apology. Anger escalates. Forgiveness de-escalates.

Just as the most intimate time of love-making can be in the aftermath of togetherness, so a marital fight can result in a time of great love and togetherness. It is the time when a couple show each other that they can be loved and lovable, 'warts and all'.

It is not necessary for the couple to resolve the issue that they were fighting about. If they do, then that is a bonus. Most of the time the issue at hand becomes irrelevant in the middle of a raging row. These are what I call 'toothpaste tube' fights. Whether the toothpaste tube is squeezed in the middle or not is, in the universal scheme of things, completely irrelevant. Toothpaste tubes become a barometer of respectful communication between two people. If one member of the duo finds (because of some anal/ obsessional problems of their own) that it is essential for their peace of mind that the toothpaste tube is squeezed from the bottom, or the cap is replaced on the tube every time it is used, then they need to communicate that to the other. If this request is repeatedly ignored then the state of the toothpaste pales into insignificance compared to the state of mutual respect that exists (or does not exist) between the two of them.

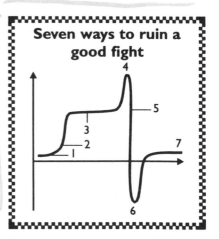

Seven ways to ruin a good fight

So this, Virginia, is how to fight. Now let me concentrate on how not to fight.

In brief, there are seven ways to ruin a good fight (check out the diagram).

1 The fight never gets off the ground.   Some people, poor sods, get through life without ever allowing themselves to own up to their own anger. They can be awfully syrupy sorts. If they choose a similarly impaired person then they can both sit around suppressing all their angst indefinitely. Trouble is they die early of peptic ulcers and heart attacks.

2 The fight begins but the brakes go on too quickly. This reminds me of a couple.

> **CASE HISTORY Ron and Jan**
>
> Jan came to see me because she was becoming a hypochondriac. She felt that every pain in her body was an as-yet-undiagnosed cancer that had spread to her bones. Every time she felt short of breath she was dying of asthma. Every headache was a stroke. In her heart she knew that all this was nonsense but it was becoming harder and harder for her GP to convince her that she did not need to worry.
>
> After a few sessions, in which she began to realise just how depressed she had been for many years, we located an important mem-ory. When she was aged seven she was admitted to hospital to have her tonsils out. Even though she was an in-patient for only a few days, she remembers it as having been a time of barely concealed terror for her. Why? Because she was all alone, without her mother for the first time. These days switched-on paediatric wards allow mothers to stay in the hospital with their sick kids, and so they should. *Johana Rihova*
>
> Jan came to associate illness with the intense isolation and loneliness that she had experienced at that time. She came to admit that she was not really afraid of illness, but of abandonment. In particular she focussed her fears upon that time of infinite aloneness that we must all one day face: the moment of death. The subconscious mind can reveal its secrets in a slow and circuitous route, but it usually produces the goods in the end.
>
> Next question. Why, in the context of her happy marriage, did she feel so alone? With some difficulty she came to realise that her marriage was not so peaches-and-cream after all. We agreed that Ron should come and join us for a few sessions.
>
> Being the dutiful husband that he was, Ron fronted up. He spoke quite honestly about his own background. His father had been a violent alcoholic.

Ron and Jan were a caring couple who obviously loved each other heaps. But they were lousy fighters. Whenever their tempers flared at each other, the fight would fall over because the brakes went on too early. Ron did it. He would simply adopt a glazed look and no matter how angry Jan became he would look at her as if she were talking to him from two blocks away. This was his instinctive response. It was a defence mechanism that he had developed in childhood. He came to admit that he always associated anger with violence. Anger induced in him a childlike terror. It transfixed him. Why not? When his father became angry he always became violent. Yet another example of how your past haunts your present.

Ron needed to be reassured that he could become angry without the situation becoming uncontrolled. It took some time and practice but in the end he even managed to raise his voice. A few more years and he will be a marital prize-fighter. Better than leaving your wife in a state of chronic abandonment.

3 Someone turns the fight off. Some people are real spoilsports. Just as a fight is becoming intense and people are getting the dirty water off their chests one of them turns around and stops the action. Note that there are three common ways to do this:

- Assume a victim role. Fighting is about attack and counter-attack. The couple take turns at being the aggressor. If one then suddenly becomes a victim then this abruptly precludes the other from the next volley. You cannot kick someone when they are down. Interestingly the sexes use different techniques to adopt the victim role. Men do it with hurt looks and sulks. Women do it with tears. Either way it stops the fight. Dead.
- Involve a third person. This is a nifty technique for defusing the nasty feelings between two people. The fighters can involve a third person as either a *mediator* ('let's ask Harry for his opinion') or a *scapegoat* ('what are we arguing about? ... it's all Harry's fault anyway'). More of this sort of stuff in Chapter 6.
- Confidently rationalise. Men are better at this than women. She comes to him with a gripe. He thinks quickly, talks quickly and rationalises the gripe away. She walks away knowing that she was angry with him but she's so confused by now that she can't remember why. More of this in the next two chapters.

4 There is not a satisfactory climax. Orgasms are about becoming so excited that you cannot hold it back any more. Climaxes in fights are about becoming so angry that you had better exit the scene before you lose control. Some women have experienced a peculiar orgasm that rolls on and on over a period of minutes. It can be quite uncomfortable for them since eventually the pleasure becomes painful. Similarly fights must have a fairly crisp climax. The neighbours whom you hear screaming at fever pitch for hours on end are, fight-wise, actually having some trouble climaxing.

The other rather catastrophic way that a fight comes to an unsatisfactory climax is when violence becomes involved. In the book of rules for fighting couples this is always *verboten*.

Psychiatrists are often accused of listening too much and speaking too little. We are often loath to offer advice. We come across as being a bit wishy-washy. There is one sure-fire way to get me speaking and that is to tell me that your spouse is violent towards you. I get into sermon mode and you get the fire and brimstone. If your partner is being violent towards you then *you must leave that relationship immediately*. Put this book down and get packing. Nothing namby-pamby about that.

5 **The fight does not have a definable conclusion.** Some couples manage to string a fight along for days or weeks. Sometimes months. After a fight they do not talk to each other for days. Usually the house becomes so tense that you could cut the air with a pretty blunt knife. The anger is expressed *passively*. It is called 'silent violence'. It can be amazingly destructive, especially to the children who observe it and feel the tension in the air.

Do your kids a favour and make up.

6 **Someone refuses to forgive.** One person reaches stage six while the other is still in stage five. The members of a couple often take different times to allow their adrenalin to calm down. You have to experiment with your partner to find a good time to approach or be approached. One of the 'rules' is also that one partner should not be stamped into the role of being the approacher and the other into being the approachee. Fair's fair.

7 **The interval between fights is either too short or too long.** Some couples have a very passionate relationship and seem to move between one 'F' (fighting) and the other 'F' (making love) with barely a pause for breath. Most of us mere mortals work on a more manageable time scale so that the passion and the rage come in more orderly waves. Some couples make the converse error: they do not fight often enough. Once

again, this is very individual. Work out your own 'F-rhythms' so that emotionally you do not suffer from either constipation or diarrhoea.

From the perspective of my psychiatric practice people do not, however, tend to come along to see me to complain about their anger. If they need to consult a professional about anger it is usually a lawyer that they see … because their anger has got them into a whole lot of trouble. Or else they have suppressed their anger so well and for so long that they sit in my office describing their *depression*. Unspoken, unresolved, unresolvable anger corrodes away at your insides. It is a perfect recipe for depression.

Enough about anger. Now let's move on.

About anxiety

O nce again let me remind you that I use anxiety as a blanket term for all the manifestations of things that you find scary, nerve-racking, intimidating or that make you feel insecure. If people find it hard to own up to their anger they find no difficulty in admitting that they can be afraid or worried. Doubt me? Then look at the following words:

- toothache, dentist, drill, fillings, no medical insurance
- tax department, shortfall, end of financial year, provisional, bank manager
- exams, too late to study now, never mind you can always do an apprenticeship
- mole, changing shape, won't go away, shouldn't you see someone about that?
- adolescence, acne, alcohol, motorbikes, your daughter in the back of a car with some creep.

See? Everyone can come clean about being anxious.

Now to analyse anxiety further. There are, in fact, four different types of anxiety (see diagram on page 67). They are the fear of death, the fear of abandonment, the fear of attack and anticipatory fear. Let me expand upon these.

The fear of death

This is the most profound, basic, primitive, animalistic fear that we all carry. Throughout our lives we maintain a healthy sense of denial about it. We know intellectually that we are all mortal, that the fun cannot go on indefinitely. But we do not dwell on it. People who do dwell on death tend to be rather melancholic sorts who do not get invited to dinner parties. Or if they are invited they tend to make the parties rather funereal.

The fear of death tends to dawn upon us slowly in that as we grow older we find that we develop more ailments and that our friends and acquaintances begin to 'pop off'. Death becomes kind of hard to ignore. Sometimes our first brush with this fear is when some serious-looking doctor announces to us in a monotone that our test results indicate that we should not bother to start reading any long novels, plan next

summer holidays or even listen in to the long-range weather forecast ... Or sometimes the fear of death is delayed until the chest pain grips us and the world becomes blurry as we find ourselves looking down a tunnel with a light at the end.

Either way, this is the most basic fear and all the others queue up behind it.

The fear of abandonment

Death is unambiguous. Abandonment needs to be loosely defined as all of the sensations of rejection, alienation, neglect and aloneness. This is the next most fundamental fear after death. Within us all is a little child who dreads being lost in the forest.

The fear of attack

For 'attack' read also criticism, judgment, humiliation, mockery, demotion and all forms of abuse.

Anticipatory fear

This is *the fear of fear itself*. This is the anxiety that many people carry that pervades their lives and stops them from taking risks.

These, then, are the four flavours of anxiety that I encounter. In my practice, however, I do not have people presenting to me complaining of a bad case of 'fear of attack'. Anxiety presents in a number of peculiar ways, such as:

Free-floating anxiety   This bewilders people. They feel frightened all the time but they often cannot immediately identify what it is that they fear. They feel jumpy and irritable, they tremble and perspire and they pray to God for a good night's sleep. Eventually, with enough time and talking, they can usually identify one or more of the four types of anxiety listed above and then they can dig deeper into trying to understand how they came to be this way.

Panic attacks with agoraphobia   A panic attack, like love, is a many splendoured thing. It comes on quickly and is associated with rapid heartbeat, palpitations, tremor, dizziness, nausea, chest pain and a choking tightness in the throat. People in the middle of a panic attack feel intensely panicky and on the verge of either going mad or dropping dead. It tends to last up to an hour and then to just as rapidly subside. The first time that a patient experiences this they are often rushed to hospital in an ambulance and extensively investigated for a heart attack. Only after they have been wired up to every machine known to medical science is the humble psychiatrist with the holey socks or laddered tights called in to proclaim the diagnosis.

Panic attacks often generalise into agoraphobia. You thought that that was the fear of wide open spaces. Right? Wrong. Agoraphobia is the fear of being *unable to escape*. It is claustrophobia and fear of flying rolled into one. People rapidly learn that when they are hit by a panic attack they must retreat to a private place and hide until it is over. Having someone with them to comfort them also becomes important so that their spouse or a member of their family must accompany them wherever they go. I dub this person the 'guardian angel' and anyone who cannot come up the elevator to my office without a 'guardian angel' in tow is an agoraphobic until proven otherwise.

Agoraphobia can manifest as the fear of going into confined spaces (such as lifts) or wide spaces (such as fields). Tunnels, bridges, trains, buses and aeroplanes also become a no-no. In its most extreme form agoraphobics cannot leave their own homes, which become their prisons. And guardian angels become heartily sick of the fuss.

Agoraphobia and panic attacks are grouped together because that is the way they occur. Agoraphobia is rarely found without panic and vice versa.

Phobias Some people develop a horror of a specific thing, such as dogs, snakes, spiders, heights, boats, etc. They go to great pains to avoid this thing, which in technical jargon is called the 'phobic stimulus'. As might be expected they avoid veterinary school, bungee-jumping and joining the navy.

Extreme shyness This is called 'social phobia'. Everyone, but everyone, experiences shyness. Only the most cocksure people rarely experience it. They are almost inhuman in this respect. Some people are incapacitated by it. The essential feature of this phobia is that people avoid any situation in which they will be scrutinised or watched for fear of making a fool of themselves. They will not make public speeches. Men who experience this will not pee in a public urinal but feel safe if they can lock themselves inside a toilet cubicle to pee in blissful solitude. They find it intolerable to have someone look over their shoulders as they write. Most interesting of all, they tend to avoid eating in restaurants as they cannot stand being watched by strangers as they eat. Social phobia is always the tip of the iceberg. Beneath it lurk major personality problems.

Post-traumatic stress disorder This is what Andrew the security guard experienced (see page 7). If you have not heard of this condition you have not read a newspaper for years. PTSD, as it is known to the *cognoscenti*, became recognised as an entity after the war in Vietnam. It relates to the fears experienced by people who have undergone an overwhelming, life-threatening trauma, such as being shot at, raped, tortured, witnessing a murder or escaping a bushfire. Becoming overdrawn in your cheque account or getting a speeding ticket do not count. The classical symptoms of PTSD are that the patient *re-lives* the horrors in dreams, hallucinations, distressing memories or flashbacks. Before the term post-traumatic stress disorder was coined, soldiers were described as having such problems as 'battle fatigue' or 'war neurosis'. Even before that, in the First World War, officers were withdrawn from the trenches to the back lines suffering from DAH, which stood for 'disordered action of the heart'. The men were not supposed to know that their leaders were terrified too ...

Obsessions and compulsions These are terribly, terribly common but often go unrecognised because they are reasonably mild. In a recent study five per cent of the population were found to suffer from obsessions and/or compulsions to some degree. So what are they? Obsessions are thoughts. Compulsions are actions. Obsessions are experienced as intrusive, unwanted thoughts that enter your mind and plague you. They might have themes of dirt, disease, contamination, the desire to be violent, sexual fantasies or blasphemy. They provoke immense anxiety. Compulsions are better known and tend to take the form of an overwhelming urge to wash your hands, count things such as cars passing your house or check that the doors of the house are locked at night again and again and again and again. Why are compulsions categorised as anxiety disorders? Because if you resist the urge to wash, count or check you will be racked with anxiety until you do.

CASE HISTORY **Jane**

When Jane came to see me she spent quite some time chatting about the weather and allied trivia. She was a nurse. And nurses who have never worked in psychiatric wards (Jane had not) are even more suspicious of psychiatrists than your average person. She was terrified that I was going to find out her deadly secret and summon the police with a stout strait-jacket so that I could lock her away forever. She was convinced that she was slowly going very, very mad. Eventually she gathered all her courage and began to spill the psychiatric beans.

For three years, no less, she had been experiencing textbook obsessions about murdering her husband. She felt the overwhelming impulse to pick up a knife and plunge it into his back. When she was driving him in their car she wanted to veer suddenly into the oncoming traffic and cause them both to perish. She knew, in a fairly rudimentary way, that schizophrenics experienced abnormal thought processes so she had diagnosed herself as suffering from that very tragic illness.

Jane was married to Anthony, who was a recovering alcoholic. (Note that alcoholics never describe themselves as being a 'recovered' alcoholic. They are wise enough to know that they have recovered only when they are put into a wooden box.) Anthony had been an utter creep for many years when he was drinking. Jane, in true martyr style, had quietly put up with his abuse, his violence, his ability to make her feel dirty and degraded. Inside she was angry as all hell. But she was such a giving, loving, caring woman, as so many nurses are, that she could not express this anger to him, let alone own up to it herself.

When her first obsession hit her she had been involved in one of their endless and futile marital arguments. She had come to the painful realisation that talking sense to a practising alcoholic is about as much use as discussing philosophy with a budgie. She noticed a pair of scissors on a sideboard and was seized with the desire to pick them up and stick them between his ribs. That started it all. Three years later she was in my office, having told no one of these obsessions, and waiting for me to call the cops. Inside my shoe I pushed my big toe through the hole in my sock and came to her rescue. I explained that her obsessions were not psychotic and she was not nuts. Relief, ah sweet relief. Psychiatry can be so satisfying at times . . .

I have described the four types of anxiety and how they are brought to me by patients with sweaty palms and bleary, sleepless eyes. Next question: how do I treat anxiety problems? Before I launch into that I must mention that anxiety phenomena are messy things that never come in ones. They are notorious for coming in batches and causing three serious complications.

Depression I have already mentioned that unresolved anger can corrode away at your feelings and cause depression. So can anxiety. Anyone who spends hours washing their hands, stifling their panic or remembering their car accident in every blood-specked detail cannot help but get down in the dumps.

Sedative and alcohol abuse Early on in the piece sufferers learn that a couple of stiff brandies can work marvels for those shaky hands. And those little blue pills that the GP down the road prescribed are the only thing that can give them a good night's sleep. These attitudes are a disaster in the making. Plenty of alcoholics and tranquilliser addicts start off with anxiety problems. Eventually they simply cannot go without the brandies or 'the little blue ones'. In the longer term sedatives and alcohol only make the situation worse since they work marvellously as the blood levels of the drug or alcohol go up but all hell breaks loose as the blood levels begin to fall. Every pill and every nip eventually induces a sort of minor withdrawal. When that happens the anxiety returns with a vengeance.

Marital and family problems Anxiety disorders ruin your sex life. Panic and passion simply do not mix. Family members who are recruited to the role of 'guardian angels' rapidly grow tired of the responsibility. Fed up, in fact. In an obtuse sort of way the agoraphobic can sometimes subconsciously allow the family to begin to revolve around her and her needs. (I say 'her' because most agoraphobics are women.) This is called 'secondary gain'. It surreptitiously encourages the sufferer to hang on to her symptoms, which allows her to avoid responsibility and to receive extra attention. The tensions within the family begin to ferment . . .

Treatment of anxiety disorders

The treatment of anxiety disorders must be tailored to the individual patient. It depends upon the type of disorder and any complications that may have arisen, as well as the intelligence, motivation and ability of the patient to be introspective. I will limit this treatise to a few generalisations.

Like anger, the treatment of anxiety involves the three steps: own it, understand it and deal with it. The importance of understanding your anxiety and where it all came from cannot be underemphasised. Despite everything that I say below, the best treatment for emotional distress is still to form a trusting bond with a therapist, work through your past and your present and feel the pain that your anxiety is trying to suppress. In other words, open that scary box called your 'subconscious' and let a bit of the distress out. Having said that, there are some specific treatments for anxiety too.

Medication

There is very little room in the treatment of anxiety disorders for medication. This is with one possible exception. The exception is a drug called phenelzine. Phenelzine stops panic attacks dead. It is the salvation of many an agoraphobic but it is a dreadful drug to use. To be on phenelzine you have to be on a special diet and avoid taking other drugs such as flu remedies or undergoing general anaesthetics. Despite all this, if you suffer from panic attacks regularly and if they are interfering with your ability to stay hale and hearty, then write the name *phenelzine* down on a piece of paper and poke it into the face of your psychiatrist. Tell him you want it pronto or you want a damned good reason why not. But please do not tell him that I told you to do this. I might meet him at a conference later this year . . .

Principles of treatment for other disorders

With phobias it is necessary to *confront the phobic stimulus*. If you are afraid of spiders you must get a pet one. If you hate snakes, get a job at the reptile house at your local zoo. If you hate heights go parachuting. For years we psychiatrists pussy-footed around with helping patients to slowly and gently confront their phobias. Now we know that it is much more efficient to drop you into a roomful of spiders and snakes and leave you there until you just get used to it. It is a technique called 'flooding'. Trouble is that you tend to flood your pants as well.

If you suffer from post-traumatic stress disorder (PTSD) it is necessary to *revisit the horror*. This is much the same as confronting the phobic stimulus. Over quite a period of time it is necessary to recall, describe and go over and over your trauma until it loses its agony for you. Easily described but awful to do.

Severe obsessive-compulsive disorder can be treated with some fairly laborious techniques that are called 'thought-stopping' (for obsessions) and 'behaviour limitation' (for compulsions). Be warned: this is long, drawn-out tedious stuff that is usually performed by a specialist therapist who would make Job look as if he were chomping at the bit. Some cognitive therapies are useful here too.

Relaxation exercises

For all of the above manifestations of anxiety, and particularly for free-floating anxiety that does not have a phobic focus, the most effective way to control the fear is by practising *relaxation exercises*. The same effect is obtained by yoga or meditation. Another method is 'biofeedback' which involves using machines that indicate to you how tense you are. You then develop techniques to make the needle on the tension gauge move down and not up. The most commonly used adjuncts to relaxation exercises that people in our civilisation use are relaxation tapes. They can be bought in shops that smell of incense, from shop assistants wearing kaftans. They are up the back next to the crystals and the tarot cards. Pardon me if my conservative cynicism is showing. I will resist the temptation to be holier-than-thou by admitting that all of these relaxation techniques can be pretty effective in winding down your baseline metabolic rate so that any anxiety problem becomes a lot more manageable. But there are three caveats here:

▪ They must induce alpha-rhythm in your brainwaves. If an EEG (electroencephalograph) is wired to your scalp then the squiggles on the read-out show that you are in that state of near-sleep that indicates that you are very relaxed.

= They must induce deep muscle relaxation. This can be indicated by the squiggles of an EMG (electromyograph) which show that the fibres deep within your muscles are having a kip.

= They must be practised daily. Learning how to relax is like getting fit. The benefits do not arise from one relaxation session or one jog around the block. You must practise relaxation exercises every day for at least three weeks before you even begin to derive some benefit. Eastern mystics practise for years. Perhaps they have not yet heard about television . . .

About sadness

I confess that I tend to use the word 'sadness' as a euphemism here. Sadness is a part of life that almost everyone can encounter and manage, without the intervention of a psychiatrist. For the most part I will be talking about that form of sadness that I see most commonly in my practice. It is *depression*. And it is *the most common presenting complaint* that I hear from patients coming to see me for the first time. Yet it is the most complex, nebulous, unfashionable and ill-understood of all the disorders that I see. If it were not such an unmitigatedly awful affliction it would inspire my great admiration. Now bend your head around the following statements:

= Depression pervades your existence.
= Depression can present simply as 'anhedonia'.
= Depression is the great mimic of modern medicine.
= Depression has a hundred faces.
= Depression is an illness.
= Depression is contagious.

Confused? Good. Read on.

What, I hear you ask, is the difference between sadness and depression? In the simplest possible differentiation, sadness is an affliction of the heart while depression is an affliction of the soul. Sadness is manageable. Often, such as in a bereavement, it is perfectly appropriate and healthy. Sadness is focussed on a particular loss or hurt.

Depression, on the other hand, pervades your very existence. When you are sad you can still find some beauty in nature, comfort in friendship and humour in the lighter side of life. When you are depressed all you can see is darkness. Poets, artists and playwrights are often very highly strung, sensitive types and they tend to be predisposed to suffering from depression. They call it 'the abyss'. Ring any bells for you?

Many years ago a wise old psychiatrist named Beck nominated the three aspects of your existence that are affected by depression. These are the three things that become coloured when you are depressed so that you see them as gloomy, helpless, hopeless and painful. The three things are:

- yourself
- the world
- the future.

That just about covers everything, doesn't it?

Depression is not, however, characterised solely by the 'down' feeling. Some people come to see me and describe the other face of depression, which is 'anhedonia' or *the inability to experience pleasure*. My patients portray this in a number of ways. They tell me that there are no kicks or thrills or fun or amusement or humour or play in their lives. The essence of the feeling is that *nothing is enjoyable or satisfying any more.* People who experience this lack of fulfilment sometimes do not even admit to feeling down. But the depression is there, embedded in their distress and camouflaged by their feelings of anhedonia. Take note. If you find that you are dragging your heels through life and that the things that used to give you pleasure are now empty or boring, if life does not give you the sort of satisfaction that it gave you last month or last year, then *you are depressed until proven otherwise.*

When I was a medical student (and I shudder to think how many years ago that was . . .) I was told by my professors that the great 'mimics' in medicine were syphilis and tuberculosis. These were the infections that could insidiously spread to any organ in the body and pretend to be just about any other illness. It was only at the patient's post-mortem that the pathologist could slice open the diseased organ and reveal that all along this heart/liver/kidney/whatever had actually been riddled with TB. The attendant physicians would be delighted that finally the diagnosis had been made. Trouble was that the patient had kicked the bucket by then so he could not share his doctors' elation.

That was the in the old days. In the Western world syphilis and TB have become something of a medical curiosity. There are other medical mimics now. Alcoholism is one. HIV infection is another. But the greatest mimic of them all is depression. I never cease to be amazed by how disguised it can be. And how so many astute doctors can miss the diagnosis. *Depression is medicine's most under-diagnosed illness.* It can present as peculiar bodily symptoms, pains, panic attacks, preoccupation with the fear of illness, obsessional thoughts, malnutrition, dehydration, unstable work history, divorce, etc. etc.

Psychiatrists have always recognised this. We talk about the 'atypical depression', the 'masked depression' and the 'smiling depression'. I work on the principle that if someone shows a significant change in personality and their brain is intact and they are not going mad, then there is only one other thing that they must be hiding: their depression.

But depression does not come in just one variety. Its forms are protean. Each sufferer, because of their own personality and life experience, has their own unique blend of depression in how, when and why their depression occurs. There are some unfortunate souls who experience recurring depressions over many years. But each recurrence is unique in its signs and symptoms and effect on the individual. While they all start to blur into each other, it is worthwhile trying to categorise the types of depression:

- *Depression as a mood* is usually not too severe and lasts for a day or two. Almost everyone has experienced such 'down' times but if they have never experienced or encountered depression as an illness they may find it difficult to believe that depression can become intense and protracted.

- *Reactive* depression has a clear precipitant such as being fired from work or learning that your dog has just been run over. Post-natal depression might fit into this group, albeit rather clumsily.

- *Organic* depression occurs because of some diagnosable biological problem, such as disease of the thyroid gland in the neck or because of the chronic toxic effects of alcohol on the brain in alcoholism.

- *Manic-depression* is a definable, diagnosable mental illness. It is characterised by *gross* mood swings, both upwards and downwards. Note the italics in 'gross'. There are some people, 'cyclothymics' they are called, who spend their lives riding something of a roller-coaster of emotions, but never quite getting to the severity of manic-depression. A mania is the event that gives away the diagnosis. It is characterised by elation, euphoria, overactivity, racing thoughts, no need to sleep and a sense of power, creativity and importance. In extreme cases the patient becomes psychotic and begins to believe all sorts of marvellous things, for example that he is God's Chosen One, a millionaire, Tom Cruise's best mate, lusted after by every member of the opposite sex and able to make a *savant* look retarded. So why do I treat someone in such a happy state? Because eventually the mania turns into a nightmare of overstimulated chaos and his wife serves divorce papers on him. That's why.

≡ *Psychotic depression* is one of the great horrors of the world. You see, there are some people who become so depressed that they actually go mad. They are usually, but not always, elderly. When people go mad with depression they develop delusions that are unfailingly bleak, persecuted and nihilistic. They come to believe that they are the devil, that the brain police follow them wherever they go, that their bowel has turned to stone and their heart is filled with worms, that they have no legs, that they are penniless and that they are guilty of every crime ever committed by mankind. This is hell on earth. Psychotic depression is one of the few conditions for which you will find psychiatrists act quickly, decisively and authoritatively in treatment. It is a psychiatric emergency.

There are two categories that are worth expanding upon. The first of these is the type of depression that lingers for months or years or even decades. It is chronic, debilitating but often disguised behind artificial smiles. The British call this 'neurotic depression' but that is a pejorative label. I like the American term. They call it 'dysthymia'.

Dysthymia is poison for your emotions. But it is a slow poison. People who suffer from dysthymia often manage to hold down a marriage and a job but they feel quietly dead inside, tired, dissatisfied and pessimistic. They can often conceal their dysthymia from even their closest friends. But when I give them a comfortable leather chair, fifty minutes of time to speak and be heard and a few tissues to cry into, it usually all comes out. Eventually.

The other type of depression that must be mentioned is Major Depression. Note the capital M and the capital D. Major Depression is serious stuff.

It is different from dysthymia in that it is briefer but more intense. It lasts, averaged out, from three to twelve months if it is left untreated. It is characterised by feelings of deep and pervasive gloom, sadness, lack of pleasure and hopelessness. Sufferers become lethargic (or sometimes quite agitated), sleep poorly, lose their appetite and isolate themselves from social activities. As a rule of thumb, anxious people have difficulty getting off to sleep while depressed people have difficulty staying asleep. They wake too early and toss and turn trying to get back to sleep. Sometimes they find that there is one particular time of day, usually the morning, that is consistently dreadful. They wake thinking 'oh no, not another day'. By that evening they are feeling better but by the next morning they are back to square one again.

Patients with a Major Depression sometimes have a particular look on their faces so that I can make the diagnosis before they even utter their first miserable word. They look concerned, dark, tortured and downcast and display the characteristic furrowed brow. They cannot hide their sense of oppression.

Almost invariably the families of these patients are becoming a bit testy by the time the sufferer is brought along to see me. Unless they have experienced this illness themselves or been educated about its nature they cannot begin to comprehend it. The family members know depression as a mood. They know that when *they* become depressed they can simply snap themselves out of it, pull their socks up and think positively. But patients with a Major Depression do not have a hope in hell of doing that. If they could, they would. One of the patient's great frustrations is that their family members become angry and frustrated by the patient's depression and begin to accuse them of being selfish, lazy, inadequate, weak, etc. These accusations are supposed to miraculously bring the patient to their senses. In reality they only intensify the misery.

That brings me to another important point. Depression is *contagious*. In fact it is probably the most contagious condition known to humans. I do not mean by that that some esoteric virus or bacterium will seep from the pores of your depressed aunt and get at you; but rather that it is almost impossible to be around a depressed person without starting to feel depressed yourself, especially if you care about the sufferer.

When you are around people who are happy it is easy to feel happy. And when you are around people who are depressed you can end up in the foulest of moods. Sometimes when I speak to patients with a masked depression I am alerted to the hidden diagnosis by this fact. They have an uncanny knack of being able to change my own emotional state from being light and breezy to being downright miserable. If you know someone who can do that to you, now you know why. Living with a depressed person is a job for saints.

Some of my colleagues in psychiatry actually sub-specialise in the treatment of depression. All day every day. Good luck to them, that's all I can say ...

Depression: its causes and treatment

I have tried to describe depression, i.e. what it *is*. This has all been pretty heavy going, so I will move on to two important questions:

- What causes depression? and
- What can be done about it?

First question first. If you thought that I had a nice simple answer to that one, you should know better by now. There are many causes of depression and I shall describe them from the most straightforward and biological to the most abstract and psychological.

In some people the most obvious cause for their depression is their *genes*. If one of your first-degree relatives (i.e. mother, father, brother, sister, son or daughter) suffers from either manic-depression or recurring Major Depression then you may have a predisposition to depression. Not *do* have, just *may* have. There is pretty clear research evidence that this effect is one of nature, not just nurture.

Major Depression is also mediated by the chemistry in your brain. I will not go into the details of this since it is about as interesting as watching paint dry. Suffice it to say that intense depression is associated with too few molecules at certain crucial places between your nerve cells. The places are called 'synapses' and they are where the electricity from one nerve cell jumps space (as a spark does in a spark plug) and sets off an impulse in the next cell. When you are very depressed your sparks are just not jumping as well as they should be. All anti-depressant medications work at this level of your brain to get you sparking again, mentally as well as chemically.

From the psychological perspective there is one solitary theme that recurs in depression. It can be summed up in one word: *impossibility*. The situation for the patient is apparently impossible. This plight is characterised by a sense of futility and he or she is powerless to change it, but is stuck, trapped, helpless. This theme can further be divided into three pathways that lead to depression. They are impossible stress, impossible loss and impossible need.

Impossible stress

Look at the triangle of emotions again (see page 54). Anger and anxiety are overstimulating. Sadness is the result of this sustained state of stimulation. It is depletion. At a biochemical level it is quite literally the depletion of the molecules that keeps your nerve cells firing. In the simplest language I state this pathway to my patients like this: *'If you are angry enough or anxious enough for long enough, you will get depressed.'*

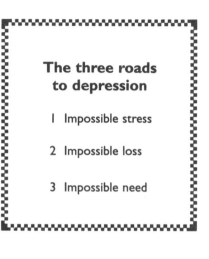

**The three roads
to depression**

1 Impossible stress

2 Impossible loss

3 Impossible need

Impossible loss

Throughout our lives we lose things. Not just our car keys or chequebook, but really Big Deal things. The diagram lists the seven big losses that everyone must inevitably face. Did you spot the thing that they all have in common? Right: aging. That is why (surprise, surprise) depression tends to be a problem of older people. Don't be fooled into thinking that kids don't suffer from depression, because they

**The seven inevitable
losses**

1 Youth

2 Independence

3 Authority

4 Generativity

5 Loved ones

6 Health

7 Life

do. They can suffer from impossible losses too and the classical situation is the parent whom they love but who has left them through their parents' divorce. Kids often show it in very disguised ways, such as withdrawal (the 'Me-out' strategy) or refusing to go to school.

If coming to terms with these losses proves to be impossible for you then you are a sitting duck for depression. You might develop a variety of techniques to avoid or deny to yourself the impact of these losses upon you. You may become a 'sugar daddy' to deny that you are old and wrinkly. You might never let anyone get close to you so that you never have to lose them. You might avoid going to the doctor so that you can never be told about the cancer that you know darned well lurks within you. But the losses are cruelly inevitable and the depression that awaits will always catch up with you in the end. And a depression that has been repressed usually strikes with a vengeance.

The chance of your becoming depressed is also increased if you find that you are *ambivalent* about the loss. Ambivalence is the process by which you value something positively and negatively at the same time. Thus I can say that I am ambivalent about my car: I love its style and colour and the gimmicks like the sunroof; but I am driven to distraction by the cost of petrol and how the driver's door rattles sometimes. This is a fairly manageable sort of ambivalence since I do not allow the fact that it runs out of petrol to overwhelm my overall impression that it is a good, practical, generally reliable car. I identify with it, rattly door and all, and if someone criticises it I will feel annoyed and take them to task.

One day if I come to find that a ten-ton truck has driven over the top of my car while I have it parked then I will be stunned, dismayed and angry. Passers-by will offer their commiserations. I will notify the police. I will lodge an insurance claim. But I will not become truly depressed. I know that I will get a big fat cheque from my insurance company and that I will soon be able to blow it on a car just like this mangled wreck that lies before me. And in the not-too-distant future I will regale guests at a dinner party with the hilarious story of how my car was turned into metal toothpicks by a ten-ton truck. My feelings towards the car are not so intense or so ambivalent that the loss of the car will bring about a depression. But if the car were a person and if my feelings were intolerably ambivalent, that would be different . . .

CASE HISTORY Stephen

Stephen came to see me four months after his father died. The old man had simply dropped dead at work. This was all very unfortunate since losing a loved one can be so much easier if you can only say goodbye. Stephen was depressed. In fact he was so depressed that at the end of our first session he left me with a little black cloud hovering over my head. He had experienced the ambivalent loss to end all ambivalent losses.

Stephen's father had been a prominent solicitor. Nice chap, but rigid and moralistic. When Stephen was a child it was easy to idealise his dad, even though the old man was hardly ever home. Life only became difficult when Stephen grew pubic hair and started to experiment with expressing his sexual urges with the girls in the neighbourhood. Dad could not handle this but to Stephen celibacy was for monks.

Stephen and his father then became locked in a lifelong power struggle. Dad spent most of his time in 'Me-up' stance and Stephen (just to keep the peace) in 'Me-down'. But no matter how hard he tried, Stephen could never be good enough or holy enough or self-controlled enough for his father.

When Stephen first began to describe his father he did so with the childlike idealisation that he had always shown as a kid. It took quite some talking before the more complex ambivalence began to emerge. Boy, was he confused. The problem was that his father had not been all moralising ogre. There had been a great softness and aspect of caring about the old guy's personality. He himself had been sent to boarding school from a young age and had never been able to admit to himself just how much this rejection had hurt him. He had always found it very difficult to show much emotional warmth. Despite this, Stephen knew in his heart that his father had been an inherently good man with a fragile armour that was controlling and intrusive.

How was Stephen to handle this powerful ambivalence now that his father's death had confronted him with it? He could not run away from the confusion. This was an impossible loss. He became very, very depressed.

It was not until Stephen could recognise and deal with the confusion that he could end this protracted, pathological bereavement. He came to be able to tease out the good elements of his father and mourn their loss while differentiating the bad elements and allowing himself to feel the anger against them.

As a rule of thumb, a 'normal' bereavement lasts about three months and rarely more than six. Protracted and intense bereavements often indicate that this was an impossible, ambivalent, loss.

Before I move on to the last Impossibility, let me confuse you further. Ambivalence in adult human relationships is a normal and necessary feature of the relationship. Ambivalence is the mature resolution of our childlike desire to *split*. Go back to the end of Chapter 1 to remind yourself of what 'splitting' is. On second thoughts, let me save all those bent pages by reminding you myself. Splitting is the defence mechanism by which you perceive someone as being either all good or all bad. It is found in children and adults who are in love. On television and in the movies the 'goodies' are all good and therefore always win. The 'baddies' are all bad and must be shot to smithereens in the last scene. Also, when you are besotted with someone you cannot and do not have any desire to see that they have protruding nasal hair, always burn the toast and are really more than a teensy bit boring. That comes later as the relationship develops. Remember?

Paradoxically, people whom you split are easy to lose. If you simply cannot stand that mean little man in the house next door because he intimidates your kids then you will make dignified noises about the unfortunate loss when he dies a hideous and painful death. But you do not get depressed and secretly you fantasise about dancing on his grave. Conversely, if the guy with the nasal hair walks out in front of a bus tomorrow you will be precipitated into a life crisis that you will simply *have to* handle. Such loss does not generally lead to a Major Depression.

All mature adult relationships involve some degree of ambivalence but this is generally manageable. You can pluck his nasal hairs, turn the dial down on the toaster and try against the odds to get him to be 'more alive, dammit'. Despite all these hassles you can still love him. Loss only becomes impossible (and therefore deeply depressing) if your ambivalence is intense, confusing and unmanageable.

Impossible need

I went into the concept of needs in the last chapter. Go ahead, bend the pages and remind yourself if you need to. In particular, remind yourself of the importance of hope. I want to put this to bed and get on to the next chapter.

The issue at stake here is how your subconscious mind handles it when your needs are not met. In particular, what happens to your feelings when your needs prove to be *impossible* to meet? The answer is that you move down the 'Cascade of D's': Desire, Disappointment, Disillusionment, Despair, Depression, Death.

Impossible needs lead to the dissipation of hope. And where hope dies, depression is sure to grow. But what are impossible needs? Needs become impossible if they reflect either the unrealistic intensity of the needer or the inability of the carer to answer that need. Thus an unloved child might have an extraordinary need for love to be demonstrated and proven by a parent who could not love the child in the first place. Vicious cycle.

Perhaps this is the 'bottom line' for depression: that people become depressed if they feel both *unloved* and *powerless*.

Now on to the second question, which is about the treatment of depression.

There is no single answer to this question since it depends upon the type of depression. Before treatment can be planned, a diagnosis must be reached. Controversial word, that. Diagnosis I mean. There are some people in paramedical fields, such as some psychologists and counsellors, who trivialise the need for diagnosis and try to blend all depressions into the one entity. This is not only arrogant, it can be dangerous. If depression is not professionally diagnosed and treated appropriately it can end in tragedy. Pills, cliffs, guns, ropes ... get my drift?

In the treatment of depression I once again return to the old three-step process: own it, understand it and deal with it. The underlying principle of ventilating the subconscious stands as well. Only a minority of the patients who present to me with depression require anti-depressant medications. Most manage to open up, get in touch with the process that got them there in the first place, feel the pain and unburden themselves of it. Having said that, there are some 'rules of thumb' in the treatment of depression.

Depression as a mood requires a hanky to cry into and a listening ear. It will get better.

Reactive depression, which is generally not too severe, requires the hanky–ear combination but with a specific focus on dealing with the issue that is oppressing the patient.

Organic depression must be diagnosed and treated by a doctor. Sometimes it requires fairly hi-tech investigations. It will not go away by itself. The treatment depends upon the underlying problem, for example thyroid disease causing the gland to secrete too little thyroid hormone responds magnificently to hormone replacement. Simple.

Manic-depression must be treated by a psychiatrist. It requires lithium or some other mood-stabilising drug and an extensive variety of other interventions, such as education and psychosocial support for both the patient and his long-suffering family.

Mivi Gajić spasiti život antidepresanti

Dysthymia is best treated by some form of fairly protracted psychotherapy. More about this in Chapter 10.

Major Depression almost always requires anti-depressant medication. This is pretty yucky stuff to use since it can have some fairly stunning side-effects and it always takes at least three weeks of faithful dosing before there is any true anti-depressant effect. But when it works (which is about seventy-five per cent of the time) it works a treat. Once again I have encountered misguided counsellors and non-medical therapists who have hung on to patients with severe depressions for too long. Usually they do this because they have some sort of misdirected aversion to drug treatment, based on a common but irrational fear that it will turn patients into zombies or control their minds. Medication is not something to be taken lightly but there are times when it is necessary for the simple reason that it is far and away the most effective treatment. Bar none.

Psychotic depression requires electro-convulsive therapy or 'ECT'. That is what used to be called 'shock treatment'. It involves passing an electric shock over the scalp of an anaesthetised patient so that they have an epileptic convulsion. That sounds absolutely dreadful, doesn't it? No wonder it is the most controversial and misunderstood modality of treatment in the entire medical world. I will not get into the pros and cons of ECT except to emphasise that, hysterical media nonsense aside, ECT is effective and safe. It works. I have seen patients respond miraculously after four or five treatments. If you get psychotic depression, you exist in a living hell. When I develop it in later life I want ECT, ASAP.

Now, before I wrap up this section on depression let me make a brief mention of one of the most tragic aspects of this affliction: suicide.

On average, every psychiatrist (no matter how good he or she is) loses one patient once a year to suicide. It is always a great human tragedy. It leaves a family who are bewildered by the intensity of the sadness of their loved one. They spend the rest of their lives feeling utterly rejected, trying to find sense in this loss, trying to find someone to blame or blaming themselves. The destructive effects of suicide sometimes begin with the death of the patient.

Let me attempt to divide people who try to commit suicide into two ill-defined groups.

suicide - Sheila regressed not supporting girlfriend

The **parasuicide** is generally performed by a young woman who is in good health but finds herself in a situation of helplessness, with no way out. She is often very angry, has been rejected by a friend, drinks alcohol and then impulsively takes an overdose of all the pills that she can find in the bathroom cabinet. Or she may take a blunt knife and superficially lacerate her wrists, consciously or subconsciously making sure that she does not cut any of the vital structures, such as nerves or arteries. Sometimes she then panics and lets someone know pronto what she has just done. She is unceremoniously dragged off to the nearest hospital where a tired and unsympathetic young intern will roll his eyes, pump her stomach, suture her wrists and then, you guessed it, summon the doctor with the holes in the socks and tights ... Sometimes she will do this repeatedly over a period of years and, if she is unlucky, end up killing herself.

The **suicide** is generally performed by an elderly man who is physically and mentally unwell. He may be in chronic pain and may have just been diagnosed as suffering from a serious condition such as cancer. He may have an overwhelming life problem, having just been caught for embezzlement or just been made bankrupt. He will tend to be either recently divorced or recently widowed, but either way he feels old and alone. He may have a history of recurring depressions and he may well be alcoholic. His mental state at the time of his death is undoubtedly seriously depressed. He harbours an intense and insidious anger within him. Eventually he demonstrates Freud's claim that 'suicide is homicide turned 180 degrees' by taking his anger and despair out on himself. He plans it well and uses a very decisive, violent method. He jumps from a cliff, hangs himself or puts the barrel of a rifle into his mouth and, making the last decision of his wretched life, pulls the trigger. No mistakes. No going back.

The division of these people into these two groups is, of course, a gross generalisation. Plenty of young people commit suicide and an alarming finding is that, in the developed world at least, adolescent suicide is on the rise. Food for thought.

Are you feeling as morose as I am? Good. Enough about your emotional world and the types of distress that you harbour there. Now on to relationships, couples, love, sex and all that ...

CHAPTER four

Two-person relationships

Couple trouble

Everyone knows that human beings tend to form couples. And everyone knows that they do this because of their great need for love and romance. Right? Wrong. Forget the mushy stuff. Couples get together so that they can bonk. Pure and simple. From the biological perspective all that courtship and poetry, all that dating and pashing, all that pursuing and conquering is about sex, procreation and the survival of the species. Am I being too simplistic here? Of course I am. But the basic principle stands. People get together in pairs because two is the exact number that is required to make a third.

So why, I hear you ask, are people not as promiscuous as most animals? Why is monogamy seldom, if ever, found in nature? Why do they not follow all that inane idealistic nonsense that was held up in the sixties ... that sex should be no more sanctified than shaking hands ... if it feels good, do it ... an orgasm a day keeps the psychiatrist away ...?

Somewhere along the way *homo so-called-sapiens* complicated the reproductive process. Emotions, morality, ceremonies, the nuclear family and sexually transmitted diseases came along. And we have been forced to handle a whole range of issues called marriage, the 'blended family', property settlements, AIDS tests, herpes, chastity belts, the back of the bicycle sheds, broken condoms and broken hearts. We sure stuffed it up. No longer can couples get together to relieve their hormonal urges. It has all become so highly emotionally charged. Ask any Iranian who has been caught committing adultery ...

In case the penny has not yet dropped, this chapter is about couples. Whenever two people get together they begin to behave in a fairly predictable way. This is epitomised by the way that married couples relate so I shall concentrate here on marriage. But you will come to see that some of these principles apply just as well to parent–child, boss–staff, friend–friend and sibling–sibling relationships, but without the sex. Read on.

The big I: intimacy

Let me begin with an over-riding observation: human beings have an extraordinary drive to *seek, establish and maintain intimacy.* That is what most of the world's poetry, literature and music is about. Falling in love, falling out of love, trying to avoid being alone, weeping unending tears, singing in the rain ... the list goes on. You will note the obvious exception to this observation: the 'Me-out' personality style. They do not really want to *avoid* intimacy, but often they are so hurt, so burned, or so damaged that they convince themselves and others that they do not need it. But I refuse to believe it. Even hermits on desert islands and gurus in caves in the snow have a deeply buried desire to share their island or their cave. Want to earn money fast? Start a dating agency.

The essence of intimacy is not really the sweet nothings and doing 'that thing you really like' to your partner. The essence of intimacy is simply the ability to be totally relaxed in each other's company. It is *trusting closeness*. It is the knowledge that this other person will do nothing to hurt you. No need for secrets to be kept from each other. No betrayal. Intimacy is about never having to put up a facade or pretending to be someone other than you really are. Care and hope can be built on the basis of that trust. That is why weddings are about public promises.

Couples get together to bonk. That is the biological reason. Commitment, exclusivity and mutual respect are the psychological reasons for couples to pair off. Quite apart from a roll in the hay and the satisfaction of our physical urges, these old-fashioned values keep us together. They provide the perfect environment for us to grow and mature as individuals. Call me wrinkly. Call me a nerd. But I see plenty of evidence in my everyday practice that if parents and children can form a nuclear family in which care, trust and hope can be expressed and shared then they are on to a winning combination. Open marriages were a quaint experiment from the days of Woodstock. Polygamy is a quirk limited to religious zealots. It is no accident that all over the world most people aspire to marry one person and to stay with that person until one of their names ends up on a headstone.

Yes, I know that one-third of marriages end in divorce. Yes, I know that there are plenty of unhappy marriages around. Yes, I know that marital infidelity happens every day. But I stick to the conservative values. Happy adults have happy marriages. Happy children know that their parents have one.

So what is this thing called a happy marriage and how do you get one?

First, let me take a moment here to consider how we decide *whom* we will marry. Usually we marry someone who has simply walked into our life at a time when we are becoming ready for this big step. More often than not that person lives within ten city blocks of where we live and not too often did we stumble upon them in discos and singles bars. They tend to be a friend of a friend or a chance acquaintance. But do not believe for a moment that our choice is arbitrary or that we could dedicate the rest of our lives to just anyone. At a deep, subconscious, childlike level we decide whom we will marry with all the cunning of the proverbial fox. We just do not know that we are doing it at the time.

There is an adage in my profession that men marry their mothers and women marry their fathers. This all sounds very Oedipal but is really quite innocuous. Sigmund Freud (why does his name keep cropping up?) suggested that we build up within our subconscious minds an image of the perfect person. This image is called the 'imago'. The process is similar to what the police do when they build up an 'identikit' picture of a suspect from the descriptions of witnesses. A square jaw is attached to thin lips and beady, close-set eyes. Throw in a receding hairline and a wart on the end of the nose and bingo! Within our own subconscious minds our imago is built up of everyone who was emotionally important to us. If we were loved enough then our imago is of a person who is loving and we are drawn to that imago. If we were continually abused then we will tend to find ourselves a replacement abuser.

The imago is more than an image. It is a hybrid of style, smell, colour, posture, temperament, humour and a hundred other qualities. When people gaze at each other across the room and experience the 'love at first sight' attraction what they are experiencing is a near-perfect matching of imagos. They seek each other out and then find somewhere private so that they can get to know each other better. Then they spend hours in intense conversation confirming that their imago has just hit its bull's-eye. Lovers often exclaim they feel as if they have known each other all their lives. This is because they have. Or at least there are things about this enchanting stranger that are deeply familiar from childhood.

It is not *de rigueur* for people to marry the first person who infatuates them. In fact, it is frowned upon since this often happens when they are pubertal and sometimes, curse the luck, it is someone of the same sex. This does not necessarily indicate developing homosexuality. It is the harmless teenage 'crush'. In our culture it is considered normal for people to pass through three or four Big Loves before they decide that this character is the one to stick with.

All right, so the young lovers have eventually found each other. Now what?

Life cycle of the human marriage

About ten years ago I got a crazy idea into my head. I decided that I would run a marathon. I know now that this idea was absurd but I am older, greyer, fatter and wiser now. Hindsight always has 20/20 vision.

You will undoubtedly have heard of how marathon runners 'hit the wall'. At about thirty kilometres or twenty miles you run out of all the energy reserves in your body and the last thirty to sixty minutes of running is done on sheer will-power and stupidity. But when you are out there with the sweat and sore knees you come to realise that actually there is not one wall, but three, and they occur at roughly ten kilometres, twenty kilometres and thirty kilometres. You also come to realise that the first few kilometres can be easy, but a bit shaky, as you warm up and your metabolism changes from aerobic to anaerobic mode.

So why am I telling you all this? Because being married is like running a marathon, that's why. No longer do people believe that marriage guarantees that you will live happily ever after. No longer is there a lot of galloping into the sunset. Marriage can be damned hard work at times and young newlyweds are not hoodwinked by all the lace and pomp. By the time people get married they have passed through that Marvellous Besotted Phase. They have had their first few fights and learned, in a rudimentary way, how to make up. She has learned about his snoring. He has learned that she always leaves the top off the toothpaste tube. But they carry on regardless.

I have already mentioned that Marvellous Besotted Phase in Chapter 1. It is the time of being so in love that you are a teensy bit psychotic with it, of escapism into the fantasy that this partner of yours will satisfy your every need unconditionally and forever. This is the time of *splitting*, of this person whom you love being infinitely wonderful and of a regression into a childlike view of your world. Bad news. This phase can last a maximum of two years, but is usually coming back into harsh reality (snoring, toothpaste tubes and all) by about one year into the relationship. With cynics it can take two or three dates.

Some people do not have the stability or maturity to move beyond it. They move from intense and transient relationship to intense and transient relationship. They like being in the Marvellous Besotted

Phase (MBP) but cannot tolerate the 'now let's get on with living' phase. They hang around the 'meat market' and the singles bars. They have plenty of one-night-stands. They are *terrified* of commitment. Worse still, the longer they avoid it, the more they become *incapable* of it.

Alas, after the MBP the couple must inevitably move into more of a plodding existence. If only we could hang on. But it is humanly impossible to maintain a healthy infatuation forever. Only 'Me-out' people do this, in their own avoidant way, by loving from afar and never having to confront the reality of the relationship.

The MBP is like the warm-up of a run. It starts off very easily but feels a bit shaky. It lasts only until your metabolism wakes up to the task at hand and realises that you had better get producing glucose for your bloodstream or you are going to fall face-down on to the pavement. So it is with the Marvellous Besotted Phase. It's just the warm-up.

Everyone has heard of the 'seven-year itch'. This is the time when marriages become stressed. Two years of MBP and five years of plodding marriage. This is the first marital crisis. What you have *not* heard about are the fourteen-, twenty-one- and twenty-eight-year itches. I don't see couples in my office with the seven-year itch. I can only presume that they either tidy up their acts or break up. What I *do* see plenty

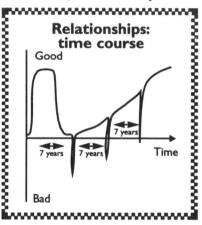

of are couples with the fourteen- and twenty-one- and even twenty-eight-year itches.

Why do marital crises happen in seven-year cycles? I have come to believe that these are simply re-adjustments in the personal development of the individuals so that they can continue to grow together, rather than apart. You see, each member of the couple continues to develop in his or her own direction. One climbs the corporate ladder and learns to escape into work. The other learns how to burp a baby and make birthday cakes that don't sag in the middle. One becomes burnt out. The other becomes bored to tears. They stop communicating. Crisis time. They both need to re-appraise their relationship and how they can help each other to feel fulfilled in life. Quickly, before one or the other has an affair. Most of all they have to learn how to work together again and rekindle the passion that got them together in the first place. Not easy, but essential. And essential, I assure you, every seven-or-so years. Just like the little 'walls' that a marathon runner hits every ten kilometres.

But please don't interpret this as being all doom and gloom. Don't give his ring back or send him a 'Dear John' letter. Also don't feel that once the MBP passes there can be no more spark or hormones or adrenalin in your marriage. Wrong, wrong, wrong. Happy couples manage to keep a twinkle in their eyes and a stirring in their groins indefinitely and they regularly inject some of these residues of the MBP into their marriage. Hell, if they didn't what would be the point of hanging around?

The yin and yang of marriage

Okay. We now have this couple moving through the years. So what is happening between them?

Essentially couples exist at any moment in time in one of three areas. In the middle is what I call the 'middle road'. This is the plodding existence of keeping each other company and looking out for each other. This is where the intimacy occurs on a day-to-day basis. Not in the boudoir, but in the living-room. This, I regret to say, is the most important aspect of marriage since this is how we spend ninety per cent of our married life. Sharing time and space. To do this and find it satisfying we need a fair bit in common with each other. It helps if we share the same opinions on politics and religion, speak the same language, like the same food and watch the sport and the soapies at different times of the day. Every little bit helps to make the plodding more peaceful.

Couples move out of the 'middle road' into one of only two other spheres of cohabitation. These are *care* or *control*. Sick of hearing about these yet? You are? That's tough.

Let me expand. For 'care' read love, passion, fondness, eroticism and all the feelings and displays of concern or attraction that couples share.

For 'control' read fights, hostility, disagreements, arguments and the power struggle.

Many years ago, while I was a general practitioner, I studied acupuncture. I came to the conclusion that it was an interesting philosophy but sticking needles in people had little place in Western medicine ... unless they were being used to inject the potent chemicals that make up modern pharmaceuticals. Why am I telling you this? Because the principles behind acupuncture are based on the ancient Chinese philosophy of Tao. According to this belief system, everything in the universe possesses one of two types of energy called *yin* and *yang*. Channels (known as 'meridians') of yin and yang run up and down the body, and all the insertion points for needles are on either a yin meridian or a yang meridian. Yin is a female force that pervades everything light, gentle and accepting. Yang is a male force that pervades everything that is dark, hard and penetrating. Thus, for example, mountains are yang and the sky is yin. In essence, yin is everything that is caring and yang is everything that is controlling. As you can see, this is all very sexist stuff and pre-dated Gloria Steinem.

The dichotomy of care and control seems to have been formalised here but pervades much of modern thought. Freud's disciple Jung called these elements of human nature 'animus' (the male part of the mind) and 'anima' (the female part). Animus was essentially controlling and anima caring. In management studies there is even a school of thought called 'situational leadership' and the dichotomy is renamed 'direction' (control) and 'support' (care).

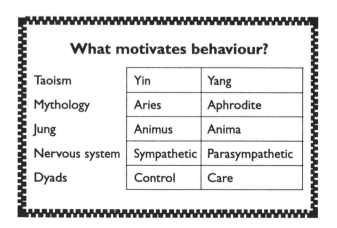

What motivates behaviour?

Taoism	Yin	Yang
Mythology	Aries	Aphrodite
Jung	Animus	Anima
Nervous system	Sympathetic	Parasympathetic
Dyads	Control	Care

In the body there are even two different types of nervous system that correspond roughly to the care and control dichotomy. The *sympathetic* nervous system runs on adrenalin. It initiates fight or flight by increasing your heart and respiratory rates and diverting blood from fairly indolent organs such as the bowel and skin to organs needed for the fight/flight response, such as the muscles. The *parasympathetic* nervous system runs on a different chemical, called acetylcholine. Parasympathetic functions are called 'vegetative' since they are associated with more nurturing and restful activities such as digestion, breastfeeding and some aspects of sexuality. Sympathetic nervous system responses are all about control and being controlled. Parasympathetic nervous system responses are all about caring and being cared for. The care/control duality in nature is being enacted in your body as you read these very words.

Now remind yourself. Couples plod along ninety per cent of the time in 'the middle road'. They deviate from this road into one of only two other areas: care and control. There are therefore three major challenges in marriage.

Challenge one: Learn how to plod

Couples must maintain their mutual interests, share time with each other and keep up the communication about even the most banal of daily experiences. While there is talk there is hope. If couples are unable to do this then they tend to lead a fairly disengaged existence. This happens to couples who come from dramatically different cultures or couples who spend a significant amount of time apart because of occupation (navy, airline flight staff) or types of escapism, such as 'workaholism'. Sometimes one member of the couple will sabotage this humble but essential plodding aspect of their marriage by executing what I call a 'wedge'. This is not a golf shot, but a ploy to block out the other partner. The most commonly used 'wedges' in our civilisation are fatigue, newspapers, work, in-laws, television and children. No communication, no plodding, no marriage.

Note also that, as I have mentioned above, there are some people who simply cannot plod. They have an emptiness and a restlessness within them that does not allow them to move from the MBP into something more mature. They leave a trail of broken hearts.

Challenge two: Maintain the care

Open displays of love and affection come to people so easily when they are in the MBP but they are, curse of curses, one of the first things to go in a committed relationship. This is a crying shame since manifestations of fondness and care are the nicest part of being together. After a while they do not come so easily, but come they must. Every couple should have a 'date' twice a month and a 'dirty weekend' twice a year. A 'date' is defined as a night out for two with no children, no talking about money worries or what is happening at work. It must involve good food, candlelight and a few of those sweet nothings that made you both so gooey all those years ago. I won't try to define a dirty weekend or what it involves. If you don't know then you've just failed Challenge two . . .

Challenge three: Manage the power struggle

For most couples this is the hardest challenge of all. When couples whose marriage is in trouble come to see me my first task is to work out where the 'power base' lies in their relationship. If one member of the couple has all the power then this marriage is in big trouble.

Essentially the power lies with the person who makes the decisions. There are a hundred decisions that each couple makes every day, but most of them become so routine that they go unnoticed. Decisions might be as trivial as 'what channel are we going to watch on TV tonight?' or as monumental as 'what should I do with all this money I just won on Lotto?'. So how do most couples try to share the power? In general, most power-sharing couples have three manoeuvres that help them to dilute the authority. I call the manoeuvres *decision-sharing, demarcation* and *flexibility*. To elaborate:

Decision sharing is just that: taking turns at making decisions. That doesn't mean that you have to have turn-about but that each partner listens to the mental warning bells that go off if he/she has either not made any decisions recently or has made too many. Some couples have a peculiar variant of decision-sharing. They organise it, quite informally, that one partner will make a thousand small-to-medium decisions while the other partner has the say in the one gigantic decision that comes along every few years.

Demarcation is the technique by which one partner claims authority over one area of their mutual experience but leaves the other partner to manage other areas. Each does not trespass into the other's area of expertise. Areas of cooking, earning, child-rearing, gardening and car maintenance tend to become the responsibility of one or other partner and never the twain shall meet. One of the most powerful areas of demarcation tends to be handling the finances and whoever gets this portfolio tends, like the minister for finance, to wield considerable power. It is rare for this area of responsibility to be truly shared. One person cops it.

In the bad old days before sexual equality it used to be straightforward, but a bit rigid. He went to work as the hunter-gatherer and she stayed at home as the bringer-upper of the offspring. And when he came home he became responsible for the outside of the house and she for the inside. Simple. But boring for both parties.

Flexibility Good power-sharers are flexible power-sharers. When unforeseen disasters arrive they have the ability to pull together. He is made redundant so they save money by taking the kids out of childcare and he plays housedad for a while. She is pregnant and finds out that a foetus can weigh more than ten bags of shopping. He takes over the shopping and distracting the bloody-minded two-year-old so that she can have a rest. He doesn't mind this because he knows that she handed him the tissues and propped him up when his mother died last year. That's flexibility.

So that's the theory of how it all goes *right*. When it all goes *wrong*, you have what I call a *Spanner*. Keep reading.

The Spanner Theory

This is called the Spanner Theory because it has a Big End and a Little End. The theory indicates how couples become caught in specific roles within a marriage so that there is no true power-sharing, no flexibility and, ultimately, no mutual respect and no happiness. Spanners are always a human disaster.

The essence of a Spanner is that the person who is the Big End is *dominating and fragile*; the person who is the Little End is *stable and submissive* (see diagram). For convenience' sake I will call the Big End 'him' and the Little End 'her'. That's an accurate portrayal of the situation in two-thirds of Spanners. In the other third the dominating partner is the woman and she is married to that wretched creature, the 'hen-pecked husband'. Men who are Big Ends tend to be dominating and their personality style is called 'narcissistic'. Women who are Big Ends tend to be fragile and their personality style is called 'histrionic'. These are, of course, pretty gross generalisations. There are plenty of dominating women and fragile men around.

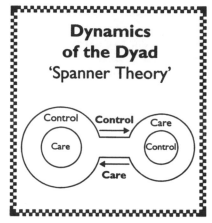

The Big End makes the decisions. His message to her is: 'I have the power. Don't challenge me or you will be punished.' Her message to him is: 'I will try to keep you happy. I will give my personal power to you. I will keep the peace. I will not disappoint you. I will walk on eggshells around you. Just don't leave me.' As you might have guessed, the Big End is always a 'Me-up' personality and the Little End is always a 'Me-down' personality. He has the control and she does all the caring.

But all is not as it might seem. Within every 'Me-up' person there hides a 'Me-down' person who does not want to be recognised. And within every 'Me-down' person there is a 'Me-up' person trying to get out. The Big End has a hard exterior that hides a soft interior. The Little End has a soft exterior that hides a hard interior. The more puffed-up and narcissistic and controlling the Big End becomes, the more he is hiding his own internal sense of dependence, vulnerability and low self-esteem. Big Ends have a very fragile shell. They can't be challenged or criticised. That brings them too close to touching their soft interior so they respond decisively to put down any rebellion. Big Ends feel real and human and dignified if they have all the power. They are lousy at compromise.

Little Ends hide within them their own hard interior. It is summed up in one word: anger. If Little Ends don't own up to their own anger then they end up coming to see me in middle age. They don't sit down with me and begin talking about the internalised rage that they have carried for so long that it is eating away at their insides. They sit down in my office and say 'Doctor, I'm depressed'. They have lived for too long with the Impossible Stress.

There is a saying in my specialty that the typical private patient is a middle-aged woman with depression and problems in a relationship. They all turn out to be Little Ends and they have great difficulty owning up to their anger. That is what the birth of the Women's Movement was all about: women who were united by their anger. Women who were fed up with being stable and submissive. Women who were fed up with the male Big Ends who kept them there.

Big Ends have a great way of chipping away at a Little End's self-esteem. They may not do this with catastrophic attacks, but often with constant, subtle pressure. Think back to the section in the last chapter about 'Seven ways to ruin a good fight'. Often Big Ends are good at turning the fight 'off' before it can get too far. They become expert at thinking quickly, talking fast and rationalising their way out of having to deal with their Little End's anger. If they do this with enough gusto and confidence they can even get the Little End to walk away thinking that there must be something wrong with *her* if she cannot see it his way. She slowly begins to feel that she really must be as unintelligent and worthless as he seems to think.

CASE HISTORY **Julian and Natalie**

Julian knew when he was on to a good thing. Natalie had 'Little End' written all over her forehead in invisible writing that only Big Ends can see. When he met her and realised that he could get her to believe just about anything he wanted her to believe he slipped a ring on her finger and took her to the nearest registry office, post-haste. Then, to ensure that he could imprison her in suburbia and bluff her into thinking that she was the luckiest woman in the world, he lost no time in getting her pregnant.

Natalie answered all his dependency needs. He never had to work on this marriage. It didn't take long before the real Julian emerged. Sarcastic, mocking, dogmatic. She recalled to me how she had fallen over on the back steps of their house when she was heavily pregnant. All Julian could do was laugh. Then off to the pub with his mates.

Natalie, in true Little End style, didn't complain. In fact it never even occurred to her that she could or should. This was her lot in life. She simply worked her spindly fingers to the bone.

She did, however, become increasingly concerned about Julian's interest in one of his workmates, Pamela, who was big and brassy. They spent an awful lot of time together. One day she plucked up all her courage and asked Julian, in a demure way, whether he and Pamela were having an affair. Of course they were, but Julian rebuked her and told her that she was simply

> being paranoid. Natalie scolded herself for being so suspicious. Of course Julian would never lie to her ... Pretty soon Julian and Pamela realised that they could flaunt their affections in front of Natalie as she could always be convinced that her concerns about Julian's infidelity were all in her head.

Now, sitting back reading this stuff you might become judgmental about Natalie's naivety. And she was naive, no doubt about it. Also there was almost certainly a part of her heart that desperately *needed* to believe that her husband was faithful to her even though a blind galah could see that he wasn't. So why did she not wake up to the fact? Because she was brainwashed, that's why.

Big Ends are good at that. And it is worth taking note of the process. This was studied in the 1950s when the USA collected all their pilots who had been shot down over North Korea after that war ended. All of them had been quite successfully brainwashed by the Koreans. When they were repatriated they had long since forgotten about the sacredness of the stars and stripes, mother and apple pie. They spouted the glories of communism and the evils of capitalism. After a few months of being home in downtown LA and endless meals of fried chicken and corn cobs they tended to come to their senses. Whistler's mother looked homely again.

The Americans learned that to brainwash someone you must follow a tried and true recipe:

Exercise: How to brainwash someone

1 Imprison them.
2 Deprive them of their identity.
3 Starve them of food, water and any outside contact; make them lose perspective. Most importantly of all, make them very, very tired.
4 Intimidate them; tell them that you have the power of life and death over them.
5 Repeat over and over to them what you want them to believe. If the brainwashee is your wife and you are a Big End, remind them continually that you are bigger, better and brighter than she is.

Brainwashing, as you will realise, was not peculiar to the North Koreans. Elements of it have been used by military organisations, religious groups and Big Ends for centuries. Did you notice the similarities between what the POWs went through and what Natalie, as the Little End, endured? Striking. The message that Julian repeated over and over again to Natalie was that he was not being unfaithful to her and, perhaps more insidiously, that he was good and she was bad. Enough indoctrination and Natalie, who had long since lost her identity and perspective, was willing to believe anything.

Sometimes, after many years of being a Little End, she will start to take heed of some sort of survival instinct that whispers in her ear: 'Get out now while you still have some sanity and self-esteem.'

Up she gets and off she goes. It takes six months of being away from the brainwashing before it dissipates from her consciousness. One day she simply wakes up and thinks 'Hey, I'm not such a bad person after all'. Then she gets in touch with her anger and becomes a staunch feminist. That is one of the most predictable things about brainwashing: it wears off if the brainwashee can simply be removed from the brainwasher. American POWs can start to warm to mother and apple pie again if they are returned to their own kind. Cult members can realise that they are not possessed by the devil after all. And Little Ends can be helped to believe in their own self-worth again.

If she stays in the relationship then it is she who comes to see me, in mid-life, carrying an awful depression. If he ever comes to see me it is because she has left him. Usually it is the Little End who leaves the Big End. That is because the relationship is set up to meet the needs of the Big End. He takes, she gives. Why would any right-minded Big End want to leave a set-up like that?

Big Ends are a predictable lot. When their Little End becomes fed up and goes, Big Ends have only three options: they must get her back, they must replace her or they must fall apart. Now one by one.

1 **Getting her back** He chases after her and gets her back. He promises her that he will change and using a million different words he tries to convince her that he can and will share power with her. If he is an alcoholic he will swear black and blue that he will stop drinking. Something within her takes pity upon this disempowered, grovelling man. She always knew that he was weak and vulnerable. She saw the sadness within him which he had to cover with his narcissistic armour of arrogance and control. In a peculiar way this vulnerability was one of the things that attracted her to him in the first place. She feels sorry for him and wants to mother him. She goes back. He is on his best behaviour for the first few weeks. He buys her a dozen roses on the way home from work. He stops drinking. Sex is terrific.

Then slowly he sinks back into the old ways. They have their first fight. He comes home from work late reeking of booze. Three weeks and two days after she comes back he hits her again. Old habits die hard. The problem is that he is still a 'Me-up' personality and she is still a 'Me-down' personality. Unless they understand themselves and the dynamics of their relationship they have little chance of even beginning to change the old ways. Turning a Spanner style of relationship, with its continual power struggle, into something that is more equitable is difficult. But not impossible.

Before I go on, let me ponder for a moment that phenomenon of modern life that is called the 'trial separation'.

CASE HISTORY **Simon and Sandra**

If you ever wondered what happened to hippies now that the sixties are thirty years behind us, meet Simon and Sandra. Hippies might age, they might cut their hair, stop smoking dope and change their children's names by deed poll from 'Zen' and 'Karma' to 'Phyllis' and 'Ralph', but they still have that peace, love and incense feel about them.

Trouble is, no amount of idealising about the meaning of life makes you exempt from the emotional vulnerability and power struggle that is inherent in any sort of intimacy. Simon and Sandra still espoused their hippy ideals but were really locked into a battle royal for control of the relationship. She slowly embraced the charms of capitalism and coerced him into getting a job. Then they were into mortgages and driving the right sort of car (with its ideologically sound, environmentally friendly unleaded petrol). To cope with the stresses he took to smoking dope again and she took to nagging him about it. The external veneer was about peace, love and incense, but in the family home the years went by with a tension in the air that could be cut with a blunt knife. Simon felt powerless to limit Sandra's demands. Eventually he left her. But he did this in a very self-controlled way, explaining to her that this would be a *trial separation*.

Sandra, being a thinly disguised Big End, freaked out. She visited him in his new one-bedroom flat pretty often. Sometimes they made love and when they did the Earth, that they had worked so hard to protect, moved. But still Simon refused to come home. And he also refused to give her any idea of how long this trial separation would last. Quite accidentally Simon found himself in a position of control. And he revelled in it. He had taken the power from her and she desperately wanted it, and him, back again. This stand-off situation lasted for months before they were both referred to me for marital counselling.

This case illustrates the two essential features of trial separations: anxiety and anger. Quite often Little Ends leave Big Ends and cannot muster the courage to make it clear that that's exactly what they are doing: leaving. They are afraid because they know full well that Big Ends are extraordinarily dependent and will simply fall apart at the seams if they realise that they have been well and truly abandoned. Simon also managed to express his anger to Sandra. She had been so demanding and nagging that she had, in Freudian terms, *castrated* him and now he had managed to re-implant his own penis. He managed to show her his new power and to punish her by being constantly and consistently passive in his anger. He knew in his heart that he could keep her hanging on indefinitely and he derived an immense amount of covert pleasure from this. So much for peace, love and incense.

My first task in helping them was to call a spade a spade. I backed Simon into a psychological corner and suggested that Sandra give him an ultimatum. If he hadn't declared his intentions within 'x' number of weeks then she would presume that the marriage was 'off' and they should both consult individual solicitors concerning a property settlement and access arrangements. The marital ball, so to speak, was back in her court.

Shortly after this the 'trial separation' game came to an end. They embarked on a course of marital therapy in which some fairly painful communication was performed at last and they struck upon a new set of rules. Then they could get back to saving the planet and knitting woolly jumpers . . .

2 Replacing her Option number two is to *replace* his Little End. Statistics show that if a couple divorces and moves on to remarry other partners, men do this after a year or two and women do it after six or even eight years. Men, and Big Ends in general, are very dependent. From the outside it appears that it is the Little End of the Spanner who is more dependent because she seems to cling to her Big End in the face of both abuse and neglect. Wrong, wrong, wrong. Big Ends can fool people into thinking that they are not dependent and often the person they fool most of all is themselves.

One way that Big Ends have of keeping their neediness and vulnerability hidden is to treat their Little Ends like car parts. When they wear out, you just replace them. Plenty more Little Ends where she came from. Sometimes men even have another Little End lined up and waiting in the wings to walk in and replace their last one. She attracts a number of labels. She is called 'the mistress' or 'the Other Woman'.

Mistresses are *always* Little Ends. What self-respecting female Big End would hang around and wait for some man to leave his wife?

Mistresses also help Big Ends to camouflage their own dependency. Men do not have to suffer at all when the marriage breaks down. Sure, it is hard to explain it all to the kids, but they never have to sleep alone or make their own beds or wash their own dirty underwear. And the big bonus is that they can flaunt their mistress in front of their estranged wife to make her feel even more rotten.

3 **Falling apart** Big Ends' third option is to fall apart, decompensate, collapse in a heap. It is not a pretty sight and the person who is often most surprised at the Big End's inability to be alone is the Big End himself. One day he is a dominating, macho, controlling male and the next day he is a screaming mess. This reminds me of one of my favourite patients.

CASE HISTORY **Bruce**

Bruce was a police sergeant. He was handsome and broad-shouldered. He was forty-something but had hung on to his hair and complemented it by a clipped, regulation moustache. He looked strong and dapper. If you were arrested half-cut and 'drunk and disorderly' and hauled in front of Bruce at the local cop-shop you would know that you were in major trouble. Bruce did not let anyone get away with much. He was respected in the force because he was very experienced and very competent.

Bruce had seen the worst aspects of humankind. He had been confronted over the decades with domestic violence, heroin overdoses and fatal car crashes. After a while all that stuff got to him. Bruce built an invisible armour around himself and tried not to listen to the little boy within him who was weeping and scared by all this brutality. Like the steel in the barrel of his handgun, he became hardened.

Bruce was married to Valerie. If you will pardon the dreadful pun, Bruce took his bewilderment home to Valerie every day and she 'copped' it day after day. He treated her like one of his junior constables. Who was the Big End? Sergeant Bruce, of course.

One day Valerie heard the coaxing voice of survival in her head and off she went. Bruce could not get her back and he did not fancy trying to shack up with someone else. So he fell apart.

Bruce was so desperate for some solace that he would come to see me during breaks in his work schedule. Because he was so senior he could be flexible with his time and did not have to account for his every working minute. He wore his uniform to my office and I wondered whether he needed to hang on to this image of his being a uniformed and respected police sergeant to offset the feelings of despair and panic that he described to me. Practicalities of police regulations dictated that he could not leave his police revolver with my secretary before sitting down with me. I'm sure she had no particular interest in baby-sitting his six-shooter anyway. So he brought his gun into the sessions, strapped to his belt as it always was. I'm sure Freud would say that he needed to hang on to this phallic symbol because he was feeling so thoroughly castrated. He sat in my leather chair session after session crying into paper tissues. I was confronted with the unnerving spectacle of a large and emotionally distraught man with a pistol on his hip and an air of desperation . . .

I met Valerie on one occasion and helped her to communicate the painful truth to Bruce. She was not coming back. She had had enough. I felt a bit more edgy about the gun.

Eventually Bruce got it together. He was a terribly likeable chap and he had the courage to reveal to me the hurt child who lived beneath the veneer of swaggering confidence. Bruce's father had been a violent alcoholic and Bruce had memories of gathering his two younger brothers in the garage of their house at night with bags packed, waiting for his parents to stop fighting and trying to decide whether it would be safer for them to go to a nearby relative's house for shelter.

In a paradoxical way, the end of Bruce's marriage marked the beginning of a painful and long-overdue introspection for Bruce. He had carried a lot of emotional pain for far too long and he managed to unburden some of it with me. The more I got to know him the less I even noticed the gun . . .

Now, the very fact that you have gone into a bookshop, browsed through the 'Personal Development' shelves and taken this book up to the counter to buy (for which I am eternally grateful) is that you are, quite simply, someone who is interested in your own personal growth. No doubt you would have read other books from the same bookshelf from which you chose this one. If you have, then you will recognise the Spanner Theory under a different name. In most of the self-help books around the type of dominant–submissive relationship that is described in the 'Spanner', it is referred to by another name: *co-dependence.* In fact ~~codep~~ you will find that about ninety per cent of the books on each side of this one are concerned with that topic. Why? Because it is one of the two buzz-words from the west coast of the USA that have filtered into our conversational jargon over the last few years. (The other great buzz-word is *dysfunctional family,* but I will describe that in a later chapter. In the meantime drop it into the chat at your next cocktail party to show how psychologically aware you are . . .)

I do not like the term *co-dependence*, so I will steadfastly avoid using it. Suffice it to say that the 'C-word' refers to the type of relationship that I have described here as being a 'Spanner': the essential features are the same. They both refer to an intense and usually slightly warped relationship that involves one person who is dominating and fragile and another person who is stable and submissive.

Why am I so disdainful about the C-word? Because as a technical term it has been bent, folded, stapled and mutilated. Its origin and pure meaning referred to the relationship between a male alcoholic (who was dependent upon alcohol) and his wife (who was dependent upon the alcoholic). With this went a slightly more insidious suggestion that the family of the alcoholic subconsciously conspired to keep the alcoholic just that: alcoholic. They colluded with his drinking by buying him the sherry and keeping him at home during his binges so that the neighbours would never see him sloshed. They made sure that some of the housekeeping money was available so that it could be spent on grog and they bailed him out of jail. They did all this for very honourable reasons. They pitied him. They found him insufferable when he was working up to a 'bender' so they learned early in the piece that the best thing for all concerned was just to let him go to it and get it over with. They were also preoccupied with keeping the shame private. In the jargon of Alcoholics Anonymous this process is referred to as 'enabling'.

The whole family became Little Ends who were trained from an early age to take responsibility for their alcoholic father. They cared for him, dusted him off when he fell over in the gutter, rescued him from the police and wiped the spew up without flinching. But by never forcing him to own up to his problem and never insisting that he take responsibility for the disastrous consequences of his drinking, they successfully managed to let him drink to his heart's (but not liver's) content.

This, then, was the original meaning of the C-word: a male alcoholic dependent and a female non-alcoholic 'co-dependent'. Unfortunately the writers of the next hundred 'pop psychology' books then managed to well and truly defile the pure meaning of the term and re-define it as just about any relationship in which one partner felt dependent, either materially or emotionally, upon the other. They made the meaning so broad that just about any relationship, no matter how benign, came to be labelled with it. They even spoke about Big Ends as being the equivalent of 'dry drunks' because they acted in the same domineering ways as alcoholics but did not necessarily display some problem with alcohol. Co-dependence became just about synonymous with dependence and both became dirty words. This was a great shame because the trend ignored a very important fact: *everyone on this Earth is dependent upon other people*, whether they care to admit it or not.

Now let me bamboozle you with a startling fact. *All relationships are Spanners.* The imbalance of power might be very, very subtle, but it is there. That is because *democracy can exist only where there are odd numbers of people.* When two people encounter a situation in which a decision must be made about whose needs will be met first then there is inevitably more compromise from one partner than the other. If God had made three sexes so that marriages occurred among three individuals then two people could out-vote the third. For couples there is just the survival of the fittest, or the bossiest person with the loudest voice. The power struggle becomes a problem only when the dependence is so one-sided or the neediness of one partner for control and the other partner for care becomes so great that they stop respecting each other.

Rubber-band relationships

Back to first principles. I work on the basic tenet that human beings go to great lengths to find intimacy. They are looking for another human being with whom they can be close, emotional and trusting. But intimacy is such a vulnerable thing. Cast your mind back to the concept of anxiety. You will recall that from day to day we human beings must try to cope with two main fears: the fear of attack and the fear of abandonment. These are the great vulnerabilities of intimacy. If we get too close we are at risk of being controlled or violated by this other person. If we get too far away we must cope with the fear of abandonment. So what do we do? The answer is found in the Bible:

'To everything there is
a season and a time
for every purpose
under heaven . . .
a time to embrace,
a time to refrain from
embracing . . .'
Ecclesiastes 3:1,5

Relationships are such dynamic things that the partners are continually moving towards or away from each other. There is a time to embrace and be loving, romantic and intimate. There is also a time to 'refrain from embracing', which means get out of each other's space pronto before the crockery, along with the Domestic Violence Act, is broken. Between these two extremes each couple works out what for them is a 'safe distance' so that each of them does not constantly feel either attacked or abandoned.

One of the saddest variations on this theme is what I call the 'Rubber-band Relationship'. These people spend years and years trying find their safe distance and sometimes never seem to find it.

CASE HISTORY Sean

Sean had a chip on his shoulder the size of a Sherman Tank. He had had a background characterised by both neglect and abuse but Sean's hurt was bigger than most: the neglect had been utter rejection by his parents and the abuse had been sexual abuse in just about all of the seven foster homes that he had grown up in. Catastrophic neglect and catastrophic abuse.

Sean had found a way of compensating for this. In his teenage years he found out, much to his surprise, that girls found him attractive. He was very tall, rugged and muscular and he had a softly-spoken boyish charm. He found out how to get girls to go to bed with him and he used it again and again. And again. His self-esteem was boosted by his ability to chase and conquer. But with the conquest came boredom. Finished with that woman; who's next? His life became a frantic search for sexier women and bigger and better orgasms. Sexual excitement could, for a while at least, ease the ache that he felt for that more secure, reliable, fulfilling sort of love that could only come from a loving parent or a devoted spouse. Repeating this seduction sequence over and over again kept the bad feelings within him at bay. The feelings? They were those old familiar ones: the feelings of being unloved, unlovable and unable to love. Except sexually. That would have been all very well for Sean's own happiness. He did not particularly care about the hurt women that he left in his wake.

Then along came a major problem in Sean's life: he became middle-aged. The nymphets stopped falling for the guy with the paunch and the gammy leg and the black dye in his greying locks. Unlucky ... Another scary thing happened to Sean. He became clucky. Sure, women have a biological clock that makes them edgy when they are childless and forty. Surprisingly enough, men often experience the same feelings. They know that they can go on producing sperm but they run out of heartbeats earlier than women and they get a bit threatened about the prospect of dealing with an adolescent son when they are sixty.

Sean decided that it was time to settle down. He met a nice, single, middle-aged doctor called Carmel. He wooed her with his inimitable charm. Of course she fell for it, paunch and gammy leg and hair dye and all. So they got married. Then the Marvellous Besotted Phase wore off.

When Carmel and Sean were together it did not take long before the vulnerability associated with intimacy became intolerable. They began to fight. Sean felt exposed and all his hidden sadness and anger came out. He threw it at Carmel with such decibels that all the neighbours knew about it. Carmel was a pretty plucky woman (that is why he was attracted to her in the first place) and she threw it back at him. But just as they were on the point of destroying each other with this hurt they found that the best (in fact the only) thing that they could do was to separate. So they did, after only three months. Then they would stew on it and become terrified of being alone. Their fear of abandonment would bring them together. For a while the reconciliation would be lovingly, erotically heavenly. Until they both reacted to the vulnerability of this closeness and the cycle of rage and forgiveness, togetherness and separateness, would start again. For the next three years they lived on the opposite ends of a Rubber-band that was continually expanding and contracting. They developed a three-monthly pattern of being together and then being apart.

Sean came to see me in a depressed state of mind. He had lost the looks and the agility of youth. He was a balding middle-aged man with an inability to let anyone get too close to him emotionally. Anyone in his life who had managed to get close to him had hurt him.

Sean had done all the positive thinking that he could stand. It helped. For about fifteen minutes. Then he was back to the sad truth: he wanted to find love but seemed to be allergic to it. His case epitomised the type of predicament that can only be adequately addressed by trying to lay to rest the ghosts of the past ... all the pain from all those people who had hurt him. In Sean's case there was a whole graveyard of them.

Did it work? No, it didn't. Sean responded to me in his habitual way. He came to three sessions, then he found that the vulnerability of describing emotions to me was intolerable. So he 'ran away' by cancelling all his other appointments. Rubber-bands exist between psychiatrists and patients too. If you are reading this Sean, come back so that we can start working on a *safe distance* between you and me.

Divorce

I have let you know how couples get together, what they must do to stay together and how it sometimes goes wrong. Now let me dwell on what happens when it goes tragically wrong. And as you read this keep in mind that one-third of modern marriages end in divorce. Before I move on to the next chapter I want to dwell on how to get out of your marriage. More than that, I am going to give you seven steps for how to make a terribly painful experience a little less painful.

Know when to let go

Do you remember those quaint old days, not so long ago, when it was really, really naughty to divorce? People of my generation went to school with one or two kids who came from families where there was a solo parent. Widows and widowers were okay but people whose marriages had failed were looked upon with a kindly but tut-tutting attitude. Those were the days when people were trapped into years of hostile, resentful dependence upon a spouse who felt equally hostile and resentful.

Thank God all that has changed. Social welfare came along to ease out the old, moralistic stance. These days the message is clear: try marital counselling first, but if that does not improve the situation or if your 'other half' does not co-operate, then you must have a long, hard look at the pros and cons of staying around. If you are in an unhappy marriage, if you have given it a good go but the situation is hopeless, if you have tried to nut out what is going wrong but no matter how hard you try you find yourself living through months or years of marital misery, *then it is time to get out of this marriage and find yourself a better life.* If you do not then you might condemn yourself to more years of unhappiness before you wake up and realise that your life has slipped past, you don't get a second chance and you are still married to that rotten sod. Learn how to let go.

There is an extra message here: if you are being exposed to physical, sexual or emotional cruelty then you must leave now. Not tomorrow, not this evening, not at the end of this chapter ... but *now*. Finish this chapter after you have bedded down at the refuge.

Call a spade a spade and an 'ex' an 'ex'

When a marriage dissolves, clear communication is essential. Not only for you and your spouse, but for kids, in-laws, extended family and friends.

Also, when you go, do it with a *stated, committed end-point.* By this I mean that you must let your spouse and your children know that as of such-and-such a time (usually when you leave or you kick out your spouse) the marriage is over, that it will never be revived and that you are committed to this action. Don't play Rubber-bands. <u>Don't keep coming back. If you do you will confuse everyone, yourself included.</u> When you let go make it clear that that is what you are doing and that you are letting go for good.

If you have kids then you must sit down with them and, in dulcet tones, give them the following messages very clearly:

- This divorce is not their fault.
- They will experience a reduction in their standard of living but they will be housed, fed, watered, educated and loved as much as before.
- You and your partner will still be in their lives, even if that involves access visits but they will come to accept that that will work well, and possibly better than family outings in the past. They are not being deserted.
- They will experience some emotional turmoil during the transition from being in a two-parent to being in a one-parent family but things often work out better in the long run because their parents are not always together in the same house fighting with each other.

- They will be told about everything that is going on and they will be consulted for their opinions on what they would like to have happen. They can also talk to you and/or your 'ex' about what is disturbing or worrying them.
- You and your spouse are not going to get back together, so don't waste any time or energy trying to engineer that.

Understand your own ambivalence

Marriages are about hope and divorces are about despair. Don't fool yourself: there is no such thing as a nice divorce. If there is then it occurs at the end of a passionless, lifeless marriage. Marriage is about public promises of eternal love. Divorces are about coming to terms with the end of forever. If a marriage ever had any love in it then it is painful to come to terms with its demise.

At the end of a marriage couples must cope with all three primary types of emotional distress: anger at the other partner; sadness at the loss of the idealised marriage and the idealised future; and anxiety about the future alone. What usually results is an intense ambivalence about your marital partner. The good parts of him or her were the parts that drew you into this marriage in the first place and the aspects of his or her personality that you found stimulating or exciting. You will miss those parts awfully. But the bad parts of your partner have led to this intolerably distressing situation and you will rejoice at being rid of them.

It is natural for couples to dump all this on to each other; in fact it is usually emotionally necessary for them to have a few ugly scenes to get the anguish out of their systems. But if you put your partner on to a purely bad 'split' and ignore or forget that he or she does have *some* saving graces then you are setting yourself up for a battle royal. Ugly court scenes, disputed custody, denial of access, accusations, counter-accusations, wealthy lawyers. I have seen this protracted legalised act of rage carried out in the most brutal and pitiful way.

Get the message: understand your ambivalence. Don't split. The good and the bad parts of your 'ex' come from the same person. Protracted divorce is a disguised form of protracted grief. Both of them stem from the profound emotional confusion that arises from feeling powerfully positive and powerfully negative about the same person at the same time. Grieve at the loss of the good parts and exalt in the riddance of the bad parts.

Friendship with your 'ex'

Don't try to make your 'ex' your friend (or at least not until the dust has settled on your divorce papers).

I hear it so often in my consulting rooms. It is said by well-intentioned spouses or perhaps people who are trying to minimise the distressing effects of divorce. They want their 'ex' to be their friend. In the early stages of separation this is not only impossible, it is inappropriate. To turn something that was once intimate and passionate into a friendship is to trivialise the intensity of what you once had. It is like enjoying *haute cuisine* but referring to it as 'good nosh'.

This is a time for anger, sadness and anxiety to be expressed and dealt with. It is hard to do that adequately to a 'friend'. So is it *ever* possible to be friends with your 'ex'? The answer is yes, but not until you have got this other person out of your heart and your head. This means that you have separated, been apart for a decent amount of time (at least months), adjusted to your new life, perceive that the kids have adjusted too and, preferably, you have both established another intimate relationship. That way you can both feel safe and trusting about opening some non-threatening channels of communication. And eventually you might even develop a real friendship. Eventually.

Beware the triangle

I have jumped the literary gun here. Triangles (or three-people relationships) are what Chapter 6 is all about. But it is worth mentioning here that the formation of triangles around the time of separation and divorce can be a very destructive process.

What happens when a couple separates is that it becomes difficult for the pair to keep their battle to themselves. Demarcation lines tend to form and, like choosing sides for basketball, opposing teams appear. On one side he stands, with his family and friends who look upon her as being an utter bitch; on the other side she amasses her own family and friends who are convinced that he should be behind bars for what he has done to her. In the middle are the poor kids who don't know whether they are on his side or hers, but manage to change sides *PDQ* depending upon who is looking after them today.

If you are separating from your other half, then you must establish the marital equivalent of the Geneva Convention: civilians (i.e. family and friends) will not be involved, and prisoners of war (i.e. the kids) will be treated with dignity and respect. On the other hand if you are trying to support a friend or family member who is undergoing a separation or divorce then you will be well-advised to try to stay as neutral as possible. Listen, empathise and shelter. But taking sides is the equivalent of donning a uniform and picking up a gun.

Mediate don't militate

I am no lawyer. I daily thank my lucky stars for this fact. I see what unscrupulous lawyers do to turn fairly healthy divorces into the adversarial stance of 'let's get him or her for everything we can'. Yes, I know that most lawyers are wise enough to advise their clients what is an appropriate settlement and when to take the money and run. Yes, I have heard the rationalisation that they are simply representing the best interests of their clients. But I have seen divorce and custody cases that have turned into living nightmares for all concerned because spouses become consumed by the narcissistic injury that is the failure of their marriage. And I have seen lawyers fan the flames.

That is why the Family Law Court, in all its judicial wisdom, has mediators. If you can sit down with an impartial third person and work out who will get the TV set, the teapot collection and the budgie, then you are well on the way to being able to get on with rebuilding your life. Make it quick, clean and fair.

Be aware also that such mediation does not have to come from court-appointed mediators (although they can second-guess what the courts might decide anyway and short-circuit a lot of courtroom wrangling). Any counsellor who is experienced in marital therapy should also be experienced in divorce therapy. Believe it or not, such a thing as 'divorce therapy' exists.

It is usually fairly short and sweet and works on a number of principles, including the need for clear communication and commitment to painful decisions. I should point out that the other important principles are:

- Divorce therapy is like some insurance policies: there is a 'no-fault' clause. We are past the time for slinging blame and anger at each other. This is not about deciding who to crucify; this is about ending the marriage with an absolute minimum of hurt for all concerned.
- Matters at hand can be divided very simplistically in two: the practical and the emotional. Practical issues are concerned with money and children. Emotional issues are concerned with

understanding that you still have both positive and negative feelings towards this other person. The gist of that exercise then becomes to accentuate and validate those negative feelings so that you can give up the positive ones. No hankering after them when they are gone. No walking back across burning bridges. Time to get on with your life.

Allow yourself some breathing space

Everyone has heard of new romances springing up 'on the rebound'. A couple splits up and before you can say 'I divorce you' three times one of them has shacked up with another partner.

Men do this more often than women. That is because your average man (if such a thing exists) is far more dependent than your average woman (ditto). In fact men are so dependent that they often tee up their next partner before they leave their last. She is called their 'mistress' and, as the word suggests, she is usually found halfway between a 'mister' and a 'mattress' . . .

If you find yourself struggling through the horrors of a divorce then you must allow yourself some emotional 'R and R' after you have split up. If you find another partner straight away and cling to him or her then you are usually starting that relationship for all the wrong reasons, i.e. for dependency rather than true love and caring. The 'breathing space' after the relationship must be to allow healing of your battered ego and your bruised feelings. Perhaps even more importantly it is a time to get an honest, objective perspective on what went wrong. If you do not do this, then you are sure to develop your next intimate relationship with all the same old unresolved myths and flaws in it.

I have a saying that sums this up: 'One divorce is a tragedy; two divorces is a symptom'. Think about it.

Before we get on with the next chapter, let me reiterate the basic principles:

- ≡ Human beings strive to find intimacy because that is the best fertiliser for personal growth.
- ≡ Marriages often begin with besotted feelings but must be developed into something that is more mature and secure.
- ≡ All good marriages have stormy times that must be weathered.
- ≡ When couples get together they live most of the time in a 'plodding' existence that is keeping company.

- They move out of this 'middle road' into one of only two areas: care and control.
- If, because of their own unresolved problems with love, trust and hope, they become locked into a dominant–submissive style of relationship then they form what I call a 'Spanner'. Spanners *never* result in the long-term happiness and fulfilment of the couple involved.
- If you are unhappy in your marriage, take a long hard look at it. It may be time to let go.

These are the principles of *marriage*, which is the most challenging dyad of them all. But they apply in many ways to every other two-person relationship. Keep that in mind.

CHAPTER five

Gender

The joy of 'Y'

Everyone knows that men are men and women are women and never the twain shall meet. At least that's the way it used to be. All that has changed now. We have gone through, and continue to go through, the gender equivalent of Future Shock. The times, as Bob Dylan said when it all began, they are a-changin'.

This chapter is going to be a short one. It is about the difference between the sexes, which is a minefield of controversy. Those I offend in the next few pages are requested to form an orderly queue outside my office door with all the other people I have already offended. Just keep the noise down because I am inside trying to be therapeutic ...

I am well aware that writers who are far more learned than I am have written screeds on gender difference and that it is a hot topic at universities. What I offer here is highly subjective. It is also written from my own perspective of having a 'Y' chromosome and an understanding of the purpose of the 'Y' in 'Y-fronts' ... I have tried to grasp what it must be like to be a woman. Imagine that. I am a skerrick under six foot two inches tall, or 188 centimetres if you prefer. I walk down dark alleys in the city without being overly concerned that I will be attacked or mugged. When I square my shoulders and lower my voice I frighten even myself. What the muggers hiding in the shadows do not realise is that I am a chicken. Glass jaw and all. My muscles are soft from under-use and the skin on my hands has not seen a callus for years. My kids know that I am a 'soft touch' for pocket money. If someone leapt from the shadows with a gun I would simply faint. But my size makes me feel safe. Clever, eh? I suppose that if I were a woman then it would be like living in a world of homosexual rapists who were all eight foot three inches tall. I cannot bend my mind around how vulnerable that would make me feel. God bless you, my 'Y' chromosomes.

On the other hand I expect that there would be some advantages. I could own up to my internal sense of emotional turmoil. I could talk to my female friends quite openly about my feelings without their looking at me as if I had gone bonkers. I would not have to measure my self-worth by my achievements. What would matter in my life would not be what I do, but who I am. I would be freed from all that back-stabbing competition and for this I would be rewarded with an extra eight years of life. Curse you, damned 'Y's.

The 'bottom line', which I shall state up front, is that I admire women and pity men.

My father was an obstetrician. He and I had a lot in common. Most of our patients were women. We both dealt with their most intimate and private problems. It's just that we worked on different ends of the body.

About three quarters of my patients are women. That is because women come to see psychiatrists and men go to jail. If I were a child psychiatrist (that is, a psychiatrist who treats children rather than a Doogie Howser who became a shrink) then I would see mostly males. If kids are going to go off the rails then most of the time they are boys.

Girls save up their emotional hurt with their characteristic stamina and stoicism and bring it along to me when they are in their thirties and forties. Perhaps this is the first observation: that males express and females suppress? Sometimes, but not always.

Now here are some statistics about the different ways that the genders experience and express their emotional pain:

- About three-quarters of all 'successful' suicides are carried out by men. Men also use more violent means of killing themselves. No mistakes.
- Despite this, women have a greater risk of developing a severe depression.
- Mental retardation is more common in males.
- Eating disorders are the realm of women. If men get eating disorders then they tend to get them more severely and have a worse prognosis.
- Women live five to ten years longer than men on average. This may explain why they have a greater incidence of senile dementia.
- Men are convicted of criminal offences nine times more commonly than women.
- The two outstanding risk factors for being a victim of domestic violence are being a woman (surprise, surprise) and being exposed to violence as a child.
- Alcoholism is about eight times more common in men than women.

There are lies, damned lies, and then there are statistics. Who said that? I forget, but it makes sense. You see one is easily lulled into the idea that women suffer more than men. If I sit in the comfort of my consulting room and wait for patients to come to me then I could come to believe that women suffer more than men. So what if you go out and actually catch people at random in the street and ask them about their psychiatric disorders. Sounds crazy? Believe it or not, a huge team of researchers in the USA did exactly that. It was called the Epidemiological Catchment Area study and a team of trained interviewers went door-knocking. Somehow, don't ask me how, they managed to interview tens of thousands of people and come up with computer-aided diagnoses. The result? If all forms of psychiatric disorder are taken into account (and this includes drug and alcohol abuse and criminal personality styles) then *men outnumber women*. It's just that they do not come to see the people with the halitosis and the holes in their socks or ladders in their tights. They see lawyers instead.

Women have a whole swag of psychiatric problems that are exclusively theirs. Premenstrual tension, post-natal psychosis and depression, the emotional consequences of termination of pregnancy, the hassles of filling your body with all sorts of hormones in order to avoid making babies, the challenge of hysterectomy, and, last but not least, that midlife crisis called 'menopause'. Most problems that are distinctly male reflect the difficulty that your average bloke has in owning up to, and dealing with, his emotional distress: drink, crime, suicide and the narcissistic personality style.

Narcissus, as students of Greek mythology will know, was the youth who happened to catch a glimpse of his own reflection in the water of a still pond and promptly fell deeply in love with himself. Most women will know what I am getting at here. It is male self-love, also referred to as the 'fragile male ego'. That is the worst thing about narcissism: its fragility. True narcissists have an inflated, but fragile, view of their own self-worth. They cannot stand for that fragility to be revealed by some pest coming along and criticising them: that shows up the cracks in their armour. Narcissists also cannot, for the life of them, empathise with the suffering of anyone other than themselves. No one could suffer as much as they do, or so they all believe. So let's get to the point here. Narcissists are a selfish lot. Are narcissists mostly male or female? Silly, silly question.

Gender roles have changed immensely over the past few decades. No one will argue with that claim. The old white picket fence ideal is now something of a museum piece. You know, the happily married, healthy, fertile young couple. He goes out to do an honest day's work. She stays home and minds the 1.7 children. When he comes home and unburdens all his woes upon her she is there

Seven male myths

1 If I'm ambitious and successful, I'm a good bloke.
2 Showing feelings is for women.
3 Male friendship is OK. Close male friendship is for poofters.
4 Give your woman an inch and she'll take a mile.
5 No red-blooded man could ever stay faithful to his wife.
6 If you show your kids you love them, you'll spoil them rotten.
7 Anyone with balls can hold his drink.

with his pipe and slippers. She has a stiff drink ready and then they and their one-and-a-bit kids sit down to a hot meal that she has prepared even in the sweltering heat of summer. Of course he sits at the head of the table. She is patient, loving, giving, caring, and long-suffering. She is a lady in public and a nymphomaniac in bed.

Did these creatures ever exist? I doubt it. Women became aware of the fact that men had all the power. Not fair. So they started the Women's Movement.

Back to the Spanner

In the last chapter I described the Spanner Theory. A Spanner is a two-person relationship in which there is a dominant, fragile person (the Big End) and a stable, submissive person (the Little End). The Big End has a hard exterior of isolative armour that hides a soft interior that contains low self-esteem, feelings of inadequacy, self-contempt, dependence and vulnerability. The Little End has a soft exterior of caring and a hard interior of anger and resentment. No prizes for guessing: Big Ends are mostly men and Little Ends are mostly women. That's why I want to expand upon these ideas in this chapter.

Have you ever noticed how men and women relate to each other when they sit down together? Women communicate and men compete. Women are into establishing a 'rapport' style of communication, men into establishing a 'report' style. Women talk about their experiences in order to gain understanding. Men do so in order to show how big, strong, clever, successful they are. No wonder women got the you-know-whats with them . . .

It was easy for women to be united by their anger. Anger is like glue, but only if people unite against a common enemy. The enemy of my enemy is my friend, and all that. The rest is history. Women's rights. Liberty and equality. Departments of women's affairs at governmental level. It is still going on but it has also tended to fizzle out in recent years. Women are still paid less than men. They still get bashed up by drunken men. They are still raped; outside of a prison shower-room that doesn't happen too often to men. So men make sick jokes about it. And blame the victim. Has the Women's Movement accomplished anything? Of course it has, but something has changed in recent years. The anger has gone out of it. Women in business stopped carrying briefcases to work as a symbol of their emancipation. They have gone back to handbags again. Shoulder pads, which made women look as menacing as men, are out. Germaine Greer has been recognised as having her own fair share of narcissism, just like the men that she rails against. The spark has gone out of the Women's Movement. Perhaps this is a good thing. There has been a quiet war between the sexes over the past two decades and, as the world has taken so long to understand, no one, but no one, 'wins' a war.

We are told that a movement has sprung up in the USA that is called the Men's Movement. In California men form groups and go off into the wilderness to support each other in their manliness. They hug trees. They beat drums. They hug each other. They forgive their fathers. They grunt in unison. Will this movement take off? Will your average bloke feel okay about hugging another bloke and expressing his feelings? Like hell he will. Or at least not yet ...

Men have it a lot tougher than women in changing. Women were united by their anger. Men must be united by our sense of emotional isolation and vulnerability. That doesn't make very good glue. Certainly not as good as anger. 'I am Man hear me weep' doesn't have a very inspiring ring to it ... And herein lies the crunch. The challenge for women was to combine softness with assertiveness, even aggression. The challenge for us men is to combine a sense of masculine strength with an acknowledgment of our feelings. Too much to ask of most men at this stage. But give us time. We are all changing all of the time. Do you remember the early feminist movement? Bra-burning and anger at men who opened a door for a woman? It was extremist. The beginnings of all important societal movements are. But then some moderates come along and breathe some common sense into whatever the extremists have started and the change can become more real and acceptable. Here's hoping that this will happen to the tree-huggers.

Now let me return to the Spanner Theory. It illustrates everything that goes wrong between men and women, presuming that the Big End is seen as male and the Little End as female. Keep in mind, though, that I have seen plenty of Big Ends who are dominating, fragile women and plenty of Little Ends who are stable, submissive men. Now let's climb into the subconscious minds of these Ends.

Deep inside the mind of the Big End we will encounter something very scary: the Big End looks upon the Little End as simply an extension of himself. There to serve his needs. Little Ends care for him even though his demands are quite unreasonable. Little Ends stabilise him when he is feeling fragile and insecure. Little Ends become like the counter-weight of a pendulum: they stop the Big End from spinning out of control. Little Ends make sure that nothing displeases or disappoints their Big End. That is why Little Ends are so filled with an anger that corrodes away at their insides and brings them to people like me after they have saved up all this anger for years and years. The result: they get depressed.

Unsure which end you are? Try these two exercises.

Exercise: Being extrapunitive

1 Get into a lift with a lot of other people. Make sure that it is a lift that is going to, say, the fiftieth storey of a skyscraper.
2 Once the lift doors are closed, light a cigar. Make sure it is a really stinky one. You enjoy the cigar and everyone else is nearly suffocated. That is called being 'extrapunitive'. If you feel okay about doing this then you are a Big End. *my hubby*
3 If you are in a lift and someone else does this and you do not complain, then you are well and truly a Little End. Get in touch *ME* with your anger and tell the selfish sod to smoke somewhere else. If he resists, stick it up his nose.

Exercise: Being intrapunitive *I am neither nor*

1 Take a sharp stone.
2 Put it into your shoe.
3 Now walk down a busy street. Feel the pain? Notice that no one else has the slightest idea that you are in pain unless you tell them. This is called being 'intrapunitive'. If this feeling, of suffering in silence, is familiar to you then you are a Little End. If you stop hobbling, complain loudly about your discomfort and expect someone to come to your rescue then you are a Big End. Or an American tourist. Or both.

Confident Rationalisation and Projection, or CRAP for short

Now think back to Chapter 3, in which I described the seven ways to ruin a good fight. One of the ways was what I call Confident Rationalisation. This is the art of thinking quickly and speaking with great confidence to utterly bamboozle someone who is angry at you. Salespeople are particularly good at it. You point out that product X, which they are selling, is shoddily made, has no warranty and anyway, you have absolutely no use for it. By the time they have finished their Confident Rationalisation you wonder how you ever survived without product X and thank them for saving you from the continued misery of not owning it . . .

Now cast your mind back to the last chapter in which I discussed the alcoholic. One of the favourite defence strategies of the alcoholic is Rationalisation and Projection. This is the process of being able to explain away all your distress by some pseudo-rational twist of logic and then project it on to (i.e. blame) someone or something else. Either way there is no way that you will accept any responsibility for anything that you have done, said or felt.

Now combine the two processes. You have Confident Rationalisation and Projection, or CRAP for short. Big Ends are really, really good at this. Keep in mind that they secretly view Little Ends as an extension of themselves. In psychiatrist-speak Little Ends are called a 'selfobject' because they are perceived by the Big End as simply being an extension of the 'self' of the Big End. Now envisage the following scene. A wife comes to her narcissistic husband, who is a Big End, with a gripe. She tentatively voices it. Her husband spends the next ten minutes harping on about the complaint. For the first nine minutes he comes up with nine good reasons why she has no reason to complain. He does this with such confidence that his wife is completely convinced that he is right. In the tenth minute he suddenly turns the whole thing around so that if there really is a problem then surely it must be her fault, not his. His wife walks away totally bewildered. She has two conflicting voices inside her head that are talking to her at once. The first voice tells her off and says that of course he is right and she is wrong. How, she asks herself, could she ever have imagined that she had a valid reason for complaint? But the other voice pipes up and says that she was right all along. She had every reason to be angry at him and all he has done has been to whitewash the problem. She ends up feeling very, very confused. And her self-esteem suffers dreadfully. Recognise the process? Brainwashing. As described in Chapter 4. After years of this, of being continually reminded of how stupid or clumsy she is, she will either get depressed or get out.

If she comes to see me then my first task is to validate her instinct. I must reassure her that the voice that reassured her was right all along and that she has, quite simply, been the victim of years of unremitting CRAP ... Confident Rationalisation and Projection. Men are full of it.

Why, I hear you ask, do Little Ends hang around? Because they are unable to relate to men at some sort of adult-to-adult, mutually respecting manner and they seek out men who are similar. Some Little Ends are compulsive mothers to their Big Ends and some of them are compulsive daughters.

Compulsive mothers

Compulsive mothers recognise the hurt and inadequacy that hides inside the armour of the Big End. The classic cases here are the wives of alcoholics who somehow know that their domineering husbands live in an almost continual state of self-degradation and shame but hide it behind their bullying. The wife is simply an extension of the husband's ego. These wives often harbour a fantasy of healing this hurt in their husbands, of being the ultimate, celestial, miracle-working mother. When you climb into the subconscious minds of these women there is often a desire (a craving, in fact) to heal the hurt that they saw in their own fathers. But along with this saviour fantasy is an immense amount of suppressed resentment about their position in life. So suppressed, in fact, that even they are not aware of it ... Until I tell them that they were right all along and then all hell breaks loose.

Compulsive daughters

Compulsive daughters mistake control for protection and dependence for love. They are looking for a man who fills a huge gap in their lives. He is a strong, masculine, protective father figure. Usually compulsive daughters have had lousy fathers. Abusive, mean, neglectful, emotionally distant men. These women have never been exposed to that wonderful mixture of care and control that is called 'protection'. When a young girl feels protected she knows the instructions that she is being given are for her benefit, not that of the instructor. This is 'don't walk along the cliff edge' stuff. When a young girl feels controlled she knows that the instructions that she is being given are for the benefit of the instructor. This is 'be smart and pretty so that I can boast to everyone about what a good father I am' stuff. Protection is for the benefit of the receiver and control is for the giver. Protection has a definite quality of care about it. And kids know that from a young age. It is deeply satisfying for them to know that there are limits to their behaviour. If there is protection there is love. In other words, someone cares enough about them to want to control them *for their own good*. Compulsive daughters have never felt protected, just controlled. So they hang around with men who control them and somehow convince themselves that they are being protected. They feel some comfort in sensing this man's strength, even if it is used to punch them in the nose from time to time. Does this seem a bit warped to you? Me too. But then, let's climb further into the subconscious minds of these compulsive daughters.

Cast your mind back to Chapter 2, when I was describing the trilogy of care, trust and hope. Now remember that care has been divided further by Dr Heinz Kohut into the need for praise, the need for security and the need for acceptance. Now let's home in on the need for security.

Human beings have a great need to believe that there is someone around who will pick them up when they fall over. 'Falling over' can be performed either physically or emotionally. The person who picks them up is someone who is strong and caring and available at the time of the fall. The picker-upper must also be aware that the faller has fallen. That may sound a bit pedantic, but you would be astounded how many parents are so switched off from their children's emotional state (and usually so absorbed in their own) that they are not even aware that, say, their polite, 'Me-down' kids are actually quietly dying inside. This is the essence of 'empathy' and we psychiatrists bandy this word around incessantly at our conferences since it is all the 'go' in psychiatry these days. Kids grow up as reasonably contented and decent human beings if they have the knowledge that their parents (or some strong, kindly, empathic adult) are there to understand that they need some picking up and get on with the job.

There are all sorts of variations on this theme. Kids, or the crazy people who dream up the cartoons, create heroes and super-heroes. Let me be the first to predict that the next development here will surely be the ultra-hero. If you have just stumbled and fallen from a cliff it is pretty comforting to know that Superman or Superwoman will (somehow) know that you are in trouble and be there to catch you before you become a hair pizza on the rocks below. Parliamentary elections are all about trying to find a hero who is good enough to be parent to the family that is called a 'nation'. None of these heroes is ever good enough and there is a national ritual that occurs every few years in which the old heroes, who by now have been discredited and degraded, to be replaced by a whole new set of heroes who will, in turn, prove to be only frail human beings and not heroes at all. There is also a scheme that is enshrined in every developed society by which heroes can be summoned by dialling just three numbers on any telephone. The caller can summon police heroes, firefighter heroes and paramedic heroes according to the type of falling-over that has occurred. And finally, when you have fallen over emotionally you come to see someone in my profession. Heroes are not supposed to have laddered tights and holes in their socks, but we do our best to prove that we are competent picker-uppers to people who often should have been picked up by a parent who did not know or care that their child had fallen over.

Everyone needs heroes and everyone loves them. Heroes are really good at picking us up when we have fallen over. Either because they love us enough or because they are paid to ... So what has all this got to do with compulsive daughters?

The compulsive daughter has not been loved enough to feel protected. She yearns for that sort of caring control but ends up with controlling control, if you get the difference. Her hero is not there to protect her but to control her. It is not until she allows herself to feel her own sense of hurt and resentment that she can even begin to know what she is missing out on. In the meantime she sticks with this damaged, controlling man and convinces herself that she is happy. Or, more sadly, she comes to realise that she is miserable yet cannot leave this man because he has successfully destroyed her self-esteem and made her believe that no one else would have her ...

So are most Little Ends compulsive mothers or compulsive daughters? All are both. All Little Ends oscillate between fantasising about healing this damaged man when they prop him up and being fooled into thinking that he is strong and protective when they cower before him.

Crumbs from the table

This peculiar phenomen is worth a special mention. Big Ends are really good at utterly <u>depriving their</u> Little Ends <u>of anything</u> <u>that is good, loving and warm</u>. But Big Ends also know how to keep their Little Ends hanging on. They drop <u>what I call 'crumbs from the table'.</u> By this I mean that they know how to enchant and flatter and they do this in short bursts, usually at times when their Little Ends are getting restless. They will say something endearing or they will reveal a little of their own internal vulnerability. Little Ends are suckers for this. In fact they experience these crumbs in a cathartic way. Big Ends let the tension induced by abuse and neglect build up until it is intolerable. Then they say something loving or endearing and the resentment felt by the Little End just melts away. Until the next time.

As an analogy of the power of this technique, consider a private in the army who has a supportive and encouraging corporal. The private then encounters the sergeant-major who is an oaf of a man. The corporal encourages the private every day. Once a year the sergeant-major's intimidating face shows the faintest glimmer of a smile and he congratulates the private on a job well done. So whose encouragement is more rewarding for the private? The sergeant-major's of course. He is so clearly an authority figure and his praising comments are few and far between. He is a Big End. And his praise is like crumbs from the table.

So what happens to Big Ends in the end?

Do Big Ends die or do they just soften up? Usually Big Ends move from Little End to Little End until they can find someone who will stabilise them and look after them indefinitely. Then they are set up for life. Or until she dies.

<u>Little Ends have a better chance of maturing and being able to move</u> away from these unstable, punishing relationships. Rather surprisingly,

sometimes Big Ends grow up too. But more often they encounter a woman who is as domineering as they are or even more domineering. At this time a peculiar thing happens to Big Ends. Like a moth and a butterfly, Big Ends can be turned into Little Ends when they encounter someone who has more personal power than they have. There should be some poetic justice in this but usually they have managed to completely stuff up the lives of a few women before they find someone who can keep them in check. Deep inside their subconscious minds they have found a mother who can contain them.

Now if all that is not confusing enough, let me pull all this together to highlight the main features of the Big End:

- Big Ends are mostly men.
- Big Ends take the good stuff for themselves and dump the bad stuff. They are good at exploiting people, especially women. The woman is there to care for them and to look good for them. She is also there to take the blame for anything that goes wrong.
- Big Ends have little self-doubt. They are infuriatingly self-righteous and they are really good at CRAP.
- Big Ends form relationships that are intense and unstable. Their only saving grace is that they are never boring. Indeed, Little Ends who finally see the light and establish a relationship with a decent man often admit that they miss the excitement and chaos of their previous relationships with Big Ends, even if they can understand that those past relationships were toxic for them.
- Big Ends are blurred around the edges. They look upon their Little End as being an extension of themselves.
- Big Ends have an internal emotional world that is chaotic. They very rarely reveal it, but inside their subconscious minds they struggle with emptiness and boredom. They demand to be entertained. Some of the most amusing patients I have encountered did their 'training' at the hands of a Big End.
- Big Ends often have few or no same-sex friends. They are often men who surround themselves with attentive women. They feel threatened by other men and often shoo them off with aggression.
- Big Ends manipulate. Usually with seduction, intimidation or guilt.
- Big Ends drop 'crumbs from the table'.
- Big Ends become Little Ends when they encounter a Bigger End.

Fathers and sons

By now you will have got my drift. Men are little boys in armour. They harbour all these feelings of vulnerability, dependence and low self-esteem but they are forbidden from showing them. They are thrown into a world of having to be ambitious and competitive. Their job in life is not to *find* a hero but to *be* a hero. Their self-esteem is judged by what they do and achieve, not who they are. Nature or nurture? A bit of both. On the one hand their testosterone and 'Y' chromosomes drive them to more aggression, but on the other hand they are bombarded with messages like 'big boys don't cry'. Remember the 'YURU' chart? Emotionally damaged women often end up in a 'Me-down' position while emotionally damaged men often swing wildly between being 'Me-up' (dominating) and 'Me-out' (avoidant). And overall *men are far more damaged than women*, hands down. It's just that, tree-huggers aside, they are not allowed to show their hurt.

So how did all this damage happen? The answer lies in the father–son relationship. Damaged fathers damage their sons and so the hurt tumbles down from generation to generation. But there is hope. Mark my words. The greatest change that must happen in the world in the next few generations is that men must love their sons and show them that they do. Bigger than the fall of communism. Bigger than a peace-keeping force. Bigger than genetic engineering. Bigger than Ben Hur and Texas combined. Father–son love. Get working on it.

Exercise for fathers: Tell your sons you love them

1 If you have a son or sons, then put this book down and do this exercise now. Not later on today after you have finished watching the TV news. Now.

2 Gather your sons together. Shoo all females from the room. If the dog is a bitch or the budgie is a hen then they must go too. This is male stuff.

3 Tell your sons that you love them. Tell them that you are sorry that you have not told them more often but that you will rectify that in the future. Tell them that big boys *do* cry and that it is all right to have emotions and to express them. Tell them that doing that does not make them a sissy, like the other boys at school try to tell them.

4 Now give them a hug. Let them feel that it is comfortable for you to give this hug so that they feel comfortable in receiving it. In

particular hug that obnoxious, pimply teenage son. He's the one who needs it most.

5   Repeat steps (1) to (4) at least once a month.

Now, just as you're managing to bend your head around how two people relate, let me complicate the situation further by looking at how three people get it together.

CHAPTER six

Three-person relationships

Messing up the tango

Everyone knows that two's company and three's a crowd. Never a truer word was said. If you thought that two-person relationships were complicated, honey, you ain't heard nothing yet. It might take two to tango. But it takes three people to make a real mess of that tango. Three-person relationships are always a bit complicated. Kinky sometimes. But always complicated.

The last chapter was all about dyads (or two-person relationships). Now I shall turn my mind to the subject of triads (or three-person relationships). And in the next chapter I will examine how human beings start to behave when they form a group of more than three. You see people start to behave and relate in rather predictable ways depending upon how many people are involved. But the two common themes through all this behaving and relating are those two tried and true issues: care and control. Yes, you *are* sick of hearing about them by now. That's tough.

'Oedipus? Didn't he have something to do with Freud?'

Before I go on I must mention Oedipus. You have heard his name before in avant-garde movies or mentioned by know-it-alls at showy cocktail parties. You want to ask 'He had something to do with Freud, didn't he?' but you dare not in case you look like the illiterate that you are. The know-it-all would look at you with smug disdain.

The reality is that Freud had something to do with Oedipus since the latter preceded the former by a couple of thousand years, if you get my drift. Oedipus was the central figure in a Greek myth that is both intriguing and distasteful. The theme of the story is one of accidental incest. It goes like this . . .

Quite a few years ago, after Moses and before Jesus, lived King Laius and Queen Jacosta, who reigned over Thebes. (Don't ask me where Thebes is, I can hardly find my way to work.) Anyway they were blessed with a son whom, unaware that his name would one day be linked with murder and incest, they called Oedipus. But then prophet number one happened upon the scene and warned Laius and Jacosta that their son would grow up to murder his father and marry his mother.

The King and Queen freaked out. They decided that they had better ditch Oedipus before he got too twitchy at his old man and flirtatious with the old girl and they left him on a mountainside to die. Heartless sods.

But the baby was rescued by shepherds and, through a series of twists of fate that seem to occur so readily in Greek fables, was brought up by the King and Queen of a different country. Along came prophet number two, who terrified his foster-parents with the old predictions that he would one day murder his father and marry his mother. Oedipus decided that he had better scarper, so he hit the road.

Some time later he happened upon an old codger on the road who annoyed the living daylights out of him. This would be the sort of situation where you and I would shake our fists at someone and mutter oaths under our breaths. Not Oedipus. He took his sword out and stabbed the old bloke. Little did he know that he had just snuffed his own father, Laius. The prophets had been right, so far.

Oedipus went on to enter Thebes where there was a great commotion. A monster, the Sphinx, had entered Thebes and spent its time posing a riddle to all the citizens. If the citizen did not know the answer then they would be promptly devoured by the Sphinx. Oedipus, foolhardy as he was, tried his luck. The riddle was: 'Which animal has four feet in the morning, two at midday and three in the evening?' Oedipus replied: 'Man, because he crawls on all fours as an infant, walks on two feet in maturity, and walks with the aid of a stick in old age.' He was spot on and the Sphinx knew it. The Sphinx then plunged into the sea and perished.

Oedipus, for saving Thebes, became the King and married the widowed Queen, Jocasta. In other words he inadvertently slept with his own mother but because they were blissfully ignorant of this they lived together happily. Until a plague hit Thebes. Then, as is the wont of soothsayers, prophet number three arrived on the scene. He proclaimed that the plague would not go away until the murderer of King Laius was found. Eventually Oedipus came to realise that when he had been busy smiting the old codger on the roadside all those years ago he had actually been smiting his own father. When the horror of this, and the fact that he had been bonking his own mother, dawned on him, he gouged out his own eyes. Jocasta promptly committed suicide.

Oedipus' blinding himself was interpreted by Freud to be analagous to our subconscious defences that try to make us 'blind' to the painful truths that we carry inside.

And that, Virginia, is the rather grotesque legend of Oedipus Rex.

There, I warned you that it would curl your toes.

So how did Freud use this garish tale to his advantage? He used it to illustrate his theories of both infantile sexuality and triangulation. I will try to summarise these rather complex theories. I had better get it right or I will get a queue of angry psychoanalysts banging on my door . . .

Freud believed that kids of about four years old begin to develop erotic feelings towards their opposite-sex parent. Little boys begin to feel stirrings towards their mothers and little girls towards their fathers. Boys were described as experiencing the 'Oedipus complex' and girls as experiencing the 'Elektra complex'. With the feelings comes a contrasting antagonism and competition against the child's same-sex parent. Classically, little boys become the rivals of their fathers for their mothers' attention.

If you think that's queer, read on.

When little boys start to compute in their puerile little minds that they are vying against the old bloke for the attentions of the woman in the house they also develop a fear that their dad will come along and *castrate them* so that they aren't much competition in the sexual stakes. This is called 'castration anxiety' and corresponds to my concept of the fear of attack. Castration, after all, is a fairly decisive sort of attack.

I hope that I have got the gist of Freud's theory right. If I have not then I ask all you angry psychoanalysts to form an orderly queue outside my office door.

The theory, in all its bizarre complexity, goes on. At around the same time, little girls develop the famous 'penis envy'. This, as far as I can see, has something to do with wanting to have a penis so that your dad can come and chop it off. I will not go into the nitty-gritty of penis envy since I do not want to open my office door tomorrow to a mixed group of angry psychoanalysts and angry feminists . . .

Freud, as you can see, had sex on the brain. Of course sons *do* compete with fathers at various stages of their development. If they do not then they have had the stuffing and the spirit knocked out of them from an early age. I suppose that that is as good as being castrated metaphorically since Freud made a direct association between penises and power. That is because, like it or not, masculinity and personal power have always been (and will always be) linked. It all comes across as being a little bit bent. No wonder Freud well and truly shocked conservative Viennese society.

The essence of the Oedipal theory I suppose is that it involves three people, a triad, and the old themes of jealousy, rivalry and fear.

Let me explore these further under the headings of my old favourites: care and control. You see, whenever *two* people start to relate to each other these factors inevitably crop up. And the same applies when *three* people start to relate to each other, but they form an arrangement that is a tad more complex than the 'Spanner'. I call them the 'Control Triangle' and the 'Care Triangle'.

The Control Triangle

L et us call the three people involved A, B and C. A happens upon B one day and gives him a really hard time. A tells B that he is a human tragedy; that his parents were never married and that they never would because one of them was a baboon; that his mother wears army boots, which is no mean feat for a baboon; and that his only useful purpose in life would be that one day he would fertilise some grass in a cemetery. B limps away from this interchange feeling, as one might expect, a bit deflated. B rapidly works out that A is twice his size so

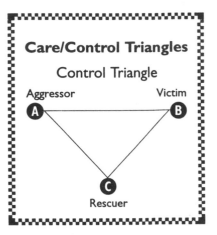

Care/Control Triangles

Control Triangle

Aggressor   Victim

A   B

C

Rescuer

bopping A on the nose might not be a wise thing. B then happens upon C and blurts out what has just happened between him and A. C, who is a skerrick taller than A but twice as broad, feels as sorry as hell for B and comforts him. He then goes and seeks out A. A greets C and is understandably surprised when C bops him on the nose. C then leaves, wiping A's blood off his hairy fists, and returns to comfort B. But alas, in the meanwhile B has been insulted by another person, D. C rolls his eyes and goes off to find D.

Now let me put a label on each of these characters. A, who is so unsubtle in his personality appraisals, is called the *aggressor*. B, for obvious reasons, is called the *victim*. C is called the *rescuer*. So who is D? D is a chap who is soon to get a broken nose, that's who D is. I suppose that he qualifies as another aggressor.

This triangle, of aggressor, victim and rescuer, is to be found in all sorts of places in your everyday life if you just look. Sometimes the players are not even people. Government welfare agencies are rescuers. The agents of the tax department are aggressors. The police can be aggressors or rescuers depending upon which side of the law you are standing on. When they get shot in the line of duty they are victims. The boss who fires you is an aggressor and you are the victim. Patients who ask me for dodgy sickness certificates are asking me to be a rescuer. That is not fair since doctors just *love* to play rescuer and when I have to say 'no' I find myself cast into the role of aggressor. People who 'turn the other cheek' are playing victim to an aggressor. Usually they get both cheeks punched. Aggressors love a sucker. And so on.

CASE HISTORY **Warren**

Warren was a panelbeater. At the end of the working day if he had grease under his fingernails, body odour under his armpits and flecks of car paint on his hands, then he had put in a good day's work. He was a big, quiet character but anyone who got to know him (and therefore managed to get past the walls of defence that he put up) found that he was a very gentle and likeable sort.

Warren took a fancy to Robyn, the new secretary in the office. Robyn was petite and demure and very, very pretty. Warren tried rather clumsily to chat her up. His blush gave him away every time.

Robyn thought that Warren's boyishness was cute. Some part of her wanted to mother him. She could see that beneath the grubby overalls beat a soft heart. She started to spend time with him and one day he summoned all his courage and asked her out. He was enraptured when she agreed.

They found that they could talk for hours. She opened up more and told him that she had a boyfriend. His stomach went into a knot. He felt sick. Fear of abandonment. Not very becoming for a macho panelbeater.

She explained that she had been knocking around with this bloke for a couple of years but that she was trying to finish the relationship with him. The knot in Warren's stomach slackened. Robyn described how her boyfriend was abusive towards her and had even been violent towards her at times. He would often use her for sex by showing up at her place after a late night out with the boys and then expect her to 'please' him. He took a lot and gave little back. Guess who was the Big End? Not Robyn.

Warren embarked on a project of convincing Robyn to dump her boyfriend. Needless to say he wanted to step into the sod's shoes but he tried not to make that so obvious ... for now. Warren was gentle and caring and Robyn became very fond of him. With his help she managed to give her nasty old boyfriend the flick and then the inevitable happened. Robyn did not seem to mind that her bedsheets were marked with iridescent purple car paint ... What a woman.

Things went along just swimmingly for a while. The happy couple were well and truly into the Marvellous Besotted Phase and Warren found that bashing those dents out of mudguards gave him more joy than ever before. Then one day Robyn told him that it was all over. She had fallen in love with another man and, surprise surprise, he was just as big a creep as that other drunk.

When Warren came to see me he was about ready to spray himself from head to toe with paint thinner and strike a match. He could not sleep, could not eat, could not think. He was very, very depressed and on the point of suicide.

A lot of time and a lot of support later his mental state improved dramatically and he managed to put this whole ghastly experience into perspective. He had become drawn into a cruel triangle by a professional victim, just as B drew C into his fights. From this he learned two painful lessons:

- Robyn was a Little End. Until she sorted herself out (and became aware of her own anger and her fear of abandonment) she would remain a Little End. She would only be attracted to Big Ends who would use and abuse her. Silly, silly Robyn.
- Robyn, like many Little Ends, was a professional victim. Some people simply make a lifestyle out of being victims. No matter how hard you try to rescue them they will always fall back into the mire and scream for someone to pull them out again. They are people who sit on huge stockpiles of untapped anger and sometimes they can be so passive in their anger that they only deal with it by infuriating anyone who tries to help them. They leave a trail of devastated rescuers in their wake.

But there was an interesting twist to the case of Warren and Robyn. Warren eventually told me about his past. His father had been a violent alcoholic. (Have you noticed how many of my patients are the adult children of violent alcoholics? Brewers brew more trouble than beer.) Warren's father would often come home drunk and rough up his mother. When Warren became a teenager he found that if his father was drunk enough he could stand between his parents and protect his mother. Then when he was a bit older still he found that he could give the old man a hiding while rescuing his mother. With Robyn, Warren was reliving a pattern of rescuing behaviour that had been deeply ingrained within him. Warren's mother had been a victim too in the days before it was okay to ditch an alcoholic husband and make a life of your own.

Warren decided to leave rescuing to lifeguards . . .

Now cast your mind back to the third chapter, the bit about anger. You will recall that sometimes one or other of two warring parties can 'turn the fight off' by involving a third person as either mediator or scapegoat. This reflects a watered-down version of this aggressor–victim–rescuer triangle that involves a fourth role: the mediator. Sometimes, if an aggressor–victim dyad can be a little civil about their rage they can involve a mediator in a reasonably constructive way. But then again some of the most namby-pamby conciliatory types I know are mediators. It only works if both aggressor and victim are highly motivated to bury the hatchet. And not in each other's skulls.

Sometimes the dynamics of the triad take an interesting twist in the phenomenon of scapegoating. In this all blame for any conflict is projected by one or two people on to a third. It is a nifty technique by which a Control Triangle becomes a Care Triangle. This is what happened during the Second World War in London. Despite the horrors of hiding in bomb shelters, never knowing whether you would emerge to find your home reduced to rubble, there was a great sense of community spirit and camaraderie during the Blitz. Two neighbours could hate each other's guts (taking turns at being Aggressor and Victim) but when the air raid sirens wailed they would help each other's families down the steps of the shelter and chat amicably as the bombs rained down above. They had both become victims of the aggression of a third party: Nazism. This then threw them together as co-victims. Then, after the war they could get back to their trivial back-fence sniping at each other.

It happens too when people shake their heads at the news of a horrific murder. 'What is society coming to?' they ask in wonderment. This nebulous thing, Society, can become the scapegoat for understanding why one individual would want to take a shotgun to another.

And if you want to see a *real* scapegoater in action just watch a good politician . . .

The Care Triangle

The Control Triangle involves anger and rescuing. The care triangle involves love, exclusion and fear of abandonment. Let's take another look at my mindless friends, A, B and C.

Imagine, if you would, the following scenario: the trio are at a party. A, who fancies himself as a bit of a lad around town, has his eyes on B (who, in case you have not guessed, is now a female letter; nothing unorthodox about A's sexuality). He spends the evening chatting her up incessantly. 'What's a nice letter like you doing in an alphabet like this?' he says. B likes the cut of his jib and the sweet talking.

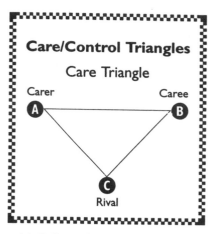

Care/Control Triangles

Care Triangle

Carer — A
Caree — B
Rival — C

Trouble is, she came to this party with C. C stumbles upon them out the back involved in a passionate embrace and making goo-goo eyes at each other. He is rapidly aware of a number of intense feelings. These are:

- an overwhelming fear that B is about to abandon and reject him in order to run into the arms of A;
- an anger at her for being so unfaithful;
- an anger at A for barging in on his girl; and
- most of all, a passionate envy, jealousy and sense of rivalry with A.

At dawn the following morning they both point muskets at each other and fire a single shot.

This is the mechanism of jealousy. A third person observes two parties who are showing signs of caring about each other. More specifically they show signs of caring more for each other than they do about the poor old third person. The jealous party sits on an immense fear of abandonment. Remember Warren the panelbeater? When he heard about the existence of Robyn's boyfriend his stomach went into a knot with this fear. It was not until Robyn assured him that she was about to dump this third person that Warren could relax. Warren was terrified that he would become the third party in a Care Triangle involving Robyn and her boyfriend. Just an observer. Always on the brink of being ejected from the triangle altogether.

As you can see, triangles are messy, messy things.

CASE HISTORY **Anne**

Anne had a bad case of jealousy. If envy is supposed to be green then Anne was a Martian.

You see Anne had a doting boyfriend called Michael, but she was still as insecure as all hell. She was slim and attractive but there were reasons for this. She was slim because her metabolism was always running at 110 per cent. She ran on fear, the continual, unrelenting fear that she was about to be abandoned, dumped, rejected, passed over for some floozie. She was attractive because she made damned sure that she was: manicured, pedicured, coiffured and stylish. Absolutely undesertable.

If the truth be known, Michael was passionately in love with her. But no matter how much love Anne received she could never be convinced that she could trust her lover; trust him to stay with her; trust him not to hurt her.

Anne's fear of abandonment reached obsessional proportions. She spent a considerable part of her day checking up on Michael. When she visited him she would surreptitiously look for the phone bill to see whether there were any long distance phone numbers that he was regularly calling. She would press the 'redial' number on his phone and wait for the caller to answer with their name. No matter who answered she would hang up. But if a woman answered then Michael would be on the receiving end of a Gestapo-style interrogation. Given the opportunity, say, when Michael was out of the room, she would quickly read through his mail. She took to phoning him from time to time on his mobile phone, listening to the background noises when Michael answered, and then hanging up on him without saying anything. She wanted to make sure that he was in the car when he said he would be and not in the pub or, worse still, someone's boudoir.

Eventually she worked out how to get a key to his house. She rang a locksmith in a dither, saying that she had lost her housekey, was locked out and needed to get in urgently. She gave Michael's address and made doubly sure that he would be at work at the time. The locksmith arrived, not thinking for a moment that this glamorous, well-spoken woman was scamming him. Using those devious means that only locksmiths and criminals know he promptly got in, leaving her with a freshly cut key to Michael's front door. Anne was horrified that she could be so underhand yet delighted with her own ingenuity.

She went on to make regular inspections of Michael's house where she could now read mail and press 'redial' buttons at her leisure. As you can see, Anne was very crafty but very neurotic. Her jealousy never quite drove her mad. Instead she nearly drove Michael crazy with it. 'Your jealousy is going to destroy our relationship' he would say. He was right of course. It did. And

Anne came   experiencing waves of
panic attacl   er that she had been
abandoned
     You wc   hat this had happened
repeatedly in Anne's life. Her jealousy, based on fear of abandonment, was a
self-fulfilling prophecy. She was so afraid of her relationships ending that she
was subconsciously ensuring that they did. No 'safe distance' for Anne. She
was either entwined in her lover's life for fear of losing him or utterly alone
because she had done just that.

Anne came from a very well-to-do background. Her father was Sir
someone-or-other and they had (as they say in those elite cliques) 'a good
address'. And what was Anne's most vivid memory from childhood? Standing
in a darkened hallway of her home at night listening at the door as her
parents quarrelled. Her father had a way of saying at the top of his voice
'Right, I'm going, and you can have the children'. Anne was devoted to her
father because he was the only source of emotional comfort. They lived in a
cold house that only seemed to warm up when Dad got home. Yet Dad kept
threatening to go. Not directly to Anne, but she heard it nevertheless.

No wonder she carried this fear into her adult life. Her father's voice was
still lodged in her subconscious mind playing over and over again those
threats.

Anne came to realise a whole lot of things about herself. When I last saw
her she had just met Roger and was doing her darnedest to trust him. She
had learned that couples need to communicate regularly and honestly and to
build up trust between them if the relationship is to survive. She was coping
with this new relationship but it was not easy. Yet.

Her father is in his seventies. I expect to see her back when he dies.

As you can see jealousy really is the one of the Seven Deadly Sins; it is
the green-eyed monster. But it is all about the fear of rejection and
abandonment. If three people are together and a closer bond forms
between two of them then the third member of the triad will inevitably
find her/himself engulfed in these feelings.

The Othello Syndrome

If you think that that sort of jealousy is bad, let me go off on something of a tangent here to describe what is in my profession a psychiatric curiosity. It is called 'delusional jealousy', 'morbid jealousy' or, for obvious reasons, 'the Othello Syndrome'. It occurs in men (often alcoholics) who become convinced that their wives are being unfaithful to them. As there is no logical reason for them to develop this suspicion, the belief rates as a true delusion. Delusions often come in bunches, like 'I am being followed by the CIA who are photographing me, going into my house when I am not there, tapping my telephone calls, steaming open my mail and trying to poison my food'. In the Othello Syndrome men have but one delusional belief: 'My wife is screwing around.' Despite all rational argument they cannot be convinced otherwise.

They become obsessed with it. They riffle through her belongings trying to find the 'evidence'. Love letters. Semen stains on her underwear. They will stop at nothing. They follow her. They eavesdrop on her telephone conversations. They pester her continually to tell them who they are seeing. Wives find this increasingly tedious.

Trouble is, men with this condition often become violent. Sometimes they murder their wives as punishment for their infidelity.

Be warned. If your old man is acting like this it is time to seek help. Lickety-split. And if he refuses to accept treatment and he has been violent to you, you know what you must do. Finish this chapter in the refuge.

Spare the kids

In the last few pages of Chapter 4 I recorded my seven ways to make a messy business, divorce, rather cleaner and less painful. Now think back to 'Beware the triangle' (see page 113). I mention this again here because it is important. It needs to be shouted from the rooftops but such behaviour is unbecoming for a greying, middle-aged psychiatrist. So I am going to repeat it here: if your marriage is breaking up then you must make sure that the conflict and tension is restricted to the dyadic relationship between you and your partner. If your rage is such that you must murder your 'ex' then please do so quickly and quietly. Most of all, spare the kids the build-up to the final scene.

There are all sorts of ways that triangles develop when a couple separates and I have mentioned them already. In particular:

- Don't set up Care Triangles by which Mother does all the donkey work while Father has the kids for trips to the amusement park and the ice-cream parlour. The kids will buy into the 'Dad's so generous and Mum's so grumpy' routine. This is so unfair on Mum who is struggling to make ends meet.
- Don't set up the triangle that makes kids the message-bearers: ' ... And tell your father that his maintenance cheque is late again ...' It is up to Mum to energise Dad into writing cheques. Not little Freddy, who would rather go hungry than get involved in all this adult hostility.
- Don't set up a Care Triangle with your new partners so that Stepfather feels left out of the action or kids feel that Mother is about to run off (just as Father did) with her new beau. Let your new partner know that you, the kids, the dog, the goldfish and the mortgage all come as a package, take it or leave it.
- Most of all, never ever ever ever make the kids the scapegoats for the breakdown of your marriage. Believe me, they will blame themselves anyway and you must take time to clearly and repeatedly let them know that this divorce had nothing to do with them.

The 'bottom line' here is that couples must shelve their anger at each other when it comes to the kids. Family and friends must stay out of the picture too. Your divorce, like your marriage, must be a two-person affair.

Extra-marital affairs

I have already remarked on what messy things triangular relationships can be. The messiness reaches staggering new proportions when it comes to extra-marital affairs.

How many marriages are tainted with affairs? I suppose that there is no real way of finding out because affairs are, by their very nature, such secretive things. Can you really ever survey marriages in the expectation that you will find an 'average' sample of marriages to study?

Can you ever expect the couples to be totally honest about that fling that they had with the handsome young lad next door or that one-night stand with a colleague from work while away at a conference? I doubt it. But taking a guess on the basis of my encountering couples both professionally and personally, I would say that most marriages are complicated by infidelity. Not a huge majority, but a majority nevertheless.

Do married men or married women have more affairs? Men, hands down. You do not need a sociologist to do a survey on that one. I do not doubt for a moment that if a member of a couple becomes involved in an affair then more often than not it is the man. Sure, married women do it too. But not half as much as men. Even in this age of gender enlightenment men are still more predatory with their sexuality. And the corollary of this phenomenon is that when a woman decides that a marriage is over, it is usually well and truly certified, embalmed and buried.

Are affairs ever beneficial for a marriage? Perhaps, but only very rarely. Sometimes a couple is on the point of breaking up and an affair from one or other partner brings about the long-overdue crisis that they have needed to wake each other up and start communicating again. Many couples *claim* that an affair, with all its sense of hurt and betrayal, has helped their marriage but I wonder whether they really feel that they can ever truly trust each other again. Simon, a patient of mine whose wife had just announced that she was having an affair, described it like this: 'My marriage is like a cracked piece of porcelain. Whenever I look at it now all I can see is the crack in it.'

Ongoing affairs are always a disaster in the making. I have encountered several patients, all women, who have been involved in affairs with married men that have lasted for years. How could these men's wives have not suspected that they were being unfaithful?

Here is a peculiar phenomenon about marital infidelity. Most women are the first to know. They sense something from the start. Their husbands do not react quite the same way to them. They are more distant or more attentive. Subtle but significant changes. Other women play out the old observation that 'the wife is always the last to know'. But I think that they have really been subconsciously denying it to themselves for years. They have not known because they have not wanted to know.

In its most bizarre form the wives do know about the affair and don't do anything to stop it. They must have had passionless marriages. Or they have had the spirit knocked out of them by a narcissistic husband. Perhaps he provides materially for her. A prestige car and some comfort become a trade-off for knowing that he is being intimate with another woman.

So why are people unfaithful to their spouses? Why do they set up this eternal triangle? Let me examine the workings of a long-term affair that one of my patients became involved in. This was the classical arrangement of a woman becoming involved with a married man. To understand why married women become involved with other men, just change 'he' for 'she' and 'him' for 'her'.

CASE HISTORY Joyce

Joyce was not a particularly attractive-looking woman. Sure, she had a wonderful personality but Joyce knew what it was like to be a wallflower at a school dance. Forever a bridesmaid. Sweet thirty-four and never been . . .

Joyce was an accountant. She became involved with a married man called Dennis while he was one of her clients. They had to 'do lunch' a few times to talk about his 'fully-franked dividends' and his 'equity-to-debt ratios', whatever the hell they are. They tucked into a couple of bottles of wine and became more personal. Despite her uncomeliness he found her personality and sense of humour attractive. One thing led to another. That is what people say when they are winking and nodding. Joyce did not know whether she seduced or was seduced but two bottles of wine and a profound sense of loneliness helped. Either way they ended up in bed. That was six years ago.

If there is such a thing as a fairly standard 'married man–single woman' affair, they had it. He lived about an hour's drive from work. He told his wife that he had to work late every Thursday night and that he had arranged to stay at his brother's house, which was only around the corner. Then he bullied his brother into going along with the alibi. Of course he spent every Thursday night with Joyce. His wife did not put up a fight; she did not even question whether he was lying. They had been in the connubial doldrums for so long that she seemed to be happy to have some time to herself. Did she suspect? Probably. But like so many men Dennis could spin a yarn with such reassuring confidence that she did not even bother to question the arrangement.

Joyce became the archetypal Other Woman. She would greet Dennis smelling of perfume and enthusiasm. She had not had much sexual experience before but she showed that she could be a hair-in-a-bun professional in the office and a sex goddess in bed at night. She would go away with him when he went on conferences by flying with him in pre-allocated side-by-side seats but she would have to check in independently of him. She tried not to look when he kissed his wife and kids goodbye at the airport.

From very early on she knew that there was something stirring in her which was uncomfortable: guilt, a fear of abandonment, a knowledge that this could not go on forever, a desperate need to have him for herself but a self-esteem that told her that someone like Dennis would never leave his wife and kids for her. She would subtly, in such a womanly way, get him to talk about the unhappiness of his marriage. It made her feel safe. It gave her hope. And Dennis seemed to relish the chance to talk of his marital misery. But then he would ruin it by trying to explain, in that typical emotionless logical way that men use when they are avoiding something, that he could not leave his wife 'because of the kids'. In a dream she saw Dennis's wife and children driving in a car that plummeted from a cliff and burst into flames. And, of course, in the dream she was there to comfort Dennis. Freud spoke about dreams as sometimes representing a 'wish fulfilment'. Now you know what he meant.

So what did she get out of this affair? As always at the start of any relationship they went through the extra-marital equivalent of the Marvellous Besotted Phase. It was erotic and exciting and possibly even more so because their love was so clandestine. 'Stolen kisses' and all that. There was also a peculiar feeling that Joyce found hard to own up to that was some sort of relief on Friday mornings when Dennis would kiss her and go back to his 'other life'. She had to admit that after all this time of being alone she needed a fair amount of space and if Dennis stayed around too long then she felt a bit crowded out. This conflicting need for intimacy yet space puzzled and distressed her. It was the extra-marital equivalent of what I have referred to as the Rubber-band aspect of the relationship: she had found a 'safe distance' from Dennis (not too much engulfing and not too much abandonment) by formalising their time together like clockwork.

But when he spoke about his unhappy marriage she delighted in the feeling of being special, the Chosen One. Would it be corny to point out that she had major problems in her relationship with her own father? Yes, it would be corny. And yes, she did have major problems with the old man. You see Joyce had been the fourth of six kids. Kids in the middle of the family so often tend to get missed out in the favouritism stakes and, to make matters worse, Joyce's younger sister was quite clearly Dad's favourite. She was cuter and bubblier. Parents can so blatantly set up this destructive sort of sibling rivalry and Joyce's father was a champion at it. So when Dennis gave Joyce the feeling of being involved in a Care Triangle in which she was the Chosen One there was a big part of her subconscious mind that exalted in that feeling. Joyce was getting back at her kid sister by trying to steal someone else's husband. See how your past haunts your present?

And what did Dennis get out of it? The worst aspects of his male ego were massaged. He felt that he could attract and lay claim to not one, but two women. Have you ever wondered why so many men fantasise about having a *menage a trois*? Now you know. It is a male ego thing: two lovers show that they are twice as attractive. You guessed right: Dennis had his problems with self-esteem too.

Like all married men in this situation he also had complete control over the agenda. Joyce could not phone him, he could choose when he wanted to phone her. Joyce could not see him when she wanted, but when he wanted. Total power. And a submissive woman whom he could string along to accept these totally unjust conditions.

But somewhere in the recesses of Dennis's subconscious mind was an even more insidious motive: Joyce was his escape clause. If his rather miserable marriage ever fell apart then he would never have to own up to his insecurities and dependence. He could fall into Joyce's arms. Better still, he could use her as a weapon to hurt his wife even more. I told you that triads were messy things . . .

So how did it all turn out? Joyce sabotaged it. She knew all along what she was doing. She got to the point where the distance between her and Dennis was not so comfortable any more. She was past the MBP and she wanted some security in her life. Dennis was starting to mean more to her that just some rollicking good sex. When the front door closed behind him on Friday mornings she felt a growing sense of panic. Fear of abandonment. And an intolerable competition with Mrs Dennis.

Her first ploy was to leave a love letter from Dennis stuffed into his jacket pocket. Mrs Dennis was supposed to find it there when she was gathering the dry cleaning. Dennis would have thought that he had inadvertently left it there and blame himself. Then he and Mrs Dennis would have a monumental fight, he would leave and come to her. But Dennis found it there and discarded it. Damn! So she went for one of the oldest in the book: perfume on his lapels. This was a signal between women. Men are so naturally odorous that Dennis did not notice the fragrance. Mrs Dennis did. Then the monumental fight. Then Dennis dumped Joyce. She suspected that that would be how it would turn out. But at least she knew now. Better than living forever in growing despair.

Joyce came to see me shortly after it ended. She had to work through the great feelings of hurt and resentment that she felt toward Dennis. 'I have been used' she kept saying. And she had. And beneath all this fresh hurt was the old stuff: a yearning desire to be special, to be the Chosen One. It came up fairly early in her therapy: she became preoccupied with my other patients. How ill were they? What sorts of problems did they bring to me? How did I treat them? She could not put into words what her real question was so I suggested it to her. She was saying 'Can you make me feel special?' Joyce was into seeing people in triangles and it was proving difficult to break the habit.

The lessons to be learned from all this?

- Married people who become involved in affairs are human booby-traps disguised as saviours. They promise the earth but they never deliver. And if they do deliver then it will only be a matter of time before they are being unfaithful to you too.

- The Mistress derives some benefits and the Married Man others. But the loser is almost invariably the Mistress.

- Call me a nerd, call me square, but I still espouse the old-fashioned principles: to achieve satisfaction and personal growth within a dyadic relationship it must be mutually respecting, trusting, committed and *exclusive*. Not easy, but absolutely essential.

This chapter has been about three-person, or triadic, relationships. Nasty, messy things. Look for the dynamics of the Care and Control Triangles whenever you see three people interacting. They are there even if they are subtle.

Unless you have been asleep you will have noticed that as I meander through this book I am building up the numbers of people involved. I started with just you, then you and your partner, then you and two others locked in all sorts of complex interchanges. Now what? Four-person relationships?

Wrong. Human beings relate in a fairly predictable way according to how many people are involved. But the subconscious mind is not good at arithmetic. It counts 'one, two, three, many ... ' Once you get beyond three people relating then you get into a whole new ball game: human systems. Let's move on.

CHAPTER seven

Human
systems

Whenever four or more of you
are gathered . . .

Everyone knows that power tends to corrupt and absolute power corrupts absolutely. Who was the original person to say these words? Who knows? Who cares? But hang on to the idea that power is the form that control assumes when it is held over a group of people. It is necessary for any human group to have some sort of control mechanism but power is also potentially dangerous. Most of the world's woes have been caused by people with too much power and not enough compassion or grey matter. Just take a look at Hitler, Amin, Hussein, some policemen, most politicians, the head of the tax department and Sister Mary Phillip, who taught me in fourth class.

Human systems
Family
Work
Neighbourhood
Church
Political party
Social club

As I predicted in the final paragraph of the last chapter, this one is about human systems. So what am I talking about when I refer to a human system? I am talking about *any group of human beings who relate together in any way in order to achieve a common goal.* Families, churches, armies, political parties, bowling clubs, boys'-nights-out, staff at the canteen, bystanders at a traffic accident, contributors to a computer bulletin board, a team of Sumo westlers, murderers on Death Row, kids playing hopscotch on the footpath, etc. etc.

Sure there are dyads and triads mingled in those groups, but when they act as a group they start to do, say, feel, believe, identify with and aspire towards a whole lot of things that are unique to the group. Cast your eyes over the diagram on page 152. It shows all the ways that human groups begin to act. Note the customary division into Control factors and Care factors. Aren't human beings so goddamned predictable?

Now let me feed a little tit-bit of information into your cerebral cortex. Mull it over. The information is, once again, a theory of that grand-daddy of all psychiatrists, Sigmund Freud. Yes, his name *does* keep cropping up, doesn't it? Anyway, Siggy came up with the idea that *the family is the prototype for all subsequent human groups.* Think about it. The structure and dynamics of a family are modelled in all of the human systems mentioned above. And it follows that if you have problems in your own family, such as a resentment towards parental authority, then you will tend to have that problem in all subsequent groups. Just ask any jail inmate.

Getting back to the factors that all human systems have in common, I shall work through them one by one.

Control factors

Hierarchy

Hierarchy is the very essence of the 'Control' factor in human groups so I shall treat it first and in most depth.

All groups have a concept of authority and groups of more than a half a dozen or so (i.e. a family that is just getting too big) tend to stratify that authority into a hierarchy in which members have power over those below but are controlled by those above. In our prototype of the family there is no way that the four-year-old will boss around the pubescent teenager and get away with it ...

Without authority there is no hierarchy. Without

Human systems
Factors in common

Control factors
Hierarchy
Roles
Rules/punishment
Entry/exit mechanisms

Care factors
Goals/rewards
Belonging —
Identity
Communication style
Tradition
Welfare

hierarchy there is no control. Without control there is no organisation. Without organisation there is chaos. With chaos there is no progress or development or growth. And no getting to that goal that you got together for in the first place, like producing a can of beans or having a good time winning at hopscotch. Human beings naturally seek out a leader.

Exercise

1 Wait until you are in a crowd, say, in a queue in a supermarket or standing at a busy bus stop.

2 Collapse. But keep your ears open and one eye open to peek at the responses of the bystanders. Hope that you are not in downtown New York, where people will respond by simply walking over you.

3 Now listen to the responses. For a few seconds there will be a startled silence while people take on board the idea that one among

them, a stranger to wit, has suddenly become supine and unresponsive. Possibly even dead.

4 The first person to make a move towards you will be some enthusiastic good-willed person like a grandmother or someone who has just done a first aid course and has been dying for something like this to happen so that they can look confident as they loosen your collar and feel for your pulse. If they were not paying attention at their first aid course then they will automatically start cardio-pulmonary resuscitation on you and break all your ribs, so you had better wake up quick-smart if that happens. The first person to react to this 'emergency' will probably become the leader of this stunned group.

5 The group will breathe a little sigh of collective relief that *someone* seems to know what they are doing. They will happily react to any commands barked by this ersatz leader: 'Lay him on his side!' 'Would someone please call an ambulance!' For all they know he might just be frisking you to find your wallet.

People fantasise about having the power that leadership brings. Trouble is, it brings a whole lot of responsibility too. In reality most people will avoid assuming that responsibility. And the cruellest blow of all is the predicament that many workers, children and housewives find themselves in: responsibility with no authority. That is a 'no-win' situation if there ever was one.

So what constitutes a good leader? The same things that make a good parent. The formula is simple: they must be both *respectable and respecting.*

Respectable people have some goodness or talent or ability that makes them engender the respect of others. They also have the confidence in their own ability that says that they will *demand* respect when it is due to them. Which leads me to one of my favourite adages: 'People respect people who have self-respect.'

Respecting people have a power that is protective rather than just authoritative. The definition of protection is that it is a *caring control.* The object of their power is not to build up their own clout, but to act as a limiting and containing influence on a human group that, without them, might get a bit chaotic or out of control. Part of this protection involves limiting people when they step out of line; but only if it is for the benefit of the stepper and not just the limiter. In a word, sometimes you must *disappoint* people in order to protect them. That is why we have to stop at red traffic lights: we might breathe a sigh of annoyance

~ who is leader.

but we are well aware that if we crash this red light we may end up under the wheels of an oncoming truck.

Lo and behold, we have stumbled upon the two words that I associated with assertiveness way back in the second chapter: demand and disappoint. I will run it past you one more time: good leaders are both respectable and respecting. Respectable people have the self-confidence to demand that their needs and expectations be met. Respecting people must protect, and this sometimes involves the need to disappoint.

Someone-or-other wrote many years ago about the three styles of leadership. Whoever it was delineated three different types of organisation as determined by their authority style: the *autocratic*, the *democratic* and the *laissez-faire.*

Autocratic leaders do not bother to listen to their underlings for their feedback or opinions. They just make decisions and if the rabble don't like it, that's tough. So tough in fact that sometimes the rabble get lined up against a wall and shot if they say that they don't like it. Autocratic leaders are not protective. Their goal in life is to look after themselves. They like the power they have and they will get more of it given half a chance. Being a dictator is so profoundly satisfying. No having to justify yourself to anyone. Trouble is autocratic leaders generate an immense amount of resentment in their rabbles. The groups that they command, whether they be nations, organisations or families, run on fear. There is a lot of buck-passing in these groups so that no one has to take the blame and get lined up against the wall. When the autocrat is finally bumped off by a sniper's well-aimed bullet there is dancing in the streets.

When the autocratic group is brought together in the name of religion then it is called by another name. It is a 'cult'. Look at David Koresh in Waco, Texas. And Jim Jones in Jonestown. No democracy there.

Laissez-faire **leaders** are wishy-washy weaklings. They are so busy trying to please everyone and look like a nice guy that they have lost the ability to disappoint. What evolves in these groups is a power vacuum. All sorts of self-appointed heirs to the throne start to jostle for the power that the wishy-washy weakling does not seem to want to claim. The groups that *laissez-faire* leaders command run on anger. And beneath the anger is an insidious contempt for the weakness of the leader.

CASE HISTORY **Paul and me**

When I was doing my training in psychiatry I had to work for a few months at a hospital in which the psychiatrist in charge of the ward was a *laissez-faire* leader. Trouble was his charge nurse, a squat figure by the name of Paul, was an autocratic leader. Technically it was my wishy-washy colleague who had the authority in the ward. But everyone knew darned well that it was Paul who had the real power.

Into this vipers' nest wandered a naive apprentice: me. Pretty early on in the piece I found that Paul was getting right up my nose. And Old Wishy-Washy was not prepared to impose some structure upon this organisation. Why would he not take control of a chaotic situation? Because he was wishy-washy, that's why. Talk about a power vacuum. Just Paul and me. The fact that I was about eighteen inches (that's about forty-five centimetres) taller than Paul made it even worse.

I learned a lot in that ward. Like how *not* to run one. What it feels like to be in a human group where there are blurred work roles, fuzzy boundaries and little demarcation. If your organisation has an unremitting sense of tension about it, is racked with in-fighting and personality clashes, then look to the leader. You will find someone like Old Wishy-Washy. And an organisation full of Pauls.

Democratic is the third type of leadership style. Actually democratic is a misnomer. Democracy implies that the group's opinion is sought for every decision. In reality a referendum is necessary only when there is an important decision to be made that will affect most members of the group. This can take the form of a poll or a family meeting or a pow-wow or whatever form of communication has been established in your particular system. The key features here are that:

- The leader is respected and respectable. He or she has dignity but is not besotted with his or her own power. He or she is approachable and human. Authority must be earned and given to a leader by the people.
- Some, but not necessarily all, decisions are made by consensus.
- There is flexibility within the system. Leaders do not have fragile egos and rules can be bent according to common sense and humanity.
- Communication within the group is such that people know where they stand, what is expected of them and what they can get in return.

All this theorising is all very well. Now let's get back to our prototype: the family. All families fall somewhere on a spectrum between the autocratic and the *laissez-faire*. In the middle is something approaching the ideal sort of 'democracy' that is described above. The factor that decides where the family will be positioned is in the leadership style of one or both of the parents. If a family wanders too far toward either end of the spectrum then it can be labelled with another dreadful buzz-word from the United States: the *dysfunctional family*. Let that term fall from your lips at cocktail parties and see how impressed all your listeners are.

Autocratic families are *enmeshed*. All the members seem to be intertwined and involved in each other's lives. From the outside they can maintain the image of being 'just one big happy family'. But inside there is a quiet, smouldering anger and barely suppressed mutiny. Autocratic families have an autocratic parent who is invariably a Big End and has a stable and submissive Little End for a spouse. But the Big End also turns all his children into Little Ends too. The pattern that emerges is, in California-speak, that at the head of every *dysfunctional family* are parents who have a relationship that is *co-dependent*, i.e. a Spanner.

Another feature of these families is that there is often a very large generation gap: parents are parents and children are children and never the twain shall meet. Sometimes children need to look up to a strong parental figure, just as soldiers need to have a leader who will make 'the command decision' and staff need to have an employer who will lay down the law when it is necessary. But not all the time. There are times when a parent and a sergeant and a boss need to 'chill out' and show that they have some humanness about them. Autocrats find it very hard to show their humanity.

Autocratic families have a very specific quality about them. It is their tension. You can sense it when you go into the homes of these families. It is not quite the same as formality or starchiness. It is the feeling that there is a touch too much discipline and a need to keep one family member (usually a fragile parent) pleased. When children grow up immersed in this state of tension they can become unaware that it is even there. But then they realise that when they go to play with little Freddy down the road, there is a different feeling about his house. It is relaxed. People smile and talk to each other. And when the child goes back home there it is again: tension. *The effect of this tension upon a child is insidious and destructive.* They grow up as nervy kids. Or resentful towards this fragile parent whom they had to keep happy. Within them burns a hurt feeling that says 'who tries to keep me happy?'

Also take note that in autocratic families there is a huge generation gap. Parents are way over there somewhere and will always be parents. Children are way over here and will forever be kids, even when they are middle-aged. There is no flexibility in this arrangement. Parents must be dour and serious and can only kick up their heels if no one is watching. Children can be given a lot of responsibility but never much authority. That is why *autocratic, enmeshed families tend to explode.* By this I mean that the adolescent children very quickly pick up the vibes that the only way that they will get any freedom will be to leave home. So they do. And they never come back. In fact sometimes they spread to the far corners of the earth in order to get away from the autocrat. But when I talk to these people in my consulting rooms they invariably describe a feeling of leaving home and feeling quite out of control for a few years. They experiment with drugs and sex more than their more well-balanced contemporaries. Sometimes they join cults — to replace the enmeshed human group from which they have just escaped. They have had so much external control that they have been unable to internalise any self-control. Just take a look at how many kids from rigid private schools fail their first year at university: they can't cope with this new-found freedom.

So how does the autocrat/Big End manage to keep this control? Basically there are three ways in which any one individual can control or manipulate another. They are:

1 intimidation,
2 seduction, and
3 guilt.

The first two are mirror images of each other. Intimidation is about the threat of punishment, and seduction is about the promise or reward. But the third is the most important of all. It is primitive, childlike, subconscious and powerful. If you want someone to jump through a flaming hoop for you, make them tap into that childlike guilt that we all carry. It is the guilt that says that you must never question the Big End. You see, Big Ends are very good at making Little Ends feel responsible. Most of all Little Ends feel responsible for keeping their Big Ends happy. Little Ends who displease their Big Ends are made to feel guilty as sin.

At the opposite end of this spectrum is the family that is *disengaged*. The political analogue of the autocratic/enmeshed family is *totalitarianism* which is the policy that within any country the individuals are unimportant; what matters is the nation as a whole and, more seriously, the welfare of the dictator at the top. In the disengaged family the political analogue is anarchy: there is no clear authority or structure. There is an emphasis on the individual but at the expense of a sense of acceptance and belonging. Disengaged families do not have much of a sense of family unity. It is not important to have the same name, values or direction. People drift into and out of these families very easily. Not many of the kids have two parents in common. And because they do not have much of a sense of guidance from above, they tend to grow up too early.

For people who come from an autocratic family this must seem like bliss. Wrong. The members of the disengaged family have a sense of alienation and lack of identity and direction that lasts for most of their lives. Unless, that is, they can create a stable family of their own in later years.

Roles

Enough about authority within human groups and now to roles. These days when you get a job the expected thing is that you are given a written job description. That means you can't answer an advertisement for a managing director and find that they really want you to clean the loos.

One of the most important functions for a human group is to allocate roles, work out demarcation issues and to clearly communicate to members what part to play. This involves letting them know what they are responsible for and when they are stepping on someone else's toes. Roles are usually given a label, like projects manager, pallbearer, hunter-gatherer, competitor, company secretary, etc. And roles remain similar between cultures, even if they are given different names, e.g. a clergyman works in a church, a chaplain in a hospital, a padre in an army, a rabbi in a synagogue and a shaman in a tribe.

In a family the roles are just as important. In the Western world we have seen some blurring of roles in that Dad is not necessarily the sole provider any more and Mum is not necessarily the carer, cleaner and nurse. Sometimes getting stuck in a role is associated with a feeling of being trapped. In the workplace the catchcry of the nineties has been 'multi-skilling', which means that if you can work a computer, make corporate decisions, drive a truck, speak Korean, balance the books and make a good cup of tea then you are more likely to get a good job. The same revolution happened years ago in the military when they realised that every soldier, from clerk to medic to storeman, needed to learn how to tote a gun as well as perform in their primary roles.

In families there are some pretty set roles. There is 'the baby' of the family who will always be Mummy's baby even when he or she is forty. Some insidious roles crop up in families too. Here are some examples.

The 'scapegoat' Scapegoats must take responsibility for everything that goes wrong. Most battered kids are scapegoats. They are, like all children, naive and innocent, but they cop the worst of their parents' anger. What happens to them when they grow up? They are re-labelled. Usually they are called a 'misfit' or a 'criminal'. Note also that family therapists have a quaint way of referring to the kid families bring along and complain about. They call this child 'the identified patient'. Dinky, don't you think? The natural conclusion is that the rest of the family are 'unidentified' patients. It all goes back to the old saying that a chain is as strong as its weakest link. A family is as solid as its most vulnerable member. And that person tends to become the scapegoat.

The parentified child If your parents are utterly incompetent or if there are so many children that strata of hierarchy form within the brood then one child, usually the oldest, will end up with a lot of responsibility. They become *parentified*. This can be a big advantage for a child since they end up with much more authority and power than the others. Trouble is they miss out on being a kid. Tough luck.

The perfect child Children who are 'perfect' tend to get less attention than their siblings. Parents are lulled into the belief that they are so well-behaved and co-operative that they must be happy and content. Right? Wrong. Every child needs to be an utter, utter brat at times. Tyrannical. Delinquent. That is their way of showing their distress and blowing off steam. If your kids are 'perfect' they have a big problem. Kids are only perfect because they have worked out that that is the only way that they can get a little morsel of love and approval. Inside they are hiding away a subconscious mind that is living in hell. You don't get to know about it until they reach adolescence. Then the hell breaks loose.

The Chosen One This is often the youngest. If not then it is the prettiest or the cleverest or the best at sport or whatever. In particular the favoured child is the one with whom the parents most want to identify now ('she got her good looks from her mother') or in the future ('he's so interested in the economy; I'm sure he'll end up a millionaire one day'). Favoured children are to a family what viruses are to a hard disk. The sibling rivalry that is set up can quietly tear a family apart. So quietly that the parents can't or don't want to see the competition and resentment that is between their children. But let's get real here. Every parent has his or her favourite child, even if they are loath to admit it. That is natural. But if that favouritism is not recognised and compensated for in some way then you are going to end up with kids who hate each other. And hate you too, for setting up this Care Triangle.

Before I go on I should also mention a couple of observations that I have made about my patients. Lots of them come from big families. Why should that be? The association with low socioeconomic status? Perhaps. The association of big families with inflexible religious beliefs? Maybe. But I think that the real answer may be more ethereal. Most of these patients from big families are either the second oldest or the second youngest. They got lost somewhere among the mob. The sad truth is that in a lot of big families there is simply not enough love to go around. If you have a whole tribe of kids at home, recognise that you have a set of individuals who have individual needs.

Rules and punishment

Rules are formalised authority. Every human group has them, even if they are unwritten. The rules might be expressed like this:

- 'Clock on in the morning and clock off in the evening.'
- 'You kids mustn't talk to Harry who lives next door. There's something strange about him.'
- 'Payment within seven days would be appreciated.'
- 'Thou shalt not covet thy neighbour's ass.'

Laissez-faire groups eventually self-destruct if they have no rules. But generally what happens, if the jostling for power runs its natural course, is that an autocrat will step into the power vacuum and simply take control.

The natural consequence of breaking the rules is that the offender is punished. Signals of impending punishment might be:

- 'You little brat, just wait until I get my hands on you.'

- 'Did you realise that you were doing thirty kilometres per hour over the speed limit?'
- 'Congratulations, Private Smith, you were the only one marching in step.'
- 'You will be taken from here to a place of execution … '
- 'If I've told you once, I've told you a hundred bloody times … '

For society there is a very complex process of rules and punishment that is called The Law. For reasons that escape me, many otherwise intelligent people choose to devote a lifetime to writing it, implementing it, debating it and then re-writing it. I don't doubt for a moment that it is necessary. I just can't imagine how anyone could find it interesting.

Within the family environment the laws are a lot more fuzzy around the edge. But discipline from parents to children is clearly necessary. Necessary to protect the child from his or her own excesses (which, in a paradoxical way, is a way of a parent respecting a child). Necessary too so that the child can respect the parent. Wishy-washy parents have out-of-control kids. Just check out the way some yuppie parents try to cajole their over-indulged brats. Everyone with half a brain can see that.

So how should parents implement discipline? Here, for what they are worth, are some guidelines:

The rules have to be spelt out.   Clear communication again. A lawyer will tell you that 'ignorance of the Law is not defence'. That doesn't apply between parents and kids. The *kinder* need to be told what they must do, what they must not do and what awful things will happen if they stuff it up. Also, don't make false threats. If you say that you are going to do it, then do it. If you don't you are setting yourself up for defiance.

Make the punishment fit the crime.   People are not sent to Australia for stealing a loaf of bread any more. In families, talking to strange old Harry next door should not be punished by ripping the kid's fingernails off. A stern telling-off should be enough most of the time. Is corporal punishment ever justified? In schools, no. In families, yes. Call that a double standard if you like. God made bottoms for two purposes: to sit on and to be smacked. Not too hard and not more than once or twice. And only in extreme circumstances, with young kids who need to be pulled back into line. There is something very just about a short, sharp unambiguous punishment like a smack, but only now and then. At least it avoids all the guilt trips, which can be so destructive to the child's self-esteem. Note too that a real hiding loses its meaning: it is for the benefit of the parent (unleashing rage) rather than the child (learning the limits of behaviour). A thrashing only serves to engender resentment by the thrashee to the thrasher, not respect.

An afterthought: if you prefer to smack adult bottoms rather than juvenile ones then you sound pretty kinky. Just make sure that the smackee enjoys it as much as the smacker.

Also let me ride one of my hobby horses here: no crime, no matter how hideous, warrants capital punishment. That is neither a punishment nor a disincentive to others who might be potential offenders. It is actually an abandonment. And a brutal one at that. No one should support capital punishment unless they personally are willing to open the trapdoor, fire the bullet, flip the switch or press the plunger on the syringe. And if they *are* then they have lost part of their own humanity.

Know when to give up.   At the end of the day, rules are made to be broken. In families they must all be flexible. In particular, as your adolescent offspring move through their teenage years you will have to come to terms with the idea that they take less and less notice of you as an authority figure and more and more notice of you as an antique. By the time they are sixteen you have lost them. They will have to live under your roof for the next few years and very occasionally (when it suits them that is) they will do as they are told. You will have to let them go, but don't worry, if you have been any good as a parent they will come back. Remember that Mark Twain said: 'When I was a boy of 14 my father was so ignorant I could hardly stand to have the old man around. But when I got to be 21, I was astonished at how much he had learned in 7 years'.

Make sure that one parent is not the executioner.   'Just wait until your father gets home and hears what you've done.' Dad becomes a real ogre. The kids imagine him wearing a black hood and carrying the biggest axe you've ever seen. Mum becomes someone who reports to Dad. A domestic supergrass. So in the kids' eyes Dad, the source of all punishment, becomes the person who has the power. He is to be revered. Mum is just someone you can give the run-around to until Dad gets home. Big mistake. Parents must not only try to share power, they must be seen to share power. There must be a unified front from the older generation to the younger. Punishment time is the time for the generation gap. Picnics, parties and playgrounds are not.

Forgiveness Punishment has a beginning and an end. Once the punishment has finished, the episode is over. *Finito.* So get the time sequence right: rules, offence, detection, judgment, explanation, punishment, resolution, end. Now everyone can get back to trying to be a unified, co-operative, mutually respecting family. Punishment that is like 'silent violence', in which the agony rolls on for days and the person being punished is ostracised or continually reminded of their wrongdoing, is very destructive, not just for the punishee but for the integrity of the family as a whole. Too much guilt just causes a festering resentment. Punishment must be short, sharp, unambiguous and then put into the past.

Entry and exit mechanisms

Every human group has procedures that signal that someone has entered the group or left the group. Entry signals are:

- 'Congratulations, it's a girl!'
- 'I do.'
- 'I'll be informing candidates of my decision next week but I must admit, you have the sort of qualifications and experience that I've been looking for.'
- 'I baptise you in the name of the Lord ... '
- 'J'ya wanna play hide-and-seek with us?'
- 'Just sign here, and here, and here, and over here. Great! You'll enjoy owning that house. It's a nice neighbourhood.'
- 'You're in the army now, son. So stop calling me "mate".'
- 'Meet you guys down at the pub.'

Exit signals are:

- 'Ashes to ashes, dust to dust.'
- 'I did, but not any more.'
- 'You're fired.'
- 'Look, I'm old enough to make my own decisions and going to church every Sunday isn't one of them ... '
- 'I'm not gonna play with you guys any more.'
- 'I've just received an offer on your house that I think you'll find quite acceptable.'
- 'Civvy street, here I come ... '
- 'Time please gentlemen. Time.'

Laissez-faire organisations don't have such crisp boundaries. Neither do disengaged families. People sort of waft into them and then just waft out again. So what is the ideal? Compromise, of course. Parents do not want their adult children to marry just anyone, but then some parents will never approve of *any* of their children's spouses. And what about the so-called 'blended family' which consists of parents, children and step-parents? Clearly there are times when the boundaries around a family must become blurred, or overlap with another family. Somewhere in the middle is a compromise between families in which birth is the only entry and death the only exit, and families in which the number and identity of the people who live under the family roof changes year by year or even month by month.

Care factors

Now think back to the old dichotomy in human relationships: care and control. The human system factors described above are all about control. I have described authority and hierarchy because those are the control issues that tend to go wrong most commonly and to cause the most damage. Now let's ease up and move on to the care issues. After all, that is what human beings get together for in the first place: to provide a safe, caring environment in which to grow, work and play.

Goals and rewards

All human groups have a goal. Workplaces are there either to create and distribute goods or to service the groups that do. The legal system creates social order. Hospitals care for ailing members of humankind. Churches provide a meaning for it all. And families manufacture and develop human beings.

Just as there is a set of goals, there is also a set of rewards to signal the achievement of those goals and the acknowledgment of a job well done. Check out the list:

≡ bonus pay
≡ an Oscar
≡ a Tidy Town Award
≡ a pat on the back

- a knighthood
- interest on savings
- a birthday present
- a better offer ...

In general, within the work environment, rewards tend to come within what I call the 'three P's': pay, promotion and positive regard.

A sense of belonging

Last, but not least, is the idea of belonging to the group and acceptance within it. Only 'Me-out' personalities shun the idea of belonging and this is usually because they have had such bad experiences with rejection that their fingers are burned. For most of us belonging and acceptance are absolutely crucial to our sense of self-worth. In particular belonging is associated with these four items:

- **A sense of group identity** Uniforms are a common way. Not just khaki and braid or a nurse's hat, but business suits and overalls are types of uniform too. Badges worn on the lapel of your suit show that you belong to Rotary. A secret handshake shows that you are a Mason. Your surname shows that you are a Smith or a Wong or an Abdullah.

- **Communication style** At the best this is language and at the worst it is jargon. At medical school I learned as many new words (like 'rhabdomyoma' and 'supratentorial') as someone learns when they become fluent in a foreign language. Be warned that doctors have a whole code of these words that they use when discussing a case in front of the patient. The poor patient doesn't have the slightest idea what they are talking about since they refer to the 'meiotic lesion' rather than the 'cancer'. When the RSM tells the NCO to get to HQ ASAP he is using a fairly inexcusable communication style. And nothing is more irritating than a mother who continues to use 'baby-talk' to her children when they are teenagers.

- **Tradition** Just as any human group has a goal (and therefore a future) they also invariably have a tradition (and therefore a past). In families the tradition is called the 'family tree' and your 'ancestors'. Nations have a tradition that is called 'history' and is not necessarily as valiant or heroic as it is portrayed in the history books. The officers' mess displays its tradition in the framed photographs and mounted firearms on the walls. Churches rely heavily on tradition. They have a variety of terms such as 'scripture' and 'the saints' and 'the Inquisition'. If you believe that people belonged to your particular human group for decades or centuries then that is far more satisfying than joining a band that was put together last week.

≡ **Welfare**   A group's humanity can be measured by how it treats its weakest members. That is why street kids concern society. Similarly tramps, who talk to the voices in their heads as they wander aimlessly in dirty clothes, seem to prick everyone's consciences. On a global scale there are organisations that purport to provide welfare to a lot of other human beings who are starving or being bombed. Closer to home there are sickness benefits, the 'dole', single parent's allowance, the St Vincent de Paul, the RSPCA and the perennial neighbourhood do-gooder who is a compulsive rescuer. A group without some formalised method of care for its ailing members is a very sad group indeed.

Think about it. When people get together they form a group and all these care and control forces come into play. Now look around the groups that you belong to and see how right I am. Human beings can be so predictable.

Now let's wrap this up and get on. I have had a look at how people interact when they are in pairs, triads and groups of more than three. Each has its own dynamics and its own problems. Recognise also that you relate every day in two-person, three-person and group situations. This is all getting pretty damned complex, isn't it? So lie back and relax. The next chapter is really quite straightforward: it is about staying healthy.

CHAPTER eight

Health

Mens sana in corpore sano

Everyone knows that fit and healthy people have a greater sense of vitality and enthusiasm than frail and sickly people. Right? You bet. *Mens sana in corpore sano.* That's Latin for "A healthy mind in a healthy body". Hope I got it right, otherwise I'll be opening my office door tomorrow to a mixed group of angry psychoanalysts, feminists and Latin scholars . . .

This chapter is a pot-pourri of items about health. Don't look upon it as being a medical textbook, just the musings of a psychiatrist who sees plenty of unhappy people who are fat, unfit, do not sleep well, and smoke and drink too much. So here are some thumbnail sketches about obesity, cholesterol, aging, sleep, chronic pain, exercise, smoking, alcohol, personal time management and, last but not least, sex. And at the end I will throw in some psychiatric curiosities about how people present to physicians with physical problems that turn out to be psychological.

Being too fat and being too thin

Ah, for a return of the Renaissance figure. You know, those podgy women who adorned the oil paintings of the time. Civilisation has just gone stark raving mad about being skinny. We all know who to blame: Twiggy. She was the model who made anorexia *chic*. Since that time the world's young women have been swept along with the idea that 'thin is in' and have subjected themselves to a variety of nasty diets and public humiliation at Weight Watchers. Even worse, I have watched young women starving themselves nearly to death to conform to some imagined social norm.

In other civilisations Twiggy would have been mistaken for a prisoner of war or a famine victim and she would have been fed endlessly to return her feminine curves. But in this society women's figures are supposed to resemble skinny boys' figures. Whatever happened to the allure of busts and bottoms? Women are supposed to be rounded. Has the world gone mad?

Is there a masculine equivalent of anorexia? First let me say that up to five per cent of anorectic patients are men. Then there was the fad for marathon running in the late seventies and early eighties that showed that men could be just as obsessionally body-conscious as women. They also managed to hurt their bodies as much as anorectic women did and they even began to look the same: really skinny. Thankfully that particular type of temporary insanity is no longer faddish. We are allowed to 'power walk' with a Walkman on these days. And the only sort of wall that we happen to hit is someone's front fence while swerving to avoid running over a poodle on the road.

These days the more common male analogue of excessive dieting is only recently becoming evident: it is excessive body-building. I have encountered Arnold Schwarzenegger look-alikes who have so many steroids floating around in their systems that they are always on the verge of psychosis. They suffer from what, in gymnasium jargon, is called the "roid rage". It is a change of personality characterised by an irrational irritability. Steroid junkies can turn from being placid, benign muscle-men into monsters in a split second. Yet they still pump all those hormones into their bodies. And they still pump iron. Why? Because they are obsessed with it, just as anorectic girls are obsessed with dieting. No matter how good they look, they never look good enough.

Nostalgia aside, I suppose that there are *some* people who really are too fat. And you don't have to be a professor of physiology to work out that obesity predisposes you to everything from high blood pressure and heart disease to varicose veins and haemorrhoids. So, I hear you ask, how fat is too fat?

In the bad old days we doctors used to work off weight-for-height tables. If you were X centimetres high and weighed more than Y kilograms then you were too heavy. But then the question arose: what about short, stocky people who did not carry a lot of fat, just buckets of muscle? For a while we turned to skinfold measurement which had to be entered into a computer program that calculated your total body fat. It looked very scientific, but not even this was really accurate.

Then someone came up with a formula that was about as simple as $E=mc^2$. It is called the Body Mass Index (or BMI). It is calculated by dividing your weight in kilograms by the square of your height *in metres*. A result of 20–25 is ideal, 25–29 is overweight and 30 or more is obese.

Fair enough. But then it all got even more complicated. Those boffins in white coats and called 'researchers' found that there was a particular type of obesity that was associated with many more physical problems: abdominal obesity. It is better to be pear-shaped than egg-shaped. The worst sort of fat of all was the 'beer gut'. So how do your quantify a 'beer gut'? In comes the waist-to-hip ratio.

Exercise

1 Find yourself a tape measure.
2 Stand with your hands on your hips. Your hands are resting on bony prominences called the *iliac crests*. Run your tape measure around your guts at the level of your iliac crests. It should pass by your

umbilicus (i.e. tummy-button in doctor-speak) and try to make it not sag around your back.

3 This is your waist measurement.

4 Now poke around in the flesh beneath your iliac crest. There is a hard bony thing there. This is your femur, or what Afro-American choruses would call your 'thigh-bone'. You are touching your femur

Overweight

1 Body Mass Index (BMI)

$$BMI = \frac{Weight\ (kg)}{[Height\ (m)]\ squared}$$

2 Waist-to-Hip Ratio (WHR)

$$\frac{Waist\ (any\ measurement)}{Hip\ (same\ measurement)}$$

just as it makes a sudden inward turn to go into your hip joint. This level is your hip level. Measure your girth here, presuming that you have enough tape to go around … The tape measure should pass around at the upper limit of your pubic hairline. So don't do this in public.

5 This is your hip measurement.

6 Now divide your hip measurement into your waist measurement. It does not matter if you have measured them in centimetres, inches, kilometres or fingerbreadths, just as long as you make both measurements using the same parameter.

7 This is your waist-to-hip ratio. For men this should be 0.9 or less. For women it should be 0.8 or less. Women must have a lower ration because they are allowed to have wider hips. *Vive la différence.*

In increasing order of risk from heart disease, etc., are four archetypal body shapes:

≡ lean pear-shaped (low BMI, low WHR)
≡ fat pear-shaped (high BMI, low WHR)
≡ lean egg-shaped (low BMI, high WHR)
≡ fat egg-shaped (high BMI, high WHR)

Next question: how do you lose weight? If you find an easy way, please let me know. Even surgery to staple up your stomach is fraught with complications and is not the miracle cure. Do I seem pessimistic? How sensitive of you to notice. But wait, there *are* a few guidelines here.

Overweight

1 BMI

20–25	Ideal
25–29	Overweight
30 or more	Obese

2 WHR

For men:	0.9 or below
For women:	0.8 or below

Your current weight is determined at least in part by a very simple formula: 'energy in' must equal 'energy out', i.e. calories consumed in food must be expended in physical activity or else they will end up contributing to your waist-to-hip ratio.

Also be aware that somewhere in the base of your brain, up behind your nose in fact, is a lump of grey matter that determines your vital bodily functions, like your breathing, thirst and hunger. Tucked among these complex structures is some mechanism that tells your body how fat it should be. This is called your 'set-point' and acts rather like the thermostat on a heater. A thermostat turns the heater off when the room gets too hot and on when the room gets too cold. Your 'set-point' gets you to eat more when you fall below a certain weight and to eat less when you go over that certain weight. In the long run, the object of the exercise is not to lose weight (since you will simply put it on again) but to alter your 'set-point'.

Many years ago, when I was younger and more foolish than I am now, I went on a crash diet. I think that the Israeli army had something to do with it. I will blame them anyway. Two days of just eggs, two days of just cheese, two days of just apples and two days of just chicken. I was transformed from the guy who was referred to as 'Hey podgy!' to someone who looked like Twiggy's cousin. On midnight of the eighth day the diet ended. I found the only diner in town that was open at that time and pigged out. Eight days later a friend of mine saw me on the street and called out 'Hey podgy!' And the moral of the story, Virginia, is that the speed of weight loss in any diet is directly proportional to the speed of weight gain after the diet ends: i.e. if you lose weight quickly you will put it on again just as quickly.

The only way to lose weight is slowly, say a kilogram a month. Throw away the calorie counters (they are for anal retentives) and the 'Before' and 'After' photos in the advertisements. Dieting is not for the next month but the next year. Use support groups like Weight Watchers if you want, but whatever you do, lose the weight slowly. That is the only way that your 'set-point' will alter.

Cholesterol

This nasty little substance deserves a special mention. Trot along to your general practitioner some time soon and ask for a cholesterol test. Your wise GP will write something on the path request form like 'fasting lipids please'. That way you will be tested for another nasty piece of work called 'triglycerides' and the lab will also produce figures for your 'high density lipoproteins' and your 'low density lipoproteins'. The former are friends and the latter are enemies. This is all very complex stuff. Leave it to your wise GP to interpret.

Your cholesterol should have a reading of 5.5 or less. If it is significantly more, then that ticking you hear is the time-bomb within you. Look at your other risk factors too. Being overweight, smoking, not exercising enough and having a family history of heart disease are all music to the Grim Reaper's mouldy old ears. Your crisp business suit with snappy tie might camouflage the clogged arteries within. If a 55-year-old business executive has a cholesterol level of 6.5 (i.e. not a *huge* reading ... I have seen them above 10), then he will have a 10 per cent chance of suffering a heart attack before the retiring age, even if there are no other risk factors involved. And heart attacks are not just for men.

Don't let the first warning of your high cholesterol be a really bad chest pain that you have never felt before and will never feel again ... Don't let the last thing you see and hear be a young paramedic saying 'We're losing him!' as he or she pounds away at your chest. Scary stuff, eh?

Aging

You know the routine. Everyone gets old. What was formerly smooth, supple skin becomes wrinkled. Your dashing black hair begins to look like salt and pepper and then just looks grey. You look back fondly on the days when you were called 'podgy' rather than 'that old codger'.

But there is good news. You see the two universal fears that most people seem to have about aging are that:

- You will lose your mind. People rate dementia as being like death and madness: things that you would prefer someone else to experience. Dementia involves a progressive loss of your thinking, cognitive, intellectual functions, beginning with short-term memory ('where *did* I put my glasses?') and developing to a complete shutdown of any ability to think, concentrate, remember, calculate, plan, navigate, organise, read or write. The last thing that you forget is your name.

- You will end up in one of those dreadful nursing homes where you will be fed corned beef sandwiches every day, washed down with lukewarm milky tea from a plastic cup with a spout. Staff who can't remember your name will call you 'dear'.

Both of these fears are unfounded for most of the population. The prevalence of dementia in people over 65 years old is about 5 per cent. It tends to increase further with age but even with the over-80s it tends to be about one-in-five. The odds are stacked in your favour that you will keep your marbles, even if you do lose your glasses from time to time.

And there is another piece of good news: only a small minority of old people end up in nursing homes. Most manage to maintain the dignity of being able to stay in their own homes until they curl up their wrinkled geriatric toes.

Sleep

'Sleep that knits up the ravelled sleeve of care.' For uncultured readers, that's Shakespeare. Problems with sleep are probably among the most common mental disturbances of all, but people do not often come to see me to complain of difficulty with sleep as an isolated problem. Why? Because most sleep disorders resolve themselves after a night or two of tossing and turning anyway.

General rules
American psychiatrists divide sleep problems into two rather neat packages: DIMS (disorders of initiating and maintaining sleep) and

DOES (disorders of excessive somnolence). In layperson's terms we are talking here about too little sleep and too much sleep, i.e. insomnia and fatigue.

Most 'insomniacs' actually sleep more than they think. I often hear the complaint 'I sleep only two hours a night and I have been doing that for months'. If such people are taken to a sleep laboratory and their sleep is monitored then most (admittedly not all) will sleep much more than they are aware of. A lot of the time spent 'lying awake' is actually spent dozing.

Sleeping pills should be regarded as toxic muck. They work wonderfully for the first week or two. Then you're hooked on them. Doubt my word? Then try to stop. You will experience a disturbing 'rebound' of insomnia and dreaming, often with vivid nightmares, and you will wish that you never started them. A sleeping pill once in the proverbial blue moon or perhaps on a long distance air flight is quite kosher. But regular sedatives become a recipe for much bigger problems later on.

The amount of sleep that you need decreases with age. Babies seem to spend their lives in the land of nod. Oldies might need only four or five hours' sleep a night and still function perfectly well during the day. Everyone has a 'set-point' with sleep too: if you have a late night out then you will probably compensate by sleeping a bit longer over the next few nights. And some people simply need more sleep than others of the same age.

Most people fall into one of two categories: morning larks and night owls. Morning larks leap out of bed and greet the rising sun with *joie de vivre*. Night owls crawl out of bed and must be avoided because they are grumpy as all hell until they begin to come alive in mid-morning. Morning larks fade early in the evening. They are rarely invited to dinner parties because they are habitual party-poopers. Somewhere in the middle of the main course they start to stifle yawns. Night owls can be found at nightclubs fandangling on the dance floor until the wee small hours. No big deal. Problems only arise when a morning lark marries a night owl. When do they ever co-ordinate their arousal mechanisms to fit in some humpy-rumpy?

The more interesting aberrations of sleep

'Hypnic jerks' These occur when you are just entering the most delectable sleep and suddenly have the sensation of falling in space.

Your body jerks as you go to save yourself, but in a split second you realise that you are in bed and your partner is giving you a funny look.

Hallucinations Some people experience quite vivid hallucinations just as they are going to sleep ('hypnogogic hallucinations') or just as they are waking up ('hypnopompic hallucinations'). The 'visions' last only a second or two and then disappear, but they can be very frightening since they are perceived as, say, a face at the bedroom window or a stranger standing at the foot of the bed. People who are recently bereaved sometimes interpret these events as being a 'visitation' from their dead relative. Don't worry, they are not going mad.

Somnambulism and somniloquy The names sound like some sort of contagious tropical infection but they are really jargon for sleep-walking and talking in your sleep. Folklore has always said that you must never wake a sleep-walker. Blame old wives for this tale, since there is no logical reason why you should not, apart from the fact that sleep-walkers are fairly hard to rouse and then might be a bit bewildered about where they are and what they are doing. What are the chances of a sleep-walker strolling off a cliff? Just about zilch. Sleep-walkers simply need to be directed back to bed and tucked up. Usually they resume their supine position and go back to counting Zs. As for sleep-*talkers* there is not much that you can do apart from put cotton wool in your ears or tape what they are saying and then blackmail them for the tape when they wake up. Are somnambulists and somniloquists emotionally disturbed? Sometimes, but not often.

Succubus, incubus, and 'old hag' These are some of the rare curiosities of the sleep world but I have had enough bewildered patients describe them to me that they are worth a mention here. All of these odd names refer to the same phenomenon. Technically they are called 'parasomnias', which only goes to prove that medicine has a jargon term for just about everything. Sufferers from the succubus feel that they have been visited by a witch or a demon in their own beds. They feel partly asleep and they are aware that they are in their own beds in their own bedrooms. But they feel terrified and often they are aware of a heavy force weighing down upon their chests. For women this can be experienced as being raped. For a long time paediatricians have described a phenomenon in children that is called *parvor nocturnis*, or *night terrors*. Kids suddenly sit bolt upright in bed, often calling out in fear, and when their parents come to see what is the matter they find a terrified child who is not fully aware of his or her environment. This, I

175

am sure, is the childhood equivalent of the succubus. Horror-movie producers have a field day on this stuff.

Common problems and possible solutions

Some of the phenomena discussed above are getting into the fine print of the sleep textbooks, so let's get back to the common problems: insomnia and excessive daytime fatigue. First some rules of thumb for insomnia:

Most insomnia is acute. Most sufferers of acute insomnia need do no more than grumble about it for a few days: the sleep cycle has a marvellous ability to sort itself out. Most people who complain of chronic insomnia are actually sleeping more than they are aware.

Sleeping pills for more than three nights in a row is a no-no. Eventually they do more harm than good.

When your emotional problems become really severe the first physical manifestation can be a sleep disturbance. As a gross generalisation, *anxiety causes difficulty in getting off to sleep and depression causes difficulty in staying asleep,* i.e. you wake up too early.

Some specific suggestions:

- Don't go to bed with a problem on your mind. Try to deal with it, or, if possible, at least talk it out with a significant person before you hit the sack.
- Don't drink caffeinated tea or coffee after 5 p.m.
- Don't lie in bed trying to get to sleep. The risk is that your bed becomes associated in your mind with tension rather than blissful slumber. Get up and read a book, watch TV (nothing with kung fu or too much passion in it) and have a cup of decaffeinated tea or coffee.
- Do some exercise during the day so that your body is physically exhausted, not just emotionally exhausted.
- Paradoxically, don't try to use alcohol as a sleeping pill. It works a treat as your blood alcohol is going up and then it tends to make you wide awake as your blood alcohol is going down again. This is a classical 'withdrawal' effect.

And what about excessive daytime fatigue? If it has been around for more than a few days then you have a problem. Have a long hard look at your health, how down in the dumps you feel, how hard you are working, how unsupported you feel and what is causing stress in your life. Then go and talk to your doctor about it. You may have some

/ sleep disturbance

undiagnosed physical problem like anaemia. You may need a physical going-over and a stern but kindly reprimand about what you are doing to both ends of your candle.

Chronic pain

P atients with chronic physical pain strike fear into the hearts of their doctors. They cause a sinking feeling in the medical stomach. Why? Because patients are supposed to get better, that's why. You see, we doctors derive most of our work satisfaction from seeing people get better. People come to us with a problem and we give them the answer. Simple. The idea of being able to rescue people appeals to some childlike fantasy that we medicos have hidden deep in our subconscious minds of being a caped crusader, someone who uses good (drugs and scalpels) over evil (infections, tumours, fractures, etc). Having a patient continually remind us of our therapeutic powerlessness is like being told that you cannot leap tall buildings after all. And that a speeding bullet would make you look as fast as a snail. We doctors do not really think that we are God. Just Superbeings.

But then there are large groups of doctors who are more humble. We do not try to heal the patient with one incision of the scalpel or one dose of wonderdrug 'X'. General practitioners follow your family's health over decades. Dermatologists all have a hard core of patients with chronic and incurable skin conditions. Diabetologists help patients to adjust to another incurable, but very treatable, disease. Rehabilitation physicians mark improvements in their patients in terms of months and years rather than days. And of course we psychiatrists plod along with patients as they slowly chip away at the invisible pain that they have carried all their lives in their subconscious minds. 'Ripe Plums' ain't that common.

Patients with chronic physical pain require this less dramatic and more supportive approach. They also confront us caped crusaders with our own limitations. They overwhelm our fantasy that we can 'cure' everyone.

I mention these patients here because of one very important observation: *chronic physical pain and chronic emotional pain eventually*

pain

pains

become blurred at the edges. In short, if you are in chronic emotional pain, such as depression, then every physical pain will be worse. When you are under severe stress and have had a huge row with your spouse you will find that your toothache has an added touch of misery to it. And people who are in chronic physical pain will invariably develop a chronic emotional pain: they become depressed. This is a defeated, depleted, burned-out sort of depression. It says that jumping off a cliff is better than having to put up with this back pain for the rest of my wretched life.

Unfortunately some of my medical colleagues prefer to view pain as *either* physical *or* emotional. The patient who does not respond to intensive physical treatment is branded as being 'neurotic' and bundled off to the psychiatrist. Wrong, my friends. All pains are an unholy blend of both physical and emotional factors. That is why pain clinics have sprung up. The idea here is that chronic pain is treated by a team that will include the surgeon who will inject your inflamed nerves to deaden them, the physician who will prescribe your painkillers, the physiotherapist who will get you up and moving again and the psychiatrist who will check out how pained your emotions are feeling. And these are but a few in a cast of, well, half a dozen or so. If you have a chronic pain that has not responded to medical treatment then go to your GP and ask for a referral to a pain clinic. Nag. Hold your breath until you turn cyanosed (that's blue in doctor-speak). He or she will probably be delighted to refer you on . . .

Smoking

In the old black-and-white movies Humphrey Bogart looked so suave when he smoked. Everyone did in those movies. It seemed at that time to be a glamorous thing to do. Not any more. Now most of the population are non-smokers. We look upon smokers as being sad but offensive people who pollute the air that everyone breathes. We see smokers for what they are: drug addicts. And they are addicted to one of the most poisonous and addictive substances known to humanity. You simply cannot have forty 'hits' a day of alcohol or heroin. But you can smoke forty-a-day and still do your job. As long as it doesn't require a lot of fitness or puff . . .

Most adult non-smokers are ex-smokers. Like me. We are a sanctimonious lot. We look down our upturned noses at smokers and say 'tch tch'. But we know how addictive those little white cylinders can be. We also know how damned hard they are to give up. In fact when I graduated from medical school (more years ago than I care to mention) my first job as a fresh-faced house doctor was in a lung cancer ward. Talk about a baptism of fire ... and smoke. My very first patients were old men who looked ashen (no pun intended) and would sit in the dayroom of the ward puffing on their last few packets of cigarettes. None of them looked like Humphrey Bogart. And none of them lived.

I gave up cigarettes then. How did I do it? I used pure, unadulterated fear, that's how. You will find that there are not too many doctors who smoke. This is not because we enjoy being sanctimonious to our patients. This is because we know what it does to you.

How do you give up smoking? If there was an easy way I would patent it. I would be a millionaire overnight. In the final analysis you just have to do it, and then it's done. It's not easy, but it is worth it.

As a rule of thumb, don't bother to wind down slowly. You are just delaying the inevitable and your enthusiasm will wane as you start to feel the grips of the nicotine withdrawal. I recommend that you go 'cold turkey'. The question is *when*. Why not now? Like, this very minute. If you are too much of a coward to take up that challenge then get cracking on the following exercise.

Exercise

1 Set a date no more than two weeks away. At one second past midnight of that date you will be a non-smoker.
2 Tell all your friends that you are giving up on that date so that you will look like a real nerd if you bum out.
3 Plan the day so that it coincides with a complete change of routine like a holiday or a house-move or a change of job. Make it a 'new broom'. Also, be away from all those stimuli that trigger your desire to smoke, like your desk or your television set after dinner.
4 Find a religious or political cause that you are powerfully opposed to. Decide upon a sum of money that will really hurt your budget. Put this sum of money *in cash* (cheques can be cancelled, cash is irreversible) into an envelope with an anonymous note saying 'this is for all your good work'. Put a stamp on the envelope, address it to this cause that you despise and seal it. Be aware that someone at this

despicable organisation might pinch the cash for themselves. That would nark you even more ...

5 Give the envelope to a non-smoking friend and instruct them that they must mail the envelope if they catch you smoking or hear of you smoking *within twenty days of your 'D-day'*. Twenty days of non-smoking does not make you 'cured' but it gives a pretty good indication of your seriousness. By then the symptoms of nicotine withdrawal should be lessening too.

6 After twenty days, get the envelope back and blow the cash on something self-indulgent. Except cigarettes.

A final comment about cigarette addiction before I move on. There are plenty of 'stop-smoking' courses around. Do they work? They all claim to, but then can their figures be trusted? Most of the statistics that they tout about their own success rates are a bit 'suss'. This is because reformed smokers can go back to their habit months or even years after stopping. The painful truth is probably that *most* graduates of these courses *do* relapse. My own observation is that *the short-term success rate of stop-smoking courses is directly proportional to their cost*. If you are willing to lay down a few hundred dollars to go to such a course then you are brimming with motivation and will almost certainly do well. In the short term at least ...

Alcohol

This is a heading that should have neon lights on it. Western society has a love–hate relationship with alcohol. Drinkers love it and the rest of society, who suffer from their excesses, hate it. What would our society be like without alcohol? A lot healthier and less violent. The roads would be safe and police would spend much more of their shifts watching Oprah Winfrey on TV. But then the moderate drinkers of this world would miss out on a great pleasure.

Now think back to Chapter 3. I wrote about how, when I was a fledgling doctor, I was taught by wrinkled old professors who had seen a lot and done a lot in their professional lifetimes. They always told me that the two greatest 'mimics' in medicine were tuberculosis and syphilis. These were the infections that could imitate any other illness. At post-mortem the diagnosis was finally made, much to the satisfaction

7 fractures & not a drop of alcohol ✓•

of the attendant physicians but a little too late to benefit the poor patient. That was in the old days. You just don't see that much TB or syphilis around any more. Today the great mimics are <u>alcoholism and depression.</u> They can imitate just about any illness. (And now there is another mimic rearing its ugly head: AIDS.)

When you drink too much you affect just about every organ system in your body. Being the simple-minded fellow that I am, I list the harmful effects of alcohol under what I call, for reasons that will rapidly become obvious, the 'List of B's':

Bowel   This item includes that offshoot of the bowel, the liver. You know the main culprits: liver disease that culminates in cirrhosis (which means that your old liver is just about to pack it in), peptic ulcers which sometimes bleed massive amounts into the bowel, etc. Nasty stuff.

Bones   In the casualty departments of all major hospitals there is a standard abbreviation for this sort of injury. On the clinical notes appear the letters <u>'PFO'. This stands for 'got pissed and fell over'.</u> When drunks come in with broken bones you can bet your bottom dollar that their X-rays will show a whole orthopaedic museumful of other broken bones in various states of healing. Once drunks start to fall over and break bones they tend to get into the habit. Young, enthusiastic doctors in starched white coats tend to rapidly run out of milk-of-human-kindness when alcoholics with broken bones appear on the scene. In fact the Americans have a rather dry acronym for these patients: they are called 'gomers', which stands for 'get out of my examination room' . . .

Blood   If you look down the microscope at healthy human blood you will see that red blood cells outnumber white blood cells. Hands down. And you will notice that healthy red blood cells look like dinky little red frisbees. The blood cells of alcoholics are a sorry sight. Big, pale and floppy. Not too good for carrying the much-needed oxygen around to their tired old tissues. Why do they look so worn out? Because most boozers have a lousy diet, that's why.

Babies   It is technically called Foetal Alcohol Syndrome. In the clinical notes it is usually recorded as another standard abbreviation: 'FLK', which stands for Funny Looking Kid. Babies who are affected in the uterus by a drinking mother tend to come out small, with small heads, a few other abnormalities and a not-too-stunning IQ as well.

Brain   Alcohol rots your brain. It causes you to be confused when you are drunk and frankly delirious when you are withdrawing. It homes in on certain nerve cells in the base of your brain that manage short-term memory, i.e. not what your fifth birthday was like, but what you had for breakfast this morning, or those three things that you were supposed to attend to yesterday, if only you could remember what they were. In the end, after years of hitting the bottle, alcohol causes you to go demented. In fact in Australia it is the third most common cause of dementia after Alzheimer's disease and problems with cerebral blood vessels.

Bastard   As if the B's listed above are not enough, let me throw in this last one to really scare you. Plenty of alcoholics undergo a personality change. All addicts, no matter what they are addicted to, tend to make that chemical the central feature of their lives. Alcoholics are just more subtle about it since they don't have to go to the seedy part of town to visit their drug dealer. But eventually they put drinking ahead of working, being a good husband and father and generally being a decent human being. Part of this is simply addictive behaviour and part of it is related to brain damage. You see alcohol tends to poison the frontal lobes of your brain in particular. They are the squidgy bits that sit on a little ledge above your eyeballs. There is an adage in my specialty that says that 'you *are* your frontal lobes', since in these blobs of tissue reside your personality, judgment, insight, social skills and a few other traits that make you a nice person and keep you out of trouble. Alcoholics tend to damage theirs. Then they disinhibit themselves some more by having a dozen doses of their favourite drug. And then they can be violent. Alcoholics can be real 'Bastards'. They wreak havoc on their families and keep disgruntled policemen busy through what should be quiet nights on duty.

So that's the list of B's. I suppose that that gin and tonic that you're drinking as you read this is beginning to taste like battery acid now …

A final note on the damage that alcohol can cause. What we are becoming more and more aware of is the particular suffering of the female alcoholic. The affliction is particularly degrading for her. Women are vulnerable to abuse. Women alcoholics are doubly so.

Let me move on to the eternal question: how much is too much? Over many years groups of psychiatric boffins have tried to answer this question. How much can you drink before you attract the diagnosis of alcoholism? The American Psychiatric Association has their definition. So does the World Health Organisation. These criteria look long and complex. What I am about to give you is Dunn's Definition. I have tried to make it as idiot-proof as possible, so that you can grasp it even if your frontal lobes passed away years ago. Quite simply, you are an alcoholic if you do the following three things: you drink too much; you get into trouble; and you can't control it.

You drink too much

An average man (often affectionately known as Stan the Standard Man) is allowed to consume 40 grams of pure alcohol per day. A woman is allowed half that, i.e. 20 grams. Forty grams converts into:

- four middies (or three cans) of beer, or
- four glasses (roughly half a bottle) of wine, or
- four nips (or one sixth of a bottle) of spirits.

Note that I said 'or', not 'and'. For women these amounts must be halved. I should also make note of the wine cask, which can be a deceptive little creature. You

Alcohol abuse

1 You drink too much
> 280g a week

< 2 Alcohol-free days (AFDs) a week

2 You get into trouble
- Health
- Marriage/family
- Work
- Drink-driving

3 You can't control it

cannot see from the outside where that silver bag is resting and giving it a shake is a bit too rough and ready. Keep in mind that one litre of wine contains 100 grams of alcohol, so that four-litre job in your fridge should last you about *two weeks* if it is just you draining it (rather than the weekend you took to polish off the last one). But hang on, Stan, there is more.

People over the years have tried to describe the different patterns of drinking and there are essentially only two: continual or episodic. Of *dipso maniacs* course most drinkers tend to combine the two somehow, e.g. six beers after work every day and then a carton of beer at a party on Saturday night. Continual drinking occurs in a stereotyped pattern every day or almost every day. It tends to rot your liver, which is under a continual barrage of toxins. It is sometimes called 'the French pattern' since the French seem to have wine with every meal yet never show overt signs blackout

+ gejũ pejũ

of drunkenness. Episodic drinking is bingeing. It rots your brain since the delicate nerve cells simply cannot stand the high concentrations of alcohol that result in the middle of a real bender. Any drinker who experiences 'blackouts' is already knocking off nerve cells. For the uninitiated, blackouts are not about fainting or losing consciousness, they are about losing memory during intoxication so that the binger wakes up and cannot remember, say, how the hell he or she ended up in this bed with this person. Episodic bingeing is sometimes called 'the English pattern' since it can be witnessed in most English pubs on Saturday evenings.

It is a big no-no to drink every day. Booze becomes a habit and then not something special or different. It is therefore important to have at least two days of the week in which you consume no alcohol at all. These days are your AFDs, or Alcohol-Free Days. They keep you on your toes.

You get into trouble

Alcohol can get you into trouble in a whole variety of ways. The list of B's simply indicates the physical damage. If your boss or your wife or your doctor or the police or your bank manager are looking worried then you had better give yourself a shake. Preferably a milkshake. In particular if your spouse nags you about the amount of alcohol that you are getting through then you had better get that wax out of your ears and, just for once, *listen*. Alcohol ruins marriages and families and careers. It makes you emotionally and financially bankrupt. And it gets you into the courts. Take note of one of my rules of thumb: one drink-driving charge might be a symptom, but two drink-driving charges make a diagnosis. If you are caught drink-driving then you are a mug and you have been warned. If you get caught again then you are an alcoholic. Nothing surer.

You can't control it

The next criterion for alcoholism is to see whether you can control your drinking. I see plenty of boozers in my practice. I challenge them that they have to prove to themselves (not to me) that they are not alcoholics by keeping their drinking in control. They smile that deceptive smile that I know so well and reassure me that reducing their alcohol intake will be 'no probs, Doc!' I know denial when I see it. They last a couple of weeks, a month tops. Then they are back to the old routine. If someone can control their drinking for *six months* then they are showing me that they are probably going to be able to control it into the foreseeable future. Probably, not definitely.

I should also mention a peculiar phenomenon that occurs in all addictions. It is called 'reinstatement', which refers to the fact that addicts can give up their drug for years and even decades. But if they ever touch it again they will rapidly (say, within three months) return to their former pattern of consumption. Like Timothy.

CASE HISTORY **Timothy**

I encountered Timothy many years ago when I was in general practice. He was a dignified old gentleman of sixty-eight, a retired executive for a large insurance company. Timothy's presentation screamed of alcoholism even though he was sober when I saw him. He came to see me, a new GP, on a Monday morning. In the waiting room he wore sunglasses and chewed peppermints. He had a gash on his elbow that should have been sutured when he fell over two days before. I examined more than his elbow. A big liver, bloodshot eyes, a fine tremor, plenty of old scars and skin covered with the peculiar little telltale signs, the so-called 'stigmata' of alcoholism. Timothy was in the early stages of withdrawal. Given enough time off alcohol he might well have gone into full-blown DTs, or *delirium tremens*. Not a pretty sight. Patients in DTs look flushed, ruddy, sweaty, confused and paranoid. They hang around the locked doors of psychiatric wards because their minds are filled with the CIA, witches, invisible fleas that crawl over their skin and their burning desire to run for the nearest pub. Left untreated maybe ten per cent of these patients die. They are found several days later in their beds in grotty back-street boarding-houses.

Timothy came clean. He still had some survival instinct left. He was admitted to hospital to receive a safe, controlled withdrawal from alcohol. Then he went straight into a rehabilitation program and re-established his links with AA.

I saw him some three months later. He looked like the dignified and venerable businessman that he was and filled in the gaps in his history. He had spent most of his twenties and thirties pissed. In the gutter in fact. Then his old friend, survival instinct, told him that he had better get his act together. So he dried out. Wasn't easy, but he did it. Plenty of AA meetings. After a while it simply became part of his routine. Orange juice at social gatherings, honest admission to anyone who asked that he was an alcoholic, avoidance of pubs and attendance at meetings.

He worked his way up the corporate ladder because he was bright and ambitious, when he was sober that is. He remained sober for some thirty years. Then the attendance at AA began to dwindle and he became complacent. Same old story. He thought that thirty years of sobriety meant that he was 'cured', so he 'picked up', as they say in AA jargon. He got away with the first drink and the second. For the first couple of weeks he could convince himself and his worried wife that it would all be okay.

It took him five weeks to reinstate. Back to the gutter. It was pre-destined to be that way from the moment that he 'picked up'. That's what reinstatement is all about. I hope that the only thing he will pick up in the future will be his grandchildren for a weekend with their ever-loving, and sober, grandfather.

Some more musing about alcohol. The alcoholic's favourite defences are denial, rationalisation and projection, as epitomised by the following statements. I hear these words so often that I can just about finish the sentence before they do:

= Denial: ' … but *I'm* not an alcoholic!'
= Rationalisation: 'I know I drink too much but I do that to forget/numb the pain/because all my mates do/I would be a real pansy if I didn't, etc. etc.'
= Projection: 'I know I drink too much but that is because of this rotten boss/that bitch of a wife/the dreadful boarding house I live in, etc. etc.'

The first step to sobriety is to overcome your own denial. The only person who can do that is you. If you need to hit Skid Row then so be it. Sometimes things can only begin to get better when they have reached rock bottom.

What do I do with patients who are alcoholic? I get them through a safe withdrawal from alcohol and I try to educate and support them in experiencing their life alcohol-free. I do not try to engage them in intense psychotherapy. Usually that does more harm than good since a newly sober alcoholic will cope with the rigours of such treatment by reverting to the most proven comforter: the bottle. After a while I start to nag them to go to an AA meeting. A support group like that can do far more than can sessions with me. No one is harder on an alcoholic than a fellow alcoholic. They know all the old rationalisations and manipulations because they have tried them all. An alcoholic who has linked in with AA tends to do far better in the long run than those who feel they 'don't need all that meetings stuff'. AA runs on pseudo-religious lines, which some people find disconcerting, but you don't get the Bible stuffed down your throat. I should also mention two AA approaches that are particularly apt. These are:

'The only one you should become sober for is you.' If you sober up to please your wife, kids, GP, bank manager or favourite police sergeant then you are setting yourself up to fail. Work on the principle that they are all frail human beings too and that they will disappoint you in some way in the future. When they do you can look upon that as your excuse to 'bust' or hit the bottle again. The only person who can be responsible for you is you. The only one who can help you is you. The person who will benefit the most in the long term will be you.

'One day at a time.' If you are an alcoholic and are confronted with the idea of remaining sober for the rest of your life then you have no hope at all. Forever is one hell of a long time when you only stopped drinking last Tuesday. When you consider the idea of not drinking year in and year out you will be overcome with a desire to give up and get on with your next binge. That is why AA suggests that you take 'one day at a time'. When you wake up in the morning you must decide that you will be sober for that day and that day only. Worry about tomorrow tomorrow. Worry about 1998 in 1998. Worry about today today.

Exercise

We all know that we need it. It's just that some of us get really good at finding reasons why we can't do it just now. One day, as the chest pain gets really bad and we feel short of breath and faint we will regret having downed all those chocolate milkshakes and watched all that midday TV on days when we should have been playing tennis or golf.

The sad truth is that exercise must be an inbuilt part of our schedules. And most people find it hard to work out just how much. The majority of the population does too little exercise and the minority does too much. This latter group can be found pounding the asphalt or checking themselves out in the mirrored walls of the gym.

We have all gone through the fads: distance running, aerobic classes and body-building have been the three most recent. Now we are beginning to understand something that is a lot more sensible: that less vigorous exercise is all that is required just as long as it is performed regularly. Walking is the best. If you must hit a little white ball around some sandpits at the same time then good on you. If you must walk with designer exercise wear and an absurd gait that makes you look as if your haemorrhoids are playing up then so be it.

Exercise

1 Train, don't strain

2 Rule of 3's: '2 on, I off'

Just as long as you get out there and do it.

My personal exercise reminder is a very large and very scruffy mongrel called Louie. The mutt has doleful eyes that scream out 'Take me for a walk or I'll phone the RSPCA'. So rather than have a canine crisis team knocking on my door I take him for his walk. We both enjoy it. I get some exercise and he manages to leave his liquid calling card all over the neighbourhood.

No matter what type of exercise you do there are some baseline rules to follow:

Exercise must be safe. If you are fat and middle-aged with a cholesterol level of thirty and you have been to a lot of family funerals recently then you had better get some medical advice before running that marathon. Also, over-use injuries such as tendonitis are nature's way of telling you that you are becoming an obsessional cripple who hasn't been watching enough midday TV recently.

Exercise must be enjoyable. Otherwise you won't go back and do it again. 'Train, don't strain' is the motto.

Exercise performed in groups, teams and classes has a better psychological effect than solitary exercise. It requires commitment to exercise for a season and our old friend, guilt, stops us from sinking into that favourite armchair to watch Oprah when we should be bashing that ball around something or other. Guilt is a very powerful motivator. Just ask Louie.

The Rule of 3's: When training for anything short of the Olympics, every third day should be a rest day. Two days on, one day off. Anything more than that makes you look like an anal retentive or someone who gets a kick out of pain.

Personal time management

Businessmen love this stuff. They attend time-management courses where they learn how to structure their day, work their little electronic personal organiser gadgets, get someone out of their office, make a meeting stick to time and end a phone call. They are promised that if they do all that then they will have time to be daydreamers, dog-walkers and good husbands and fathers. But then they always look pretty stressed and ragged when I meet them . . .

Everyone needs to stocktake their personal time management every so often. I have a very simple formula . . .

Exercise: The 100 hours analysis
1 Get yourself a big sheet of paper.
2 Make five columns on it. They should be headed *Work*, *Spouse/partner*, *Kids*, *Friends/family* and *Me*.
3 A seven-day week has 168 hours in it. Let's allow for eight hours' sleep per night on average. That's 56 hours counting Zs. Now let's presume that you spend two hours per day doing things that are regular, solitary and unavoidable. These are showering, powdering your nose, commuting, etc. That leaves us with about 100 hours per week, in round figures.
4 Now record in the columns on your paper how you think that you spent last week's 100 hours. The heading *Work* includes all manifestations of work in and around the house that you do *not* consider pleasurable, such as painting the laundry ceiling or cleaning out cupboards. The heading *Friends/family* relates to time spent with anyone beyond your immediate family or partner and offspring, presuming that you live in some kind of nuclear family. The heading *Me* relates to time spent by yourself and for yourself. Watching TV is a *Me* exercise even if it is done with the family, since little or no real communication goes on in its eerie glow. Family dinner-table time will have to be divided between partner and kids depending upon who does most of the talking. Put a guestimate in

each column of the number of hours spent in each area so that all the figures add up to 100 hours.

5 Get your partner (and kids too if they are old enough) to do the same.

6 Repeat the exercise at the end of next week and see how that 100 hours went.

7 Compare findings. You will encounter two scary realisations:

- You really don't know where all that time went; and
- One or two of the five personal time-management areas will be missing out, usually with time hogged by one or two other areas. *Work* time usually predominates and the area that tends to be sadly lacking, especially for parents, is *Me* time. Also take a long look at *Kids* time. Remember how you missed out on time with your parents and how you swore that you would never do that to your own kids? Well you're doing it. And get the message too that everyone needs time for themselves ... sacrosanct, self-indulgent, private time.

Sex

I will not try to make this like those sex manuals with the really interesting pictures. I will simply try to outline some over-riding principles.

The first of these is that most sex therapy is about getting women to come and stopping men from coming. In other words when it comes to formal sex therapy, women's most common sexual problem is *anorgasmia* (difficulty in achieving orgasm) and men's is premature ejaculation (i.e. ejaculation that occurs before your partner is satisfied). Each of these problems occurs in the early stages of experimenting with sexuality and developing relationships. Both tend to resolve spontaneously with time, communication and a desire to get back into bed and try again. Most women in a regular sexual relationship begin to experience orgasms during most sexual encounters. Most men in a regular sexual relationship manage to control their degree of excitement and to delay their ejaculation until their partner is satisfied. But both these problems do not always simply settle down. And that is when professional help should be sought.

Sex changes as the relationship progresses. In the Marvellous Besotted Phase you can experience the earth moving, and fireworks go off with every orgasm. A few years down the track you have to breathe some life back into your sex life and that requires some mutual enthusiasm, an ability to let your partner know your fantasies and enough energy after a hard day's/week's/month's work to hang off the chandeliers. Perhaps the most common sexual problem of all is not anorgasmia or premature ejaculation at all, but an insidious tendency to boredom or complacency about sex that has to be spoken about and dealt with or one of you is going to end up having an affair. Dirty weekends, blue movies, sensual massage, the back seat of the family station wagon (just to remind you of that night in the Volkswagen when you first started going out together) and finding out a few positions that the Kamasutra missed out on: these are all ways of getting some spark back into that fire in your loins.

It is said that men reach their sexual peak at twenty and women at forty. Why, oh why, did nature get that aspect of timing so horribly confused? Perhaps so that they can have lots of whoopee in their thirties when their libidos are starting to become equal?

Be aware also that as you become more geriatric your sex life does not have to be a dewy-eyed memory. About three-quarters of men over seventy will experience relative or absolute impotence. What most of them do not know is that our knowledge about impotence and its assessment and treatment has really forged ahead over the past few years so that most impotence in most men is treatable, even if the treatment can be a little, shall I say, colourful. Be that as it may, impotent men should have the courage to do themselves and their partners a favour by at least having their impotence assessed by a specialist in the field. They will be able to find out that their impotence is primarily a problem of nerves or blood vessels or psychological factors. A rule of thumb here is that most impotence is caused by the three A's: arteries, anxiety and alcohol. Then they can learn about what treatment is on offer and make an informed decision about what options they would like to pursue.

Note that there is an unwritten law within couples that it is almost impossible for two people to have exactly the same amount of libido. And, furthermore, *the person with less libido is the person who controls the sex life.* The person with more libido is left to find out ways of pushing along the sex drive of the other. A person who is ultra-horny and falls in love with a person who likes it every other month is condemning himself or herself to a life of frustration unless there can be some sort of negotiated compromise.

As a general rule the most common difficulty that couples have in invigorating their sex lives is in communication. Harken to the story of Charles and Jane. This really happened, which is sad when you consider how enlightened we think society is and yet how constrained some people feel.

CASE HISTORY **Charles and Jane**

Jane presented to her GP complaining of infertility. She and Charles had been married for eighteen years, were both involved in their respective careers and were both very successful. The biological clock kept on ticking and Jane, who was thirty-eight, was beginning to get a bit testy about having kids before her ovaries gave up the ghost. Her GP went through all the usual questions about her periods and their medical history. It was only after she had kept a menstrual diary for a couple of months and Charles had had a sperm test (all of which showed that everything should be in good working order) that Jane had the courage to speak the truth. During their eighteen years of marriage they were respected and successful and impressed their friends as being a loving couple devoted to each other. But they had never had intercourse. Not once.

Early on in the piece Charles had had a few goes at it. Performance anxiety and premature ejaculation well and truly put him off. But then he was a pretty uptight character who was overwhelmed by these problems; so overwhelmed in fact that he simply refused to talk about it. Jane tried to broach the subject a number of times but Charles became edgy and blushed so much that she eased off and let it be. For nearly twenty years.

The first hurdle in uniting his sperm and her ovum was to get him to even talk about the problems. Rather poignantly he expressed some tearful relief at the chance to get all this off his chest since it had been plaguing him quietly for years. Corroding away at his self-esteem and his sense of masculinity. It took time and patience. But eventually he learned how to do that thing that most of us take for granted as being an instinctive behaviour. Being randy is instinctive. Satisfying a partner requires some considerable skill.

Exercise A

1 Put this book down.
2 Find your sexual partner.
3 Presuming that you are not riding on a train or cutting the cake at a kid's birthday party, show your partner your genitalia.
4 Women must demonstrate their clitoris. Men are notorious for being deft at finding a pub but lousy at finding a clitoris. Show the poor sod where it is, what it looks like, what it feels like, how it must be touched and how it can be rubbed to elicit sexual pleasure.
5 Men must do the same with their penises.

If this initiates a mutually satisfying sexual encounter then that's a bonus. Either way, you can now move on to the next exercise.

Exercise B

1 Find two large pieces of paper.
2 Give one to your sexual partner.
3 Individually and privately write down the answers to the following questions:

- What physically turns you on? What parts of your body do you like stroked or caressed? What parts of your genitals do you like touched and how?
- What are your most common sexual fantasies? Presuming that they do not involve electricity, blood-letting or farmyard animals, how would you like your partner to act out these fantasies for you?
- What visually turns you on? What are the parts of your partner's body that you like to see? What parts of your body do you like to show off?
- How often do you want and need to make love? Where?
- How can you provide something different, challenging or naughty in your sex life?

4 Add your own questions if you want. When you have finished, put your answers into an envelope and give them to your partner. Exchange envelopes so that you have your partner's answers and he/she has yours.
5 Read your partner's answers as they were written: individually and privately. Do not do this in the same room. Gasps and giggles can be disconcerting. Then destroy the paper so that your mother-in-law

doesn't stumble upon it. All information given and obtained is to be treated with dignity and confidentiality.

6 Mull over the results for twenty-four hours before discussing them with your partner. Then use this information to give your sex life one hell of a kick.

Okay, so you have tried your best and you are not getting anywhere. She can't come. He comes too quickly. She is horny all the time and he would rather read Plato. She becomes a little tired of the fact that he can only do it if he is watching from inside the wardrobe and wearing nappies. So what now? Get help, that's what.

If people find it hard to drag themselves to see a psychiatrist, then people find it doubly hard to get themselves to a sex therapist. When they get there they find someone with holey socks or ladders in their tights and only then can they throw off the stereotype of sex therapists as being people who wear kaftans, smoke too much marijuana and organise orgies. If your sex therapist does look like that then consider finding someone who is a little more (dare I say it?) conservative. Sex therapy is a very personal and private affair. You must find someone who is competent and professional. Not a space cadet.

Psychosomatic disorders

Last but not least comes a mention of this group of disorders. They are worth mentioning because there are so many misunderstandings about them. People say 'it's all in your mind'. They believe that positive thinking will cure your cancer when what you really need is chemotherapy, a good wig and some strong painkillers.

In the 1940s psychoanalysts went a bit mad and began to claim that almost all physical illness was the result of unresolved emotional problems lodged deep in the subconscious mind. This belief has not stood the test of time and plenty of those illnesses that were thought to be 'in your head' are now known to be well and truly in your blood vessels or your immune system. There are a few exceptions to this blanket statement. We do know that stress can give you (or at least help to give you) your peptic ulcers and your coronary artery disease. It can raise your blood pressure by a few notches so that when you go to that holiday resort your blood vessels get a good rest too. And every student knows that the closer they get to exams the more time they spend in the loo . . .

Get the message clear. I am talking here about how *emotions cause illness*, which is a controversial area. Probably *most* illnesses are worsened to some extent by stress. The converse association, how *illnesses cause emotional difficulties*, is quite straightforward. Usually minor illnesses cause minor stress and major illnesses get your emotions doing overtime. Being told you have a wart is associated with a sense of annoyance and a sigh of 'ho-hum'. Being told you have cancer is major breakdown material.

There are also some curious syndromes that develop when the mind interacts with the body.

Somatisation   This occurs when emotional difficulties are expressed with physical symptoms. The classical case is the little old Italian woman who becomes depressed. She will never say 'I am depressed'; she will say 'I have this dreadful pain in my back and neck and stomach'. All sorts of examinations and investigations fail to find the cause of her pain. When the depression is treated, lo and behold, the pain goes away . . . I have never encountered a depressed Italian woman who has *not* somatised. It is simply a culturally acceptable way of expressing emotional pain. Don't be surprised. There is a universally entrenched belief in most cultures that physical pain is more valid than emotional pain. I have patients who live in a quiet state of emotional agony and never tell anyone. They do not feel that their torment is as acceptable as, say, a broken leg in a plaster of Paris cast, even though the latter is far, far less painful than their panic attacks and depression.

Hypochondriasis   Hypochondriacs become convinced that they have *illnesses*. Note the difference between them and somatisers, who have *symptoms*. Hypochondriacs' most common 'disease' is cancer, which they get twice a week. And that's a good week. Any symptom, from a cough to the release of flatus, only goes to confirm in their minds that they are terminally ill. When I show them their pathology results and explain in painstaking detail what all those names like 'gamma-glutamyl-transpeptidase' and 'packed cell volume' mean and that they are as healthy as any marathon contestant they look relieved and thank me profusely. Then they are back four days later with that cough and flatus again. But this time they have also found a pimple on their navel and they are worried as all hell. Mention the term 'hypochondriac' to most doctors and they will suddenly develop a nervous tic … If I can ever climb into the subconscious minds of these people I often find that they are classical 'Me-down' types who have a 'bad' part of themselves that they want to have amputated. The 'bad' part is a whole lot of self-contempt and childhood guilt. Somewhere between the subconscious and the conscious parts of the mind these feelings assume a different identity; they become a malignant tumour and they must be cut out with a scalpel rather than wept out with tears.

Dysmorphophobia   What a marvellous word. Now say it backwards. Dysmorphophobia is the preoccupation that a part of your body is ugly or misshapen. Plastic surgeons know these people well and try to avoid them like the plague. They come for nasal reconstruction, convinced that they have a huge red hooter. But then they show you this cute little button nose that looks like a ski-jump and would make Claudia Schiffer green with envy. Or they think that their perfectly normal ears make them look like a wing-nut. Once again, deep inside, is a lot of self-hatred that is manifested by their feeling ugly.

Psychogenic pain disorder   This is a subtype of somatisation. Here there is a clear emotional precedent to the onset of pain and no obvious organic cause. These are the persistent headaches that come on at Dad's funeral. Or the 'angina' that turns up the day after the widow's chihuahua is run over by a ten-ton truck.

Conversion reactions   I have mentioned these in Chapter 1 with the case of Moyra, who lost her voice when she wanted to tell her daughter's fiance that she loved him. I have seen patients having full-blown epileptic fits while the reading from their electroencephalogram (which monitors brainwaves) shows that there is no epileptic activity in their brains. This is the disorder that gets soldiers carried from the field because their legs are 'paralysed'. They are not malingerers. They are not 'bunging it on'. At a deep subconscious level they have dissociated their physical ability from some emotional state that is causing them impossible distress.   Mary blind

We psychiatrists are no fools. We like to stay out of malpractice lawsuits as much as we possibly can. That is why we investigate all of the above complaints as much as we possibly can before we apply any of the above labels. Otherwise we will miss out on diagnosing the Italian woman with sciatica and the hypochondriac who really does have cancer. And the widow who lost the chihuahua will have a heart attack because we ignored her very real angina. The shrink who forgets that he is a doctor will end up with egg on his face. Confucius said that. I think.

Enough about health, from a psychiatrist's viewpoint. Having waded through the previous chapters you will now be an apprentice psychiatrist. On the other hand you might also be beginning to realise that you have always carried a lot of distress: sadness or anger or anxiety. Or a combination of all three. If the time has come to do something about it then you had better keep reading. The next chapter is about how to find help.

Getting help

Is there a psychotherapist in the house?

Everyone knows that only mad people go to see psychiatrists. Do these words sound familiar? That's because I started the first chapter with them and it seems only appropriate that I start the last chapter with them too. One of the main points I want to make in this book is that this popular idea is wrong, wrong, wrong. Sure, I have plenty of patients who suffer from ongoing mental illnesses such as manic-depression, but I have tried to show that psychiatrists deal not only with madness. We work with the whole gamut of mental and emotional suffering, just as most other doctors focus on physical suffering.

Everyone carries an invisible suitcase. Inside it is their emotional baggage. Coming to see someone in my profession involves prying open the rusted locks of that suitcase and looking inside. The objective of that process is to make the suitcase lighter. But be warned that there are two disadvantages to the process:

1 **It hurts.** In particular it makes you feel extremely vulnerable so you can only do it with someone you trust.

2 **It takes time.** Not too many people are the 'Ripe Plums' that I described in Chapter 1. For most people, opening the suitcase takes not hours or days but months or years. Brief interventions give brief results. If this were not so then we would all have dumped the contents of our invisible suitcases years ago. Giving yourself an emotional spring-clean requires determination, strength and patience.

So who should seek professional help for an emotional problem? How big does a problem have to be to warrant going to see a psychiatrist? Most importantly of all, how do you find one of these people with holes in their socks or tights and how do you find one with whom you feel comfortable? That is what this chapter is all about. If you are poised on a cliff edge grasping a suicide note and reading this, then it would be an advantage to be a speed-reader. People with other less acute problems can put their feet up and mull over this before seeking help.

In a very general sense, you should take your emotional problems to a psychiatrist when they start to interfere with your ability to find life enjoyable, satisfying and fulfilling. Your invisible suitcase must be opened when it is so heavy that it is intruding upon your ability to function in life in any sphere, be it personal, academic or occupational. The 'barometer' for how well you are functioning emotionally can be found in the harmony of your intimate relationships. When these go down you will follow fairly shortly. Guaranteed.

Glossary

Before I move on, let me deal with some of the terms that I will use in this chapter:

Counselling This implies simple supportive techniques that help people to get talking and express their feelings. Learning the techniques takes a weekend. Learning what all these feelings actually mean and what to do with them takes years.

Therapy or **psychotherapy** In this chapter they are synonymous. The meanings of these words have become so fudged that all sorts of crackpots do all sorts of things with their clients (victims, more likely) and call this 'psychotherapy'. The essence of the meaning is that there is some verbal interaction between a therapist and his/her client that is aimed at easing the distress of the client.

Psychologist Someone who has a degree in psychology. Even though I sound a bit snooty about them in this chapter I have to admit that they are generally good sorts.

Psychiatrist A medical practitioner who has specialised in psychological medicine. As a general rule psychologists claim authority over 'normal' psychology and psychiatrists over 'abnormal' psychology but this is by no means always the case. Clinical psychologists often do very similar work to that of psychiatrists but cannot prescribe medication.

Psychotherapist Anyone who practises psychotherapy. They may be a psychologist or a psychiatrist but formal qualifications are not a prerequisite.

Psychoanalyst A psychotherapist who follows a particular school of thought founded by Breuer and subsequently developed by Freud and his followers. Their clients are called 'analysands'.

Help-giver A word that I will use in this chapter to refer to any person who tries to give professional emotional help. I use this word because help-givers call themselves by so many different names that I had better use an umbrella term. It covers the entire spectrum from the most incompetent and unethical to the most competent and professional. human worker

Finding the right therapist

L et us presume that obtaining relief from your emotional distress is a three-step process:

- Own it.
- Understand it.
- Deal with it.

You have just got past step one. You own your distress. Or more specifically, you own up to it. You also recognise that you have the problem. Not everyone around you. Not your boss or your partner or your kids. You. You also understand that this distress is such that it is interfering with your ability to get on with life and to think that life is a worthwhile experience. You have tried to nut out the problems yourself. You have thought positively. You have given yourself a break. You have wept into your claret so much that it is tasting salty and your drinking friends are drifting away because they cannot cope with 'old misery guts' any more. So where to now?

You have a variety of sources of help which I will describe below. You will pretty soon pick up on my belief that there are a lot of idiots who work in the field of counselling and psychotherapy. There are also a lot of people who have impressive letters after their names (some of these qualifications are really, really easy to get!) but plenty of them are educated fools. Having said that, I ask the competent and ethical counsellors out there, and there are plenty of them too, to forgive me for this most recent burst of unbridled cynicism.

I also confess from the outset to a certain bias here because I have my own trumpet to blow. Despite this I will try not to portray the world of professionals who provide emotional help as a pyramid with psychiatrists stuck near the top, just below God.

My dentist's name is Karen. When I open my mouth for her I have a reasonable degree of trust that she knows what she's doing. I would not bare my carious teeth to anyone who did not have a framed university degree on the wall because I would presume that these precious pieces of ivory would be drilled in the wrong places for the wrong reasons. I tried two other dentists before I got to Karen. One was too old and doddery and the other charged like a wounded bull. Then I found Karen. Charming, efficient, professional.

Not too cheap and not too expensive. I pay her an honest dollar for an honest filling and she keeps me informed about the state of my caries.

Surely most people respect their own teeth enough to do the same: to seek out a dentist whom they can trust. What staggers me is how many people trust their minds to the machinations of counsellors who are incompetent. Be aware that anyone can call themselves a counsellor, a therapist or a psychotherapist. Anyone can hang out a brass plate with such an epithet on it. There is no legal requirement for a person who calls themselves any of those three titles to have any qualifications in the field at all. None. Zero. Zilch. You might think that you would make a good psychotherapist because you have read a couple of books just like this one. If you do and you want to set up your own business as a psychotherapist then there is nothing to stop you. The poor sods who bring their misery to you might never realise that you are completely out of your depth. And doing more harm than good. I often find myself trying to undo their damage.

How much training do most counsellors or therapists have? Some have read a few books. Some have been to weekend training courses over a few months. Some have a degree in one of the humanities subjects, such as social work or nursing. Sometimes this last group go on to do quite reputable professional training in one or other school of psychotherapy or psychoanalysis.

Psychologists must generally have a degree that takes four years at university and they must then work under supervision for another two years to become registered. Psychiatrists have a degree in medicine (i.e. six years at university) then at least one more year to get medical registration and some post-graduate medical experience. Only *then* do they undertake their medical specialty training which takes an absolute minimum of another five years.

The moral of the story is that if you are going to entrust a stranger with the most private aspects of your existence apart from your genitals then you had better find someone who, primarily, has some qualifications and experience. You must also be aware that not too many varieties of help-givers work within the confines of a governing body that determines professional standards. Psychologists and psychiatrists are the only ones that come to mind. If you go to see any other counsellor who is not working within the rules of some regulatory body that ensures their competence then you are taking some degree of risk.

No regulation, no guarantee of standards, no comeback if it all goes wrong.

So what attributes does your ideal counsellor/therapist possess, as well as qualifications and experience? Read on.

Attributes of the suitable help-giver

Your ideal help-giver, this person whom you will seek out, must have the following five attributes. Make this a checklist. If your own help-giver lacks just one of these then you might have to think again.

1 Your help-giver must be ethical

This is the most important attribute of all. It is also the attribute the people think of least of all before they go to see their help-giver for the first time. Bless their naive little hearts.

Matters between you and your help-giver must be strictly confidential. No chatting to your neighbour about you. Records of the therapy must be kept in a secured place. Information divulged to any other source (with the possible exception of your GP if you see a psychiatrist) must be with your written consent.

Your help-giver must maintain a professional distance and respect the boundaries of the relationship. It is not appropriate for them to be your sister-in-law or your old school-friend. It is not appropriate for you to 'do lunch' with them over a couple of bottles of wine. It is not appropriate for you to buy a car from them. It is not appropriate that you know too much about them or their personal lives. It is not appropriate that they tell you about *their* miseries too. This may sound all very peculiar, but for the two of you to develop a therapeutic relationship your help-giver must be *an intimate stranger.*

Most important of all, it is not appropriate for you to have sex with your help-giver. I know it happens and probably it happens all too often. And it is always an unmitigated disaster. The intimacy and the caring emotionality of the relationship becomes blurred with eroticism and, unless your help-giver is ethical enough to respect the boundaries of the professional relationship, he (or sometimes she) will take advantage of you sexually.

2 Your help-giver must be personable

This is more a personality variable than the result of training. You don't learn how to be charming or inspire confidence at medical school or in psychiatric training. You either have it or you don't.

Psychiatry is a huge field. There are psychiatrists who work exclusively with psychotic patients committed to psychiatric hospitals, some who specialise in working with children and families, some who work with only old people, some who do forensic work (i.e. court reports in both civil and criminal cases), some who sub-specialise in long-term psychotherapy and some (like me) who try to do a bit of everything. If a psychiatrist does not want to work with privately referred patients with a variety of personal and emotional problems then there are plenty of other areas to choose from where the personable qualities are not so needed. Forensic psychiatrists, for example, tend to be pretty tough, straight-talking types so that they can stand up to ruthless cross-examination by some QC.

Rather paradoxically, for reasons already outlined, you do not want a help-giver who is *too* personable. Your professional is just that, a professional, not a pal. But overall you want someone who displays a bit of human compassion and is not too *distanced*.

3 Your help-giver must know what he/she is doing

This implies plenty of skill and knowledge. Preferably years of study and plenty of supervised counselling or therapy before they are let loose on the unsuspecting public. It also implies a lot of common sense. One of the hardest things that a counsellor must learn is how to shut up. It requires patience and empathy to get people speaking. It also requires common sense to know when to pipe up, to offer some feedback, a new perspective, an interpretation of events in the client's life or in the therapy and, rarely, some good old-fashioned advice.

They must also be able to be empathic. This means that they try to understand what it is like to be you, in your shoes. Not how they would feel if they were in your shoes. Note that this implies an ability to see you as an individual with your own personality and life experience, your own feelings and family. Not one who wants to put you into a pigeon-hole of some theory that they are pushing.

Psychiatrists use the medical model, which implies that they work through the signs and symptoms in a methodical way, come to a diagnosis and, on the basis of that, plan a treatment. Seems fair enough. But there are critics of this approach. They claim that doctors 'label' people. The critics claim that if you call someone a psychopath then you are guaranteeing that that person will act like one. Probably there is some merit in that theory too. Psychiatrists actually stray from the medical model as well. In assessing a patient, we work towards two ideas: diagnosis and formulation. A diagnosis groups people. All people with signs X and symptoms Y are given diagnosis Z. Diagnosis is important because it indicates two things: treatment and prognosis, i.e. what we should do with the patient and what to expect in the future. Formulation, on the other hand, is a summary of this particular patient's personality, background and circumstances. Formulation emphasises individuality. Both are necessary to get the best possible understanding of this patient and his or her problems.

Good therapists must be eclectic, according to the problems, needs and abilities of the client. They must be able to use a bit of this treatment and a bit of that one, according to what is indicated and what is working. If you go to an acupuncturist you will get needles, no matter what your complaint. If you go to a help-giver you should find one who has a broad armamentarium of therapeutic tools: individual therapy, couples therapy, group therapy, etc. Even medication if it is indicated.

If a trusting relationship is to develop between you and your therapist it is imperative that you believe that they are honest. They must let you know what they can and cannot do for you. They must not hit you with all sorts of promises and optimism and compliments in the hope of boosting you up. You like hearing it but in your heart you know that it's not true. Or, if you can convince yourself that this therapist will provide the answer to all your emotional needs then you will be in for a big fat bout of disappointment when you realise that they are frail human beings, just like you.

Indeed, many of the problems that my patients bring me are, quite simply, insoluble. I can't bring their dead child back. I can't make the barren fertile. I can't make the narcissist eternally youthful. And most of all I can't give them any promises that I can make the impossible possible, even if they beg me to.

4 Your help-giver must be reasonably available

It's far from ideal if your help-giver has an office that is fifty kilometres away, can see you in four months' time for an initial assessment and then can provide only a half-hour appointment every other week. On the other hand the last patient referred to me in my private practice phoned me and asked to be seen after office hours in a consulting room near her work and for free, or nearly free. I politely explained that I could not meet her requests. What I wanted to say was for her to 'get real'.

What often develops between a help-giver and a client is a subtle battle over how much contact there should and can be. How often should the sessions be? And how long? Can the client phone you outside session-time? How long will you be able to spend on the phone? Is there provision for extra sessions if a life crisis comes along? The client often realises at head level that their help-giver cannot give all this attention at the exact moment that it is needed, unconditionally and for free. But at heart level the client still wants this, just as he or she wanted unconditional parental love but didn't get it. A certain degree of disappointment is an inherent part of the process. Very needy clients who can't stand to be disappointed tend to exhaust untrained or poorly trained help-givers pretty early in the piece. It is necessary for them to accept the inevitable limitations of the therapeutic process. This is called 'containment' and it requires special patience and an understanding of the process by the help-giver.

Quite paradoxically, it is also necessary for the help-giver to be reasonably *unavailable* since that situation mimics life. No client ever had perfect parents or perfect friends or perfect partners who were available to them exactly when they needed them. Having a bit of this 'controlled neglect' foisted upon a client actually increases their individuality and independence if they can cope with it.

Sounds all very confusing? Go into therapy. You'll find out pretty quickly what I mean.

5 Your help-giver must be affordable

In general the public health system will help you to cope with diagnosable mental illnesses and life crises. Mental health workers in the public system who disagree with that claim are invited to join the rabble outside my office. If you are seeking a more long-term process to help you with ongoing emotional problems then chances are you will end up in the private system. And you will end up paying for the help that you receive. People who feel the sense of entitlement that all their health-related professional help should be free have their heads in the clouds. In fact payment is an essential part of the therapeutic relationship between client and help-giver.

Payment for therapy, like any service, boils down to the old issues of supply and demand and paying for quality. If you pay peanuts, you get monkeys. You must work out what sort of therapeutic help you can afford and go for it.

It is also a matter of priorities. Some people will pay a fortune to have the paint job on their car fixed but grumble about paying someone to help fix their internal emotional world. Often the people who come to see me have come to some stage in their lives in which they realise that they only get one crack at this mortal coil and they had better make it as satisfying as they possibly can. The paint on their car will only become more cracked and faded. But their enjoyment of life might simply get better and better. Paying for your therapy shows that you are working out what the real values in life are all about.

In Australia we view ourselves as being descendants of hardy pioneering stock. We are people who sweat and swear. We have a laconic sense of humour and drink far too much beer in the hot, hot sun. We view Americans as being introspective and neurotic and we believe that all Americans have their own 'analyst'. What most Australians don't realise is that we have a very generous health funding system in Medicare and that it covers most of psychiatrists' fees. Psychiatrists are, after all, first and foremost medical practitioners. This means that most of the fees paid to a psychiatrist are refunded. A former federal Minister for Health once questioned this arrangement. He had been a 'counsellor' in the past and he felt that all human problems should be manageable in, say, ten sessions. He had no idea. Ten sessions is fine for 'band-aid' treatment, not for true personal growth.

Attributes of the suitable patient

So far so good. But is long-term, in-depth, introspective psychotherapy for everyone? Are there some patients for whom there is no point? There sure are.

My ideal patient has his or her own four essential attributes. This is a checklist for you to apply to yourself. If you are missing one or more of these then you had better re-think whether psychotherapy is the right way to go for you.

1 Suitable patients are motivated

Ideal patients are not half-hearted and window-shopping. Also they are not expecting me to do all the work.

When you see a surgeon your role is quite straightforward. You go to sleep and when you wake up the work has all been done for you. Then your role is to put up with the injections of morphine while your body does its own healing. When you come to see a psychiatrist you have to do your own emotional surgery with only a mild anaesthetic in the form of emotional support from your therapist.

Once you undertake to become involved in therapy you must accept that you are not there to chat for a few sessions and then disappear again into miserable suburbia. Like most therapists I lay down 'rules' to my patients and if they can't accept them then they are wasting time for us both. The 'rules' are such things as the need for a commitment, an agreement on fees, the need to be punctual and to attend once or twice a week, a prohibition on cancelling sessions at short notice or without good reason, and an agreement on how we will decide together when the therapy should finish. If there is no motivation then there is no commitment, no rules, no containment, no boundaries, no trust and no therapy.

I should also mention that patients come to see me seeking psychotherapy when they have one of two feelings about their lives. They come to see me when it is *unsafe* to come or when it is *safe* to come. People present to me when it is *unsafe* because their life is turning to custard. They have lost someone very important to them, they are emotionally isolated, they wonder whether there is any point in going on. They are getting to the point that if they don't get some help quick-smart then they are going to see what it's like to be a bird and launch themselves off a nearby cliff.

On the other hand people who come to see me when it is *safe* to come do so when their life is going very well. They are supported in a loving relationship, they derive considerable satisfaction from their job or their parenting role and planet Earth is, all in all, a good place to be. It's just that there has been something that has been annoying them for years and they had better get it sorted out: a rage against their father, which they know kicked off that depressed time three years ago; a vague memory of childhood sexual abuse by someone whose face they can't visualise . . . yet; a lifelong resentment about being a twin and feeling that their co-twin was more favoured.

2 Suitable patients are able to withstand the rigours of therapy

Plenty of people have this whimsical fantasy that being in therapy is like having a captive audience that you can moan and complain to. Right? Wrong, wrong, wrong. Being in therapy is just bloody hard yakka. Trying to prise open your emotional suitcase is one of the hardest things that you will ever do. You will find that demons will leap out at you that you thought were dead. They will threaten to devour you. If therapy does not have a huge component of emotional pain in it then it is too polite, contrived and superficial. Therapy may begin as a sophisticated chat between two adults but if it is going to get anywhere it must become an outpouring of pain within a trusting and professional environment. You can't make an omelette without cracking eggs; you can't lance a boil without breaking the skin and you can't open an emotional suitcase without strain and pain.

Patients are not suitable for psychotherapy if we get to some really tense, juicy piece of emotional pain and they run away.

3 Suitable patients are verbal

Psychotherapy is talking therapy. The suitable patient must be able to talk and talk freely. That sounds a bit simple, but some of my patients (mostly the ones who look upon me as an emotional surgeon) just sit there and wait for me to lead the way. Sitting there in mutual silence strikes me as being a waste of good psychotherapeutic time. Sometimes it takes a while for them to grasp that this is their time, not mine. They pay me for it. They set the agenda. They lead the way. And they do most of the talking.

I might also mention an interesting cross-cultural aspect of psychotherapy here. In general this process is viewed as being an upper middle-class Anglo-Saxon-Celtic phenomenon. To some degree that observation is quite correct. But this is mainly because there are many languages in the world that do not have words to describe the nuances of emotions that the languages of the developed world have. Many cultures, for example, do not have a word to describe what we call or anxiety even more!,

'depression'. This is pretty mind-blowing when you consider that most of my patients present to me with just that complaint. I do not for a moment believe that people from all these other cultures do not suffer from depression; I am convinced that that is a universal phenomenon. But perhaps they do not have words that adequately describe it.

4 Suitable patients are psychologically minded

By this I refer to patients' ability to be insightful about how they tick. Some people have a natural curiosity about the dynamics of their relationships and feelings. Women excel in this, but a psychologically minded man is a pleasure to work with.

Unfortunately there are some people who find this introspection to be beyond their ability. Some people can't do maths; some people can't spell; some people are tone-deaf and others can't appreciate the pleasure of good art. Some people just can't grasp or describe what they are feeling and they can't put together all these abstract, ethereal models of what makes up the thing that they call 'me'. They are not, in the jargon of psychotherapists, *psychologically minded*.

You don't have to be an Einstein to become involved in psychotherapy but you need to have a bit of grey matter to understand yourself. Rest assured that if you have been able to wade through this book and understand some of the basic concepts then you have more than enough neurones.

People who *are* psychologically minded may do well in psycho-therapy. But there are two interesting aspects of how they develop a psychological awareness of their own situation. They must do it slowly and in their own way. I can sit down and barrage them with my perspective of who they are, where they came from, what their problem is and what to do about it. But in this journey of personal exploration it is far better if they do most of it for themselves. My perspectives may be mostly irrelevant to them. I did not live inside their heads for all of their lives. *They* did. And they must work out how they work.

How to find a help-giver

You are now well and truly convinced that you have a personal problem that you would like to deal with. This problem is emotional, not just body odour or really bad dress-sense. You have exhausted your family and ostracised your friends. Time to seek professional help. Where to now?

The first step is to try to work out what sort of help-giver you will consult. You will be all too aware by now that I am fairly pro-psychiatry and anti-all-the-others, but not to the point (I hope) of insufferable elitism. In fairness I should state that I am sure that many non-medical counsellors are excellent. But you can also waste a lot of time consulting charming crackpots. I must also point out that the greatest amount of professional counselling that goes on in our society is not performed by psychiatrists or psychologists but by general practitioners. I should know. I used to be one before I became a psychiatrist.

The best way to find a help-giver is to be recommended to one by someone who knows the market-place. Preferably even someone who has sought the professional help of the person whom they have recommended. If you have contacts or friends in the medical or psychological fields then contact them and tell them the sort of help that you think you might need. Ask them if they can recommend someone or even recommend someone who can recommend someone else . . .

If you have no joy there, the next step is to go to see your GP. Spill your guts, or that portion of your guts that you are prepared to let your GP have a look at, and ask for a referral. Your GP may be skilled at counselling and many GPs are. But their limitations are the same limitations that drove me from general practice into the long, arduous road of specialising: time constraints and limited training. To any GPs whom I have just insulted: you know where to queue.

Another source of information on local resources is your local Community Health Centre. Phone them (usually under 'Community' in the telephone directory) and ask them for the name of a reputable local help-giver. If you have any preference for counsellor, psychologist, psychiatrist, etc. then state that. They may ask to see you themselves. Go along and check them out if you like. But don't settle for anything less than what you want and feel that you need.

If you can't find a good recommendation and if you want to see a non-medical counsellor then all you have to do, as they say in the advertisements, is to let your fingers do the walking. Look them up in the Yellow Pages under 'Counsellors'. But be aware that by doing this you are taking a certain amount of 'pot luck' no matter how professional the ads look.

My personal opinion is that, as a generalisation, if you have been consistently hurt by some person in your life then it is a good idea to go to a help-giver who is of the same sex as the hurter. Women who have been raped, for example, should go to an ethical and reputable male therapist. If you have fallen off a horse it is important to get back on to a horse, not an elephant or a motorcycle. Get my drift?

Okay, you have their name and phone number. Ring and make an appointment. Don't make decisions until you have seen them, sat down with them, spoken to them, revealed a little of your pain and encountered their reaction. Once you get to see this help-giver, never lose sight of the fact that you are the customer and you can choose how you should spend your money.

Within the restriction that no help-giver, like no parent, can be perfect (we all strive simply to be 'good enough'), you must work out whether this person 'feels' right for you. Do you trust them or do the hairs on the back of your neck tell you that you are getting a creepy feeling? Can you talk to them easily? Are you on the same wave-length? Have you established a rapport while at the same time maintaining a safe professional distance?

Somewhere in your subconscious mind the hurt child within you must be reassured that this is a person who can cope with the intensity of your distress if you come to be able to reveal it to them. And yourself. You end up asking yourself the question: could you become enraged at them for not being the perfect parent/therapist for you and feel that your rage is manageable by both you and them?

But now comes a challenge: if you have been to see three or four help-givers and feel that none of them was right for you, if you have seen a counsellor, a couple of psychologists and a psychiatrist, and none of them seems 'good enough', then is this a problem in them or a problem in you? Are you approaching this quest with unreal expectations of the process and the outcome? I say this because I have learned by bitter experience that patients who inform me that I am the sixth psychiatrist that they have seen in four years always give me a sinking feeling. I cannot escape the impression that I am standing at the end of a queue and I am about to be criticised for some failure of understanding or not giving my unending attention to the patient. People who endlessly 'window-shop' for emotional help are either avoiding getting down to the nitty-gritty of working through their pain or else they are deriving some subconscious pleasure from disempowering their psychiatrists.

I have no fantasies of being able to leap over a tall clinic while wearing a red cape with the letter 'P' emblazoned upon it. If the patient continuously fails to establish a therapeutic rapport then that is, for the most part, their problem. They may try to make me feel responsible for them ('Me-up' people are good at this) but I know the realities of their game. And I know when they are trying to drag me into it.

Next step. You have found a help-giver. You have a rapport. You have the beginnings of some trust (don't fool yourself: it can take months to develop a real trust) and you are beginning to open up. What happens now?

What is your psychiatrist thinking?

I can speak only from my own perspective. If you go to see a psychiatrist you will be busy going through your checklist and he or she will be busy going through theirs. So I will give you an insight from the other side of the leather couch and tell you what goes through the mind of your psychiatrist.

Essentially the process is that I gather information, come to some sort of idea of what is going wrong, come up with some treatment options and see whether the patient is willing and/or able to go along with them. All through this I use a 'checklist' that is called the *biopsychosocial* model. That means that I am trying to view the patient from three different perspectives.

Biological perspective   *important part ↵*

All feelings stem, after all, from the electrochemical computer that is called the 'brain'. The organ requires the *corpus sanum* ('healthy body') that I highlighted in Chapter 8. Is your fatigue really because your thyroid gland is not functioning as well as it should? Or because you are anaemic? Have you lost so much blood from your heavy periods or from the as-yet-undiagnosed cancer in your bowel that has been bleeding for the past two years? Are you drinking so much that you have damaged your liver? Are you confused because you have had a stroke or the HIV infection that you didn't even know that you had has now got to your brain? If your complaints are mostly of bodily symptoms is this because you are somatising or being a hypochondriac or is it that you really do have some rare physical illness with insidious onset, such as multiple sclerosis? No wonder we psychiatrists are expected to struggle through all those years of medical school. It helps us to fully assess our patients. And not to confuse the mental with the physical and vice versa.

Psychological perspective

This refers to everything that I have written in this book so far, and then some. How does this person think, feel, and relate? How do they find care, trust and hope? Where did all these habitual ways of thinking and relating come from? Are there repeating patterns in their life that need to be investigated?

Social perspective

What are their relationships like? How do they seek and maintain intimacy? To what groups of human beings do they belong? How do all these other people impinge on their lives?

As I speak to a patient I gather information. Signs and symptoms. First there are symptoms. These are what the patient tells me. Then there are signs. That is what I observe. Sometimes they are quite incongruous. There is, for example, the 'smiling depression'. They are the people who surprise everyone by committing suicide 'out of the blue'. But really they have hidden away their intense despair from everyone around them.

Then I gather more information. Their medical history from their GP. Blood tests and X-rays. From time to time, with their express permission, I speak to their partner or their parents so that I can broaden the perspective of my impression.

Then I come up with a formulation and a diagnosis. Sometimes it is more accurately called a 'problem list' since the summation of the distress of a human being can rarely be expressed in a few words.

※ In THAT case you are not on the
same page = any of your patients.

Getting help

Next I negotiate with the patient about whether my perspectives match theirs or whether we can agree on a mutually acceptable way of viewing the problems. Then I have to negotiate what is the best way of trying to solve the problems. If the patient and I cannot come away from this assessment process feeling that we are both 'on-line' (as a computer buff would say) then we are each wasting the other's time. If a patient comes to see me because their partner feels it would be a good idea but he/she doesn't then I am dealing with the wrong patient. If a patient perceives his/her distress as being a result of harsh upbringing and I believe that it is because he/she is an unrepentant alcoholic then we are definitely 'off-line'. For the most part, however, patients leave my consulting room after the first appointment feeling that they and I are speaking the same language and working in the same direction. This is all done by a process of negotiation. Gone are the days of 'doctor's orders'.

Both are true!

The sole exception to that last statement is the highly unpleasant situation in which a person is either very psychotic or very depressed or both. In these cases, where there is a risk of their doing harm to themselves or to others and they have no intention of complying with treatment (usually because they do not understand their own mental state) I am forced to legally 'commit' them to hospital. I do this very rarely, perhaps once every few years, and I do it with a considerable degree of paranoia. You see, I hate lawyers. They terrify me. And I try to avoid any situation in which I can be sued for wrongfully committing someone who does not need it. On the other hand I might also be sued for neglecting to commit someone who needed to be committed. On those rare occasions when I am confronted with a dangerously mad person or a very suicidal person and I cannot convince them to accept treatment then my usual policy is 'commit now and ask questions later'.

Types of treatment

So what sorts of treatments do I use? Once again that word *biopsychosocial* crops up. We will look at these in turn.

disappointments are universal

1 Biological treatments

Most often biological treatments are drugs. I prefer to call them 'medications' because it makes them sound a little less like cocaine and angel dust. We 'shrinks' take a lot of flak for prescribing medications and, I admit, a few of my colleagues may find it hard to resist reaching for their prescription pads. But it is easy to lose sight of the fact that medications often constitute the cornerstone of some patients' treatment.

In particular, patients who have severe depression are best treated with a supportive style of psychotherapy in combination with anti-depressant medications. These are patients whose depression has crossed that fine line that says that it has stopped being a mood and started being an illness. Patients who have depression as an illness have a characteristic set of signs and symptoms. Their distress is severe. They have little or no pleasure in life. They have a characteristically negative view of life such that they, their world and their future all look black. They sleep poorly, often waking too early in the morning. Their mood changes during the day, usually with mornings being intolerable and evenings a little easier to manage. If they are not treated assertively with anti-depressant medications then there is a high chance that they will eventually try to do that bird thing with the cliffs.

Similarly, patients who are psychotic need medications. They and I can talk each other blue in the face but it is not going to stop their being mad. They need a chemical change in their brains and the only way to induce that is to prescribe antipsychotic medications. *Tout de suite.*

> **CASE HISTORY Mad Madeleine**
>
> Madeleine was a 19-year-old woman with a shock of red hair. At school she had been nick-named 'Maddy'. Unfortunately the nick-name proved to be a little too accurate and in her late teenage years she slipped into a chronic psychotic illness from which she has never quite fully recovered. Diagnosis: schizophrenia.
>
> Madeleine was a very memorable patient because her parents were Scientologists. Now you may or may not be aware that Scientologists and psychiatrists simply do not get on together.
>
> Madeleine's parents tried to perform upon her the standard Scientological technique which is called 're-programming'. Don't ask me what goes on with this procedure but it has something to do with challenging ways

of thinking. Needless to say it did not help Madeleine's psychosis a lot. In fact it got her so confused that I think she even got worse. It was not until Madeleine appeared at the local police station that anyone outside the family knew that anything was wrong. She had 'escaped' from home, where she had been all but imprisoned for several months of 're-programming' and gone to the police station because God had told her to. She heard God's voice inside her head. She informed the bemused duty sergeant that God had sent her to have sex with all the policemen in the station, plus anyone in the cells. The sergeant declined Madeleine's offer and instructed a couple of his constables to transport her forthwith to the nearest psychiatric hospital.

Here Madeleine was promptly committed. Her parents tried to 'rescue' her from the hospital but when they found out about the police station incident even they were shaken up. Only then did some proper treatment start. Medications. Pretty unsophisticated stuff, with side-effects and slow action, but generally reasonably effective. God's voice dwindled away. Madeleine's schizophrenia had a poor prognosis and the medications were not a 'cure'. But without them she might have been a lot worse off.

2 Psychological treatments

Most psychotherapy carried out by counsellors, psychologists and psychiatrists falls within the rubric of what might be called 'supportive psychotherapy'. This is what I called 'band-aid' therapy and I do that without too much disparagement. Plenty of the patients who are referred to me simply do not satisfy the criteria for the type of patient who would do well in long-term psychotherapy and, to be honest, plenty of them have absolutely no interest in hanging around for that long. So they come to see me simply to be propped up during a time of stress in their lives. Fair enough.

The difference between supportive psychotherapy and more intense forms of therapy is that the former are aimed at supporting the patient through some current life situation while the latter is about changing deeply held lifelong ways of feeling and relating. Supportive psychotherapy is about easing symptoms while long-term psychotherapy is about remodelling your defences.

In between these two extremes is cognitive therapy which I spoke of quite critically in Chapter 1. I then had to 'come clean' and admit that I used cognitive therapy from time to time. The gist of cognitive therapy is that it looks at your habitual ways of thinking and challenges them. It is, you will recall, particularly applicable to the treatment of depression

CBT

because that is when patients develop very characteristic 'cognitive distortions' which can be identified and challenged. The distortions might be:

- drawing the most pessimistic conclusions from any situation;
- focussing on the worst aspects of a situation;
- using one experience to draw unrealistic conclusions about one's worthlessness or incompetence;
- minimising successful experiences and maximising one's failures.

Cognitive therapy can be very useful with some patients. They must be motivated and organised enough to go through with the process, which involves, among other things, keeping a diary and reviewing it regularly with the therapist.

Last but not least of the psychological treatments comes the sort of long-term 'psychodynamic' therapy that I have been harping on about for most of this book. You have already guessed that this is my main interest.

I shall not intellectualise too much about this process. It is not an academic process, but an experiential one. When you learn how to drive a car it is best done by getting into the car with someone who knows how to do it and giving it a go. Reading books about driving a car is not nearly as useful as getting behind a steering wheel. In fact reading the book might just make you more confused. The same applies to this psychodynamic therapy. But I should point out a few of the obstacles that you might encounter on the way.

Every therapist has a certain bent. Some follow one school of psychotherapeutic thought and others follow another school. Some are more formal than others. Your therapist may have a grounding in Jungian psychoanalysis and your brother-in-law's friend may be seeing someone who is a Kohutian Self-psychologist. All schools have a number of things in common. They all allow for:

- a confidential, trusting relationship between therapist and patient;
- the expression of emotional distress;
- a 'rationale' or 'myth' to explain the patient's distress (the words of an American psychiatrist Dr Jerome Frank);
- a long-term commitment to promote trust and to allow the patient time for true personal growth. Significant, permanent, worthwhile change takes time. Are you sick of hearing this yet?

In the process a number of things happen:

'Transference'   This is the way in which the patient comes to relate to the therapist, as in the way they habitually relate to important, caring people in their lives. This may sound a bit wonky and the only people who can really get a grasp of this important concept are people who have experienced it. The classical 'transference' is of course 'erotic transference', in which the patient becomes sexually attracted to the therapist. If the therapist is short on ethics and long on hormones then this can lead to a disaster. Thankfully, the vast majority can keep their own sexual needs to themselves.

'Counter-transference'   This is the tendency of the therapist to relate to the patient in some way that he or she is pre-programmed to by his or her own life experience. It is not your problem, it is the therapist's. That's why most psychotherapists have had their own therapy: so that they understand themselves and their own reactions to their patients. Keep this in mind when you want to drive a wooden stake through the heart of your therapist: there were times when they wanted to do the same to their own therapist.

'Resistance'   This is an inevitable and crucial part of psychotherapy. Therapy can be a hard, frustrating, drawn-out process. Usually when it is hardest to go along to your session and hardest to bear the pain then it is doing the most good. Simplistic but true. Patients signal their resistance in a variety of ways: they begin to miss appointments or to show up late. They 'forget' their cheque-books or they pay their accounts weeks late. They sit in sullen, passive silence. Anything to express their anger and frustration other than verbalising it.

Enough already with the intellectualising about psychotherapy. If you really want to know about psychotherapy then it is time to find a therapist and get on with it. Get behind the steering wheel of your very heart and soul.

I might mention too that the role that I play in all this varies very much according to the type of treatment that I am using. When I prescribe I am a doctor. When I provide supportive psychotherapy I am a confidant, an adviser and a provider of an endless supply of paper tissues to weep into. When I provide cognitive therapy I am a teacher. I teach the right ways to think. But when I am a psychotherapist in that sort of intensive, dynamic, long-term psychotherapy I am a co-explorer and sometimes a guide on the journey. I have been this way before.

3 Social treatments *That is why I wanted do to see sh*

If a patient's distress is directly attributable to difficulties within a *sh* relationship then it is sometimes appropriate to bring the other person or people in that relationship into the consulting room. That way the difficulties can be thrashed out in an 'open forum' situation.

The common types of therapy are couples therapy, family therapy and group therapy. I won't try to intellectualise too much about these forms of treatment here. I can see the end to this book in sight so I will have to get you to ask your own therapist about them.

The end

Congratulations. You have bravely ploughed through this book. I hope that you've learned something in these pages and I'll be thoroughly disappointed if you haven't.

What you have read here are my perspectives. Lots of this stuff is described as models that I have generated for my own practice and found helpful, such as the 'YURU' chart. You won't find a lot of it in any other writing. This is how I see the human mind, feelings, relationships, health and even the meaning of life.

If you have been psychologically minded and curious enough to get to this point then you are undoubtedly a wonderful candidate for psychotherapy. And interested enough in all this to do something about it. I recommend now that just reading books has exhausted its potential to be helpful for you. You need a therapist. Put this book down and get working on finding someone to see. You know what you must do.

So what are you waiting for?